Mastering

Blender 4.4

The Ultimate Guide for Beginners and Professionals with Step-by-Step Tutorials, Advanced Techniques, and Industry Insights to Create, Animate, and Innovate

Cassius Peregrine

TABLE OF CONTENTS

INTRODUCTION

Are you struggling to navigate Blender's vast toolset, unsure where to start, or searching for ways to refine your 3D skills? Do you find online tutorials too fragmented or lacking the depth needed to truly master Blender 4.4? Whether you're a beginner aiming to understand the fundamentals or a professional seeking to harness Blender's latest advancements, this book is your definitive guide.

"Mastering Blender 4.4" is designed to provide a **structured, in-depth, and professional approach** to mastering Blender's capabilities. With the rapid evolution of 3D design, animation, and game development, staying ahead requires not only technical proficiency but also an understanding of the latest features and workflows. This book bridges the gap between foundational learning and advanced techniques, ensuring you build both **confidence and competence** in Blender 4.4.

Inside, you will find:

✔ **Step-by-Step Tutorials** – A clear and structured learning path, breaking down complex concepts into actionable steps.

✔ **Advanced Techniques & Industry Insights** – Practical guidance on professional workflows used in animation, visual effects, and game development.

✔ **Comprehensive Coverage of Blender 4.4's New Features** – Stay up to date with the latest enhancements and improvements.

✔ **Efficient Workflow Strategies** – Master shortcuts, optimizations, and productivity techniques to enhance your creative process.

✔ **Real-World Applications** – Whether for **3D modeling, rendering, animation, or VFX**, gain the skills to apply Blender in professional projects.

Blender is more than just a tool; it is a powerful platform for **creative professionals, game designers, animators, and 3D artists**. This book ensures that **whether you are starting fresh or refining your expertise, you will have a comprehensive, professional, and structured guide** to **unlocking the full potential of Blender 4.4**.

Now is the time to take your 3D skills to the next level—are you ready to master Blender?

CHAPTER 1
OVERVIEW OF BLENDER

Animators, designers, and artists all utilize Blender, an open-source 3D creation program, to give life to their imaginative visions. You can create, shape, and animate objects for use in films, games, architecture, art, and even virtual reality projects. It's like having your digital workshop. The ability to work in three dimensions is fundamental to Blender, allowing you to simulate real-world lighting, shadows, and textures while also creating realistic objects that can be viewed from any angle and rotated. Blender stands out because of its versatility. It is an all-in-one tool that can build the shape of an object, animate it, and then render it. Moreover, it can handle advanced tasks like video editing and visual effects.

The main features of Blender are as follows:

1. **3D Modeling:** Shapes and structures can be created using 3D modeling. Whether it's an automobile, a person, or a structure, Blender equips you with the means to shape and mold these ideas through processes such as extruding (the act of stretching a surface to add depth) and sculpting (the act of molding clay).
2. **Animation:** After you've made a model, you can give it movement to give it life. Animation of a character's gait, expressions on their face, or even the bouncing of a ball could fall under this category.
3. **Texturing and Materials:** Blender lets you give your objects color, pattern, and surface features. You can give something the sheen of metal, the smoothness of linen, or the roughness of stone.
4. **Rendering:** Rendering is the last step in creating a final product from your 3D scene. The in-built rendering engines of Blender, such as Cycles and Eevee, mimic real-world lighting and shadows to give your projects a polished appearance.
5. **Physics and Simulations:** Blender can mimic real-world effects like fire, smoke, water, and cloth. Think of a seaside scene with crashing waves or a windswept flag as some examples.
6. **Video Editing:** To put your animations and clips together, you don't need any additional software. Cut, arrange, and add effects to your videos using Blender's video editor.
7. **Visual Effects (VFX):** Blender can be used to add effects like explosions or even integrate 3D components with live-action video if you are working on films or media projects.
8. **Game Design and VR:** Blender is also commonly used to make VR and game assets. It works with programs that let you create dynamic worlds and then export your models to game engines like Unity or Unreal.

The fact that anyone can use Blender is one of its many outstanding features. You can use it for free because it's open source, and it has a large community of artists and developers who work on making it better and sharing what they've learned. There is always someone online to help you out, so even if you're just starting, you won't be alone.

The extensive set of tools and capabilities in Blender gives it a reputation for a steep first learning curve. Nevertheless, it turns out to be a very useful tool if you master the fundamentals. People in small studios creating indie games and movies utilize it, as do professionals at major companies creating box office hits. Blender is an all-in-one solution that offers everything you need to make 3D art, from basic models to intricate animations and simulations.

Blender 4.4 Key Updates and New Features

The Blender Foundation has officially launched the first beta builds of **Blender 4.4**, the next iteration of its powerful open-source 3D software used in **VFX, animation, game development, and visualization**. Unlike previous versions, which introduced groundbreaking features like **Eevee Next in Blender 4.2** and **Grease Pencil 3 in Blender 4.3**, this update focuses primarily on **workflow improvements and bug fixes** rather than major new tools.

That said, **Blender 4.4** still brings notable enhancements. We've highlighted five key updates, including **refinements to animation tools, a complete overhaul of the compositor, and crucial bug fixes** that improve stability and performance.

Additionally, at the end of this article, you'll find a **roundup of updates** across other essential toolsets, including **sculpting, Geometry Nodes, the Cycles and Eevee renderers, and the Video Sequencer**.

Blender 4.4 is set for an official release in **March**, and while minor tweaks may still be made, no major features are expected to be added before the final version rolls out. Stay tuned for updates!

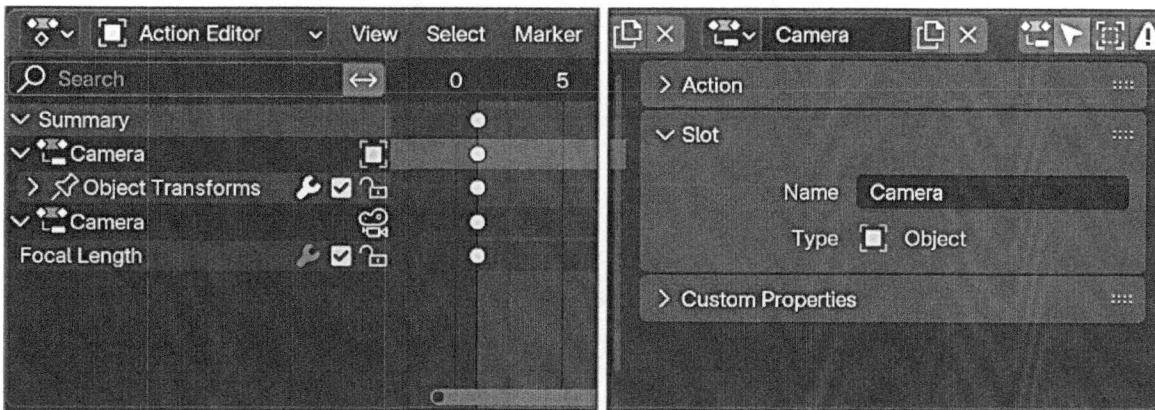

Blender 4.4 introduces a **revamped structure** for **Action data-blocks**, which are responsible for storing animation data. In this new system, each Action can now have multiple **Slots**, allowing for a more organized and flexible way to manage animation.

For instance, in the example provided, the **Action** contains **two Slots**: one assigned to the **Camera Object** and another linked to the **Camera Data**. This separation enhances clarity and makes it easier to manage complex animations, particularly when dealing with objects that have multiple animated properties.

1. Animation: Slotted Actions Streamline Workflow

Blender 4.4 brings **a major structural update** to animation by **introducing Slots in Actions**, the data-blocks used to store animation data. This enhancement allows a **single Action to hold multiple types of animation data**, offering greater flexibility and control.

For example, an object that **moves while changing color** can now have **separate slots** for **position** and **material animation**, making complex animations **easier to manage and edit**. This improvement is particularly useful for **cameras**, where different slots can be assigned to **camera movement and lens settings**, as well as for **materials**, where the material itself and its **shader node tree** can have distinct slots.

Additionally, Blender 4.4 introduces the ability to **merge animations from multiple objects into a single Action** or **split an Action into multiple slots**, providing **more control and flexibility** when animating complex scenes.

This update is a key step in the **Animation 2025 Project**, Blender's ongoing effort to modernize its **character rigging and animation tools**. While the original proposal aimed to replace Actions with a new **Animation data-block type**, the introduction of **Slots** has proven to be an effective evolution of the existing system.

To support this change, Blender 4.4 also introduces a **new Python API**. However, it's important to note that **this update is not fully backward-compatible**, though existing **.blend files will be automatically converted** when imported into Blender 4.4.

Backend	Test	Duration
OpenGL	Cold start (no subprocesses)	1:47
OpenGL	Warm start (no subprocesses)	0:06
OpenGL	Cold start (8 subprocesses)	0:56
OpenGL	Warm start (8 subprocesses)	0:06
Vulkan	Cold start	0:30
Vulkan	Warm start	0:03

Although the **new Vulkan backend**—designed for **real-time rendering**—is still classified as an **experimental feature** in **Blender 4.4**, its **performance has notably improved** compared to the default **OpenGL backend**. These enhancements bring **better efficiency and responsiveness**, making Vulkan a more viable option for future Blender updates.

2. Viewport Rendering: Major Performance Boost for Vulkan Backend

The **Vulkan backend**, first introduced in **Blender 4.1** for **UI and viewport rendering**, receives a **significant upgrade in Blender 4.4**, delivering **better performance, stability, and compatibility**.

One of the most noticeable improvements is in **startup times**. When opening a scene, **Vulkan now loads the viewport up to 5x faster than OpenGL on a cold start** and **2x faster on a warm start**, making the workflow much more responsive.

Additionally, Vulkan is now used to **display the rendered output of Cycles**, Blender's high-end production renderer. However, it does **not yet run Cycles itself**, as Blender's official documentation still considers this "not viable."

Despite these improvements, Vulkan remains an **experimental feature**. While it supports **older GPUs—** including **NVIDIA's GTX 900 Series (2015) and AMD's Radeon 400 Series (2016) on Windows and Linux—** it still **lacks support** for essential features like **OpenXR and OpenSubdiv**, and **animation performance requires further optimization**.

As development continues, Vulkan's enhanced **efficiency and speed** position it as a promising **future default** for Blender's real-time rendering pipeline.

New 4.4 CPU Compositor

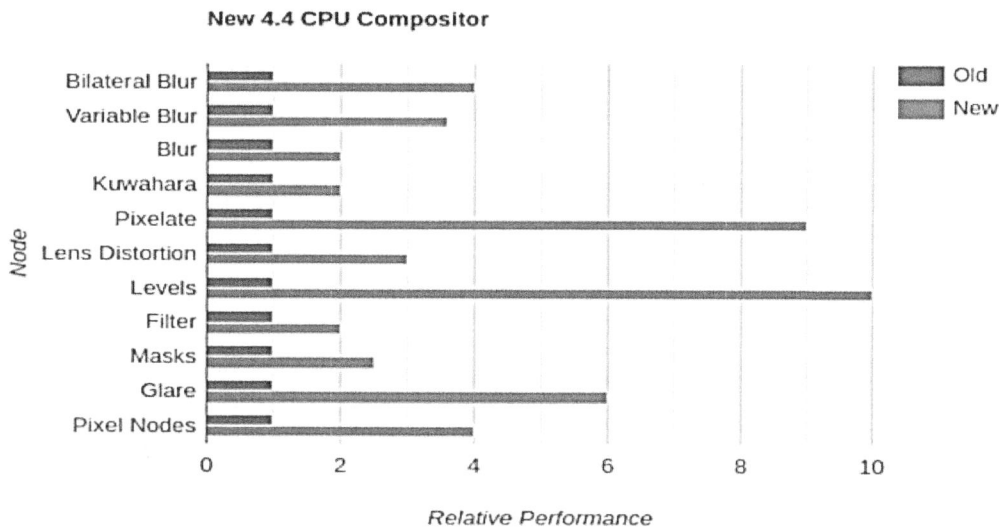

The CPU Compositor has been rewritten in Blender 4.4, improving the performance of key nodes, and revamping the Glare node used to add glows and lens flares to images.

3. Compositing: Faster CPU Processing and an Enhanced Glare Node

Blender 4.4 brings a **major rewrite** to its **CPU Compositor**, the original compositing system (not to be confused with the **Viewport Compositor** introduced in **Blender 3.5**). While this overhaul lays the groundwork for future development, it also delivers **immediate speed improvements**, making compositing workflows **much faster and more efficient**.

Key compositor nodes, including **Blur, Filter, and Mask nodes**, now operate **2–10x faster**, significantly reducing processing time for complex scenes.

Additionally, the **Glare node**—responsible for adding **lens flares and glow effects**—has been **redesigned for better usability**, offering **more refined control** and improved results. For an in-depth breakdown of these enhancements, **VFX artist Rob Dickinson** has shared a detailed overview on his **Decoded YouTube channel**.

These upgrades make **Blender's compositing pipeline more powerful**, setting the stage for even more **performance optimizations and feature expansions** in future versions.

VFX REFERENCE PLATFORM

Blender 4.4 updates key libraries, including OpenColorIO, OpenEXR and OpenVDB, to match the new CY2025 specification for the VFX Reference Platform.

4. Pipeline Integration: CY2025 Compliance for VFX Workflows

For **visual effects and animation studios**, a crucial update in **Blender 4.4** is its **full compliance with the CY2025 specification** for the **VFX Reference Platform**.

This industry-standard specification, overseen by the **Visual Effects Society**, ensures that all tools used in professional **VFX production pipelines** rely on the **same versions of key software libraries**, improving compatibility and stability across different applications.

Although the **Blender Foundation** had previously considered moving away from the **VFX Reference Platform**, it ultimately reversed course in **2022**, restoring full compliance with **Blender 4.0**. Now, with **Blender 4.4**, the software remains aligned with industry expectations, making it easier for studios to integrate Blender into their **existing production pipelines** without compatibility issues.

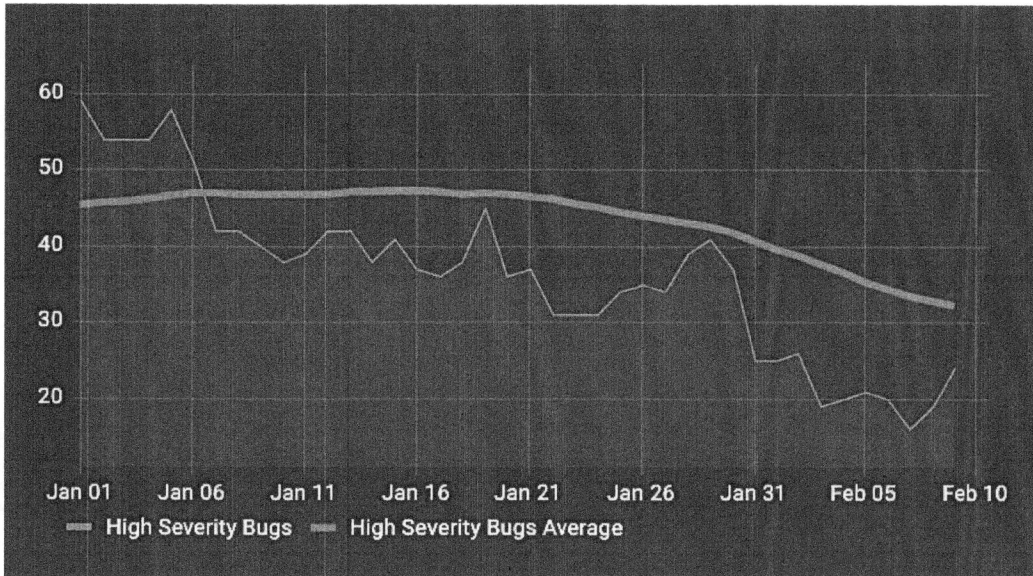

A key focus during the development of Blender 4.4 has simply been to fix bugs, with more than 500 reported issues fixed during January 2025 alone.

5. Bug Fixes: Stability and Refinement Across the Board

One of the **main priorities** for **Blender 4.4** wasn't to introduce **groundbreaking new tools**, but rather to **fine-tune existing features**—which is why **bug fixes** are one of the biggest highlights of this release.

As part of the **'Winter of Quality' initiative**, Blender's development team focused on improving stability and reliability. According to a recent **Blender Developer Blog post**, **over 500 reported issues were fixed in January alone**.

Among the areas receiving the most attention:

- **Grease Pencil**, Blender's **2D animation and storyboarding tool**, saw the highest number of fixes, following its **major overhaul in Blender 4.3**.
- The **user interface, viewport, and Geometry Nodes framework** each received **over 70 fixes**, improving overall usability and performance.

With this focus on **polishing and refining Blender's core functionality**, Blender 4.4 delivers a **smoother, more stable** experience—setting a strong foundation for future updates.

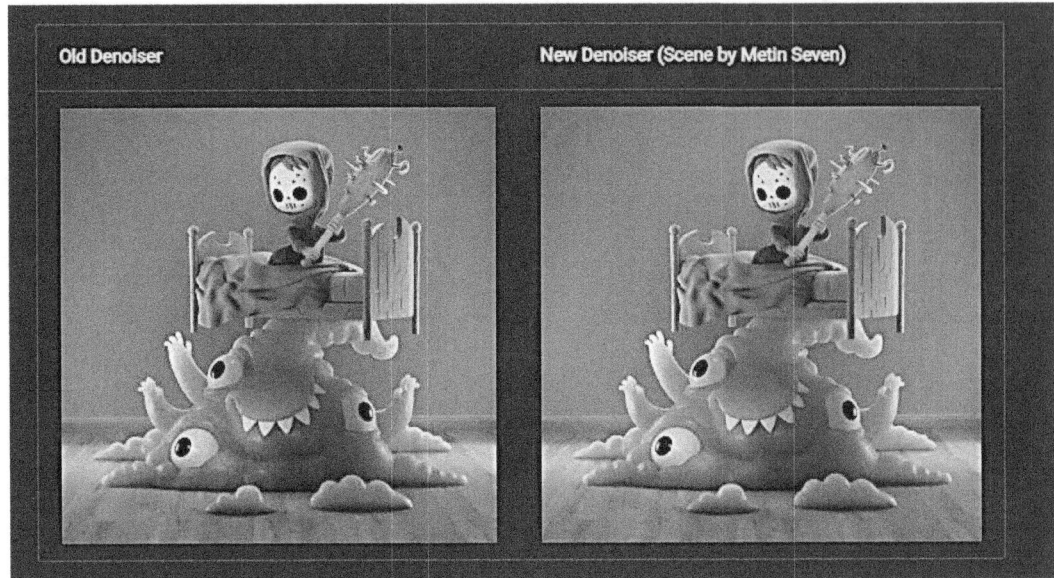

Changes to Blender's other key toolsets in Blender 4.4 include an update to the OptiX denoiser used in the Cycles render engine, improving consistency of denoising on NVIDIA GPUs.

Other Key Updates Across Blender's Toolsets

Blender 4.4 isn't just about **workflow improvements and bug fixes**—it also brings **refinements** to various key toolsets, making the software **more intuitive, efficient, and powerful**. Here's what's new:

- **User Interface (UI) Enhancements**

  - Updates to **UI fonts, tooltips, common panels, and dialogs** for a smoother experience.
  - The **Status Bar now highlights warnings** for common issues, such as **negative scale values** on objects.

- **3D Modeling Improvements**

  - New options to **select all three- and five-pole vertices** in a mesh.
  - Improved **'Join Tris to Quads'** function, now favoring a more even **quad grid topology**.

- **Sculpting Updates**

  - The **Flatten, Fill, and Scrape** brushes have been merged into a **single, more versatile 'Plane' brush**.

- **Geometry Nodes & Physics Enhancements**

  - New **Collection and Object input nodes** for better workflow integration.

- **Character Rigging & Animation**

  - **Bone collections** now mirror properly when **symmetrizing an armature**.
  - The **Pose Library** can now **export pose assets as external libraries,** making it easier to **reuse animations across projects**.

- **Cycles Renderer Updates**

  - Now uses an **updated version of NVIDIA's OptiX denoiser,** improving **denoising consistency—** especially for users with **older GPU drivers**.

- **Grease Pencil (2D Animation)**

  - Restores **features that were removed** during the **Blender 4.3 overhaul,** improving the 2D animation experience.

- **Video Sequencer Improvements**

  - Now supports **H.265/HEVC video codec,** an industry-standard format for **high-quality video compression**.
  - Supports **10- and 12-bit-per-channel video formats** (though **HDR video handling isn't fully implemented yet**).
  - Videos rendered from Blender now explicitly use the **BT.709 color space,** ensuring **proper HDTV compatibility**.

- **Pipeline Integration & USD Enhancements**

  - **AAC audio format** is now supported.

  - Improved **USD export workflows,** including:
    - **Better handling of animated volumes & instanced non-mesh objects** (e.g., point clouds, curves).
    - **Support for displacement in UsdPreviewSurface,** enhancing shading in USD-based projects.

With these updates, **Blender 4.4** further refines both **creative and technical workflows,** making it a **more robust tool for artists, animators, and VFX professionals alike.** 🚀

System Requirements and Installation

Make sure your computer can run Blender smoothly before installing it. Even though Blender can function on relatively low-end hardware, upgrading will allow you to run more complicated and large-scale projects without stuttering or crashing. Everything you'll need is outlined below:

Minimum Requirements

These specs allow you to run Blender, but you might experience slower performance with detailed projects:

- **Operating System:** Windows 8.1, macOS 10.13, or any Linux-based system with updated libraries.
- **Processor:** Dual-core 64-bit processor (2 GHz).
- **RAM:** At least 4 GB (8 GB is recommended for practical use).
- **Graphics Card:** A GPU with at least 1 GB of video memory, supporting OpenGL 4.4or higher.
- **Storage:** 500 MB of free disk space for installation.
- **Monitor Resolution:** 1280x768 pixels.

Recommended Requirements

For a smoother experience, especially if you're working with animations or detailed simulations:

- **Operating System:** Windows 10 or 11, macOS 11.0+, or Linux with newer kernels.
- **Processor:** Quad-core or higher, with support for AVX (Advanced Vector Extensions).
- **RAM:** 16 GB or more.
- **Graphics Card:** A dedicated GPU like NVIDIA GeForce GTX 10-series or AMD Radeon RX-series with at least 4 GB VRAM. NVIDIA RTX cards are ideal for faster rendering with CUDA or OptiX.
- **Storage:** An SSD for faster project load and save time.
- **Monitor Resolution:** Full HD (1920x1080) or higher for better workspace visibility.

For Advanced Users

If you're working on very large projects, heavy simulations, or professional-grade animations, aim for:

- 32 GB or more of RAM.
- High-end GPUs like NVIDIA RTX 30/40-series or AMD Radeon RX 7000-series.
- Multi-core CPUs like AMD Ryzen Threadripper or Intel Xeon processors.

Installing Blender

You can proceed with the installation of Blender now that you know your PC is capable of running it:

1. **Download Blender**
- Visit https://www.blender.org, the official Blender website.
- The website will recognize your operating system automatically when you click the **Download** button.

- Just scroll down to the options if you're looking for a particular version or OS.
2. **Choose the Installation Type**

You can install Blender in two primary ways:

- **Installer Version (Standard):** This is the most typical option. Just like any other program, it installs Blender and adds shortcuts to your system.
- **Portable Version:** If you'd rather not install Blender on your computer, you can get the portable version by downloading the ZIP file. You can now launch Blender without installing it at all by running it directly from the folder.
3. **Install Blender (Standard Method)**
- Open the installation file after the download is complete (it will typically be located in your Downloads folder).
- Pick a location to install Blender by following the on-screen prompts. It will usually end up in the Program Files folder on your computer.
- In only a few minutes, when you click **Install**, the procedure should be complete.
4. **Run Blender**
- The Blender icon will appear on your Windows desktop or start menu after installation. Press it to launch the application. When you initially start Blender, it may prompt you to set up some defaults, like a theme and keymap. This is optional; you can modify it or skip it entirely.
5. **(Optional) Update Your Drivers**
- Outdated graphics drivers are usually at blame when Blender crashes or runs poorly. For the most up-to-date drivers, visit the official website of your graphics processing unit (GPU) manufacturer, be it NVIDIA, AMD, or Intel.

For Portable Version Users

- Use an archive extractor such as WinRAR, 7-Zip, or the one that comes with macOS or Linux to unpack the ZIP file that you downloaded.
- Open the extracted folder and double-click the blender.exe file (or the equivalent file for macOS/Linux).
- You can move this folder anywhere on your computer or even run Blender from a USB drive.

Additional Tips

- **Check for Updates:** Blender is always getting updates that add new features and repair bugs. Under **Help > Check for Updates**, you can check for updates right inside the program.
- **Addons and Plugins:** There are a plethora of add-ons and plugins available for Blender that extend its capability. There is a Preferences menu item where you can activate these.
- **Community Help:** Blender is a vibrant community that is always willing to lend a hand if you run into problems. If you're looking for assistance, you can get it on Blender Artists or the Blender subreddit.

CHAPTER 2
GETTING STARTED
Navigating the Blender Interface

The Blender window will resemble the image below after you have started Blender and dismissed the Splash Screen.

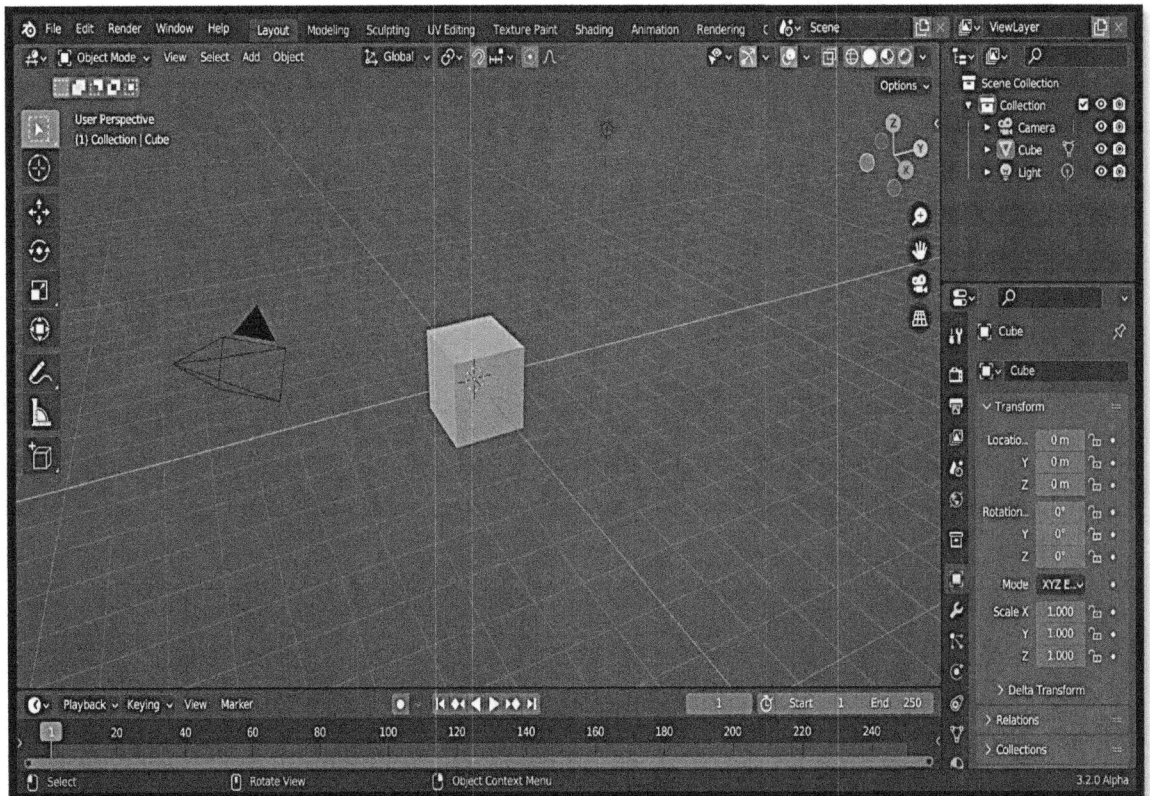

There are primarily three sections to the Blender interface:

- **Top bar**: The main menu, which can be used for several tasks including rendering, saving, importing and exporting files, and setting up preferences, is located in the top bar at the very top.
- **Areas**: The central areas, which serve as the primary workspace
- **Status Bar:** The status bar below gives you suggestions for handy shortcuts and shows you relevant facts.

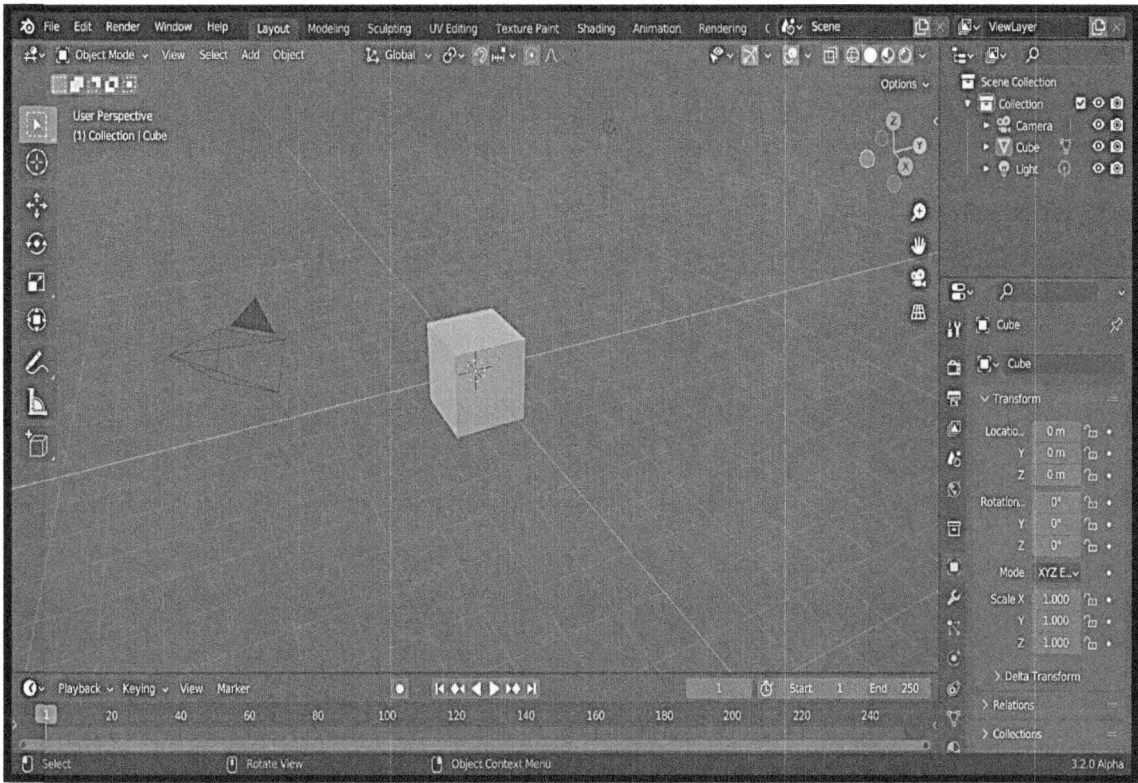

Splash Screen

The splash screen will be front and center in Blender as you open it. You can start fresh projects or access ones you've already finished using it.

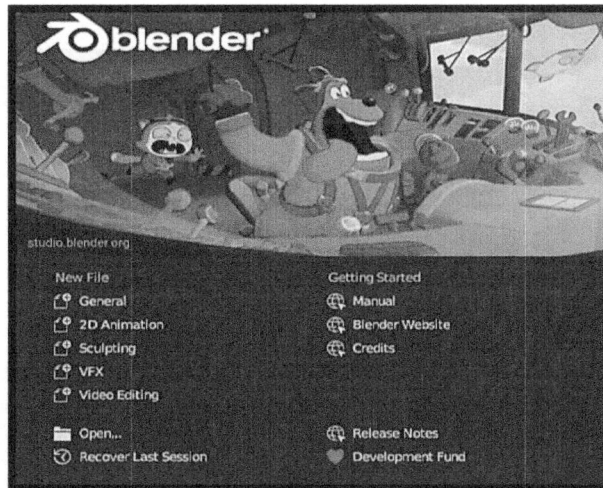

You can start a new project by clicking anywhere outside the splash screen in Blender's window or by using the **Esc key**. As soon as the splash screen disappears, the default screen will be shown. For a quick return to the splash screen, simply click the **Blender icon** in the top bar and then choose the **Splash Screen** option. One feature of Blender's **"interactive region"** is a Quick setup process that is available on the initial launch or installation of new versions.

- **Splash Image:** The splash image and the Blender version are both visible in the top right corner of the splash screen.
- **Interactive Region:** The interactive region is located in the lower portion of the splash screen.
- **New File**: Start a fresh project by utilizing a template that has already been designed.
- **Recent Files**: Blend files that you have recently opened are listed here. You may easily and quickly access your most recent projects in this way.
- **Open**: Enables the option to open a pre-existing blend-file.
- **Recover Last Session:** Blender tries to retrieve the last session by utilizing temporary files.
- **Donate**: Blender's Development Fund can be accessed on their website.
- **What's New**: View the notes from the latest release.

Top Bar
Menu Options

Blender Menu

Splash Screen: It opens the Splash Screen.

About Blender

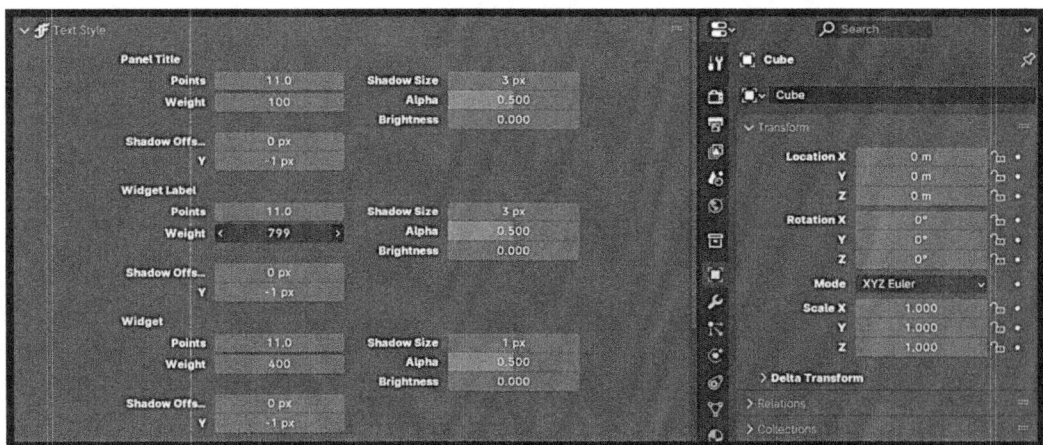

Presenting a menu that highlights Blender's detailed information:

- **Version**: The Blender version.
- **Date**: The date of compilation for Blender.
- **Git Hash**: The unique identifier of the build. This can help provide support personnel when troubleshooting an issue.
- **Branch**: You can include an optional branch name.
- **Windowing Environment:** The Linux version of Blender will display either Wayland or X11, depending on the windowing environment it is running on.
- **Donate**: Consider donating to the Blender Development Fund by visiting their website.
- **What's New**: Check out the latest release notes for updates?
- **Credits**: Open the credits webpage.
- **License**: visit the license webpage for more information.
- **Install Application Template**: Install a new application template.

File Menu

Here are the available file management options:

- **New Ctrl-N:** Press **Ctrl-N** to create a new document.
- **Open Ctrl-O**: Opens a blend-file.
- **Open Recent Shift-Ctrl-O**: Pressing **Shift+Ctrl+O** brings up a list of all the blend files that have been opened recently. A preview and information about the blend-file will be shown when you hover over things. To open the blend-file, choose it from the list.

Remove Recent Files List

Clears the list of all items.

Revert

Reopens the current file to its most recent saved version.

Recover

Recover Last Session

- This opens a blend-file that Blender saves automatically before closing. For example, if you close Blender by accident, you can restore your prior work session using this feature.

Recover AutoSave

- Retrieving a file that was stored automatically.

Save Ctrl-S

- Save the current blend-file.

Save Incremental Ctrl-Alt-S

- Ensure that the current **Blender file** is saved with a name that is incremented numerically, avoiding any potential overwriting of existing files.

Save As... Shift-Ctrl-S

- Starts the File Browser where you can choose the name of the file and where to save it.

Save Copy…

- Saves a copy of the current file.

Link

- Establishes a connection between the desired one and data stored in an external blend-file (library). Only the external library can be used for editing that data. You can use Append and Link to bring in parts of another file one by one.

Append

- It incorporates data from an external blend-file into the existing one. After being transferred from the external file, the new data is now fully autonomous from it.

Data Previews

- Tools that allow for the efficient management of previews of data blocks.

Import

- Blender can use data from numerous file types generated by different graphics tools.

Export

- The option to export your work to a format that is compatible with other graph graphics tools is available. Work is often saved in a blend-file.

Automatically pack into .blend

- This function makes the file compression feature available. When this option is turned on, any external files will be included in the blend-file with each save.

Pack all into .blend

- Include all used external files within the blend-file.

Unpack Into Files

- Save each compressed file separately after extracting it from this blend-file.

Make All Paths Relative

- Make sure that the current blend-file is the starting point for any relative paths to external files.

Make All Paths Absolute

- Make sure that any path pointing to external files is absolute, which means that it includes the complete path starting from the root of the system.

Report Missing Files

- You can use this function to check if there are any links to unpacked files that might not be available anymore. When you select this option, a warning notice will be shown in the Info editor's header. It means that all external files are there and taken care of if no warning is shown.

Locate Lost Documents

- With the help of this guide, you can fix the problem of broken links in a blend-file. It will bring up a file browser. If you select a directory or a file inside it, a search will be run over all the directories it contains. The search will result in the restoration of all missing files. Absolute pathways will be used to accomplish recoveries. **Make All pathways Relative** is the option to select to employ relative pathways.

It may be necessary to reload restored files. To achieve this, you can either reload each external file one by one or save the blend-file and then reload it to make sure everything is reloaded at once.

Clean Up

Unused Data-Blocks

- Eliminate any unnecessary data-blocks from both the current blend-file and any Linked Data. This action cannot be reversed.

Recursive Unused Data-Blocks

- Remove any data blocks that are not needed from the current blend file and any linked data. This includes data blocks that are used indirectly, including those that are only utilized by data blocks that are not currently being used.

Unused Linked Data-Blocks

- Eliminate any unused data-blocks exclusively from Linked Data.

Recursive Unused Linked Data-Blocks

- Get rid of any data blocks that aren't needed from the Linked Data, even those that are indirectly utilized but depend on other blocks that aren't being used.

Defaults

Save Startup File

- Save the current blend-file as the startup file.

Load Factory Settings

- Resets the default startup file and preferences.

The following operators are shown when an application template is used:

Load Default Settings for Blender

- Restores the default settings to the original Blender configuration, disregarding any modifications made from the current application template.

Quit Ctrl-Q

- Close Blender. Blender will save the current scene to a file called "**quit.blend**" in the program's temporary directory. On the "**File Paths**" tab of the Preferences, you can see where the temporary directory is located.

Edit Menu

- **Undo, Redo, Undo History:** Undo, redo, and access your undo history.
- **Adjust Last Operation, Repeat Last, Repeat History**: Make adjustments to the previous operation, repeat the last action, or revisit the entire history of actions.
- **Menu Search:** Locate a menu by its name.
- **Operator Search**: Perform an operator based on its name.
- **Rename Active Item:** Change the name of the active object or node.
- **Batch Rename**: Batch Rename tool allows you to conveniently rename multiple data types simultaneously.

Lock Object Modes

Ensures that only objects in the current mode can be selected. Unintended mode changes can be prevented with this feature. For instance, it stops you from accidentally going to Object Mode when you pick a background object in Pose Mode instead of a bone. In cases where you need to weigh rigged objects or participate in sculpting/painting while switching between objects in different modes, disabling **Lock Object Modes** can be handy.

Preferences Ctrl-Comma

- Access the Preferences window.

Render Menu

- **Render Image F12**: Carry out the rendering procedure for the active scene's current frame.
- **Render Animation Ctrl-F12**: Complete the animation for the current scene.
- **Audio Rendering**: Expertly combine the sounds of the scene into a high-quality sound file.
- **View Render F11**: Brings up the Render window. (To go back to Blender's main window, press again.)
- **View Animation Ctrl-F11**: View the rendered animation in a special player.
- **Lock Interface:** It is advised to lock the interface when rendering to provide the renderer with extra memory.

Window Menu

- **Next Workspace:** Move to the next workspace.
- **Previous Workspace:** Go back to the previous workspace.
- **Show Status Bar:** Decide if you want to display the Status Bar at the bottom of the window.
- **Save Screenshot**: Take a photo of the current Blender window. A file browser will open for you to select the destination for saving the screenshot.
- **Save Screenshot (Editor):** Take a photo of the chosen editor. Click within the area of the Editor after running the operator to select it. A file browser will open to select the destination for saving the screenshot.

Workspaces

Users will appreciate the ease with which this collection of tabs allows them to switch between Workspaces and the many window styles they offer.

Scenes & Layers

Users can select the current Scene and View Layer from these data-block options.

Status Bar

The Blender window's Status Bar can be accessed from the bottom. Messages, statistics, and keyboard shortcuts are all part of the contextual information it offers. The Status Bar can be hidden by dragging it down from the top border or by deactivating the option to Show the Status Bar in the Window menu.

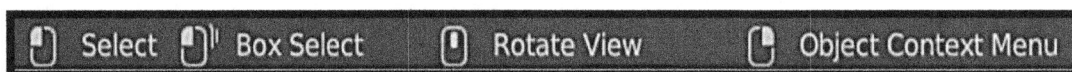

Keymap Information

The Status Bar on the left side provides information about mouse button shortcuts and the keymap of the active tool. When utilizing editors with a toolbar, you can quickly switch between tools by pressing **Alt** (or **Option** on macOS), which is located on the toolbar. Adjusting the **Alt Click Tool Prompt preference** in the Keymap Preferences gives you the option to disable this functionality.

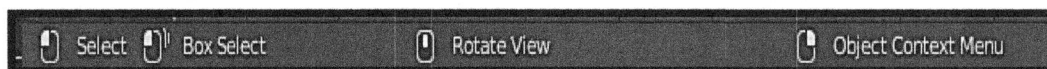

Status Messages

Messages regarding currently running processes are displayed in the Status Bar's central section.

- **Running Task:** Displays the current state of the running task, like rendering or baking. The progress bar will show you an estimated time when you move the mouse over it. To end the current action, just click the "**cancel**" button (the X icon).
- **Report Message**: After saving a file, for example, you may receive a report message that provides helpful information. They disappear after a short while. To see the full content in the Info Editor, click on the messages.

Setting Up Your Workspace

Workspaces provide an organized and productive work environment through the use of pre-arranged window layouts. Areas that hold Editors make up each Workspace, and each Workspace is tailored to a specific job, such as modeling, animation, or scripting. When working on a project, it's normal to move between different workspaces.

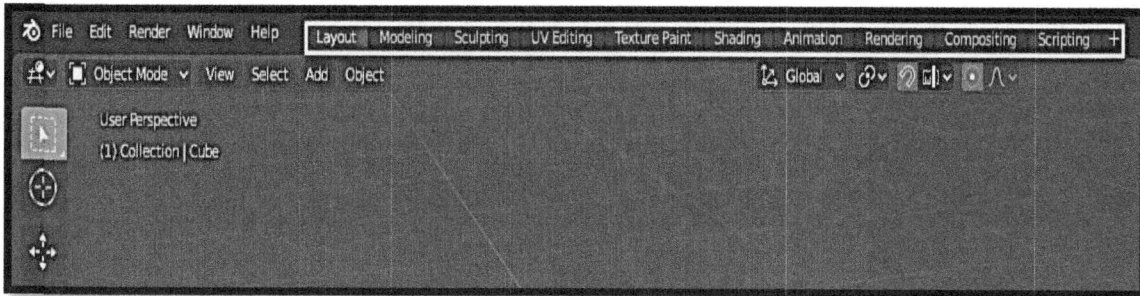

You can access workspaces from the top bar.

Controls

- **Tabs**: To switch between workspaces, click on the tabs. On top of that, you may use keyboard shortcuts like **Ctrl-PageUp** and **Ctrl-PageDown**. Renaming the workspace is as easy as double-clicking on a tab.
- **Add +:** Select the **Add button**.
- **Context menu RMB**: The context menu offers various options for duplicating, deleting, and reordering workspaces.

Default Workspaces

When you initially launch Blender, the main area will show the "**Layout**" workspace. **You can preview your scene with the use of this workspace's extensive range of editors:**

- The **3D Viewport** is located in the top left corner.
- **The Outliner** is located in the top right corner.
- **Properties** are located in the bottom right corner.
- **The timeline** is located at the bottom left.

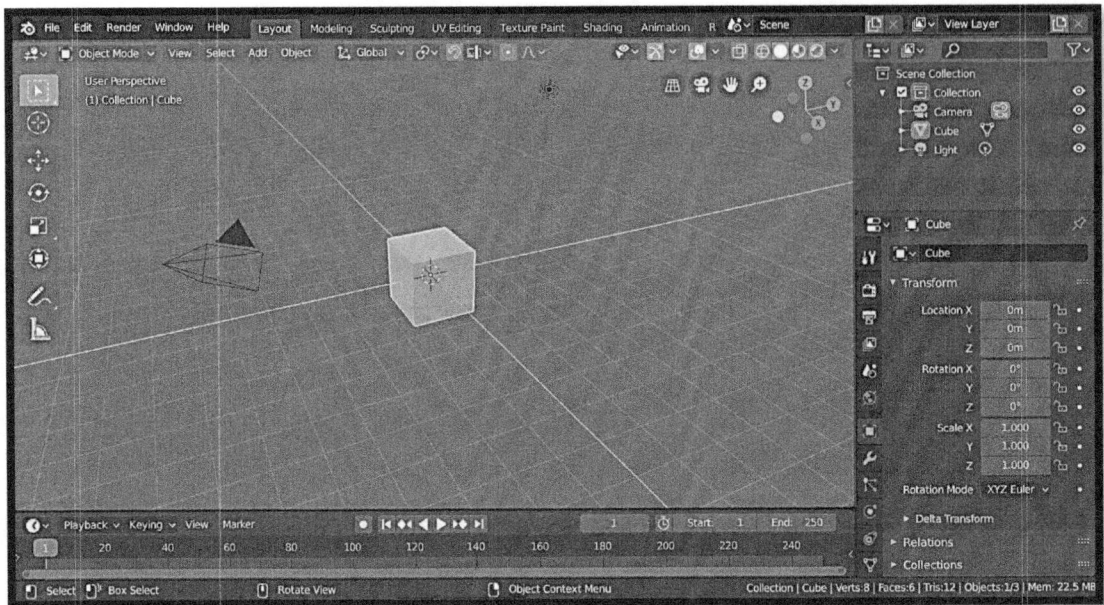

The **'Layout'** Workspace in Blender is designed to make your workflow more effective with its four editors. The 3D Viewport is highlighted in yellow, the Outliner in green, the Properties in blue, and the Timeline in red. **On top of that, Blender has many different workspaces already installed:**

- **Modeling**: For altering the shape using modeling tools.
- **Sculpting**: For enhancing meshes using sculpting tools.
- **UV Editing:** To convert the coordinates of picture textures to 3D surfaces.
- **Texture Paint**: To improve the look of image textures in the 3D Viewport.
- **Animation**: Animation is used to make objects' attributes change over time.
- **Rendering**: Created to see and analyze rendering outcomes.
- **Compositing**: For combining and manipulating images as well as modifying rendering data.
- **Scripting**: To make the most of the Python API in Blender and to create scripts.

Additional Workspaces

While making a new Workspace in Blender, you have a few more options to choose from:

- **2D Animation**: A versatile workspace for using Grease Pencil.
- **2D Full Canvas**: It's like "**2D Animation**" but with a much larger canvas.

VFX

- **Masking**: The production of 2D masks for use in compositing or video editing is the specialty of masking.
- **Motion Tracking**: To accurately calculate camera motion and stabilize video footage smoothly.

Video Editing

- **Video Editing:** For putting together different types of media into a unified whole.
- **Save and Override:** The workspaces are stored in the blend-file. When opening a file, selecting Load UI in the File Browser will instruct Blender to use the file's screen layout instead of the current one. You have the option to save a personalized collection of workspaces as part of the Defaults.

Regions

Different sections make up each Editor in Blender. Tabs and panels are tiny structural elements that can be used to organize regions. These panels and tabs can hold widgets, controls, and buttons.

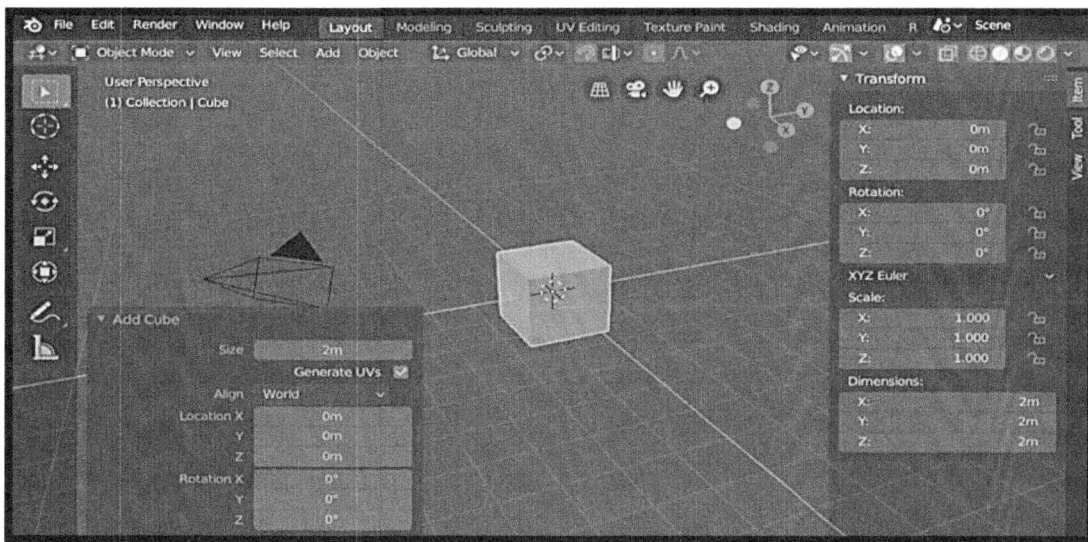

The 3D Viewport's Sidebar and the Adjust Last Operation panel will be shown in the regions after you add a Cube.

Main Region

One region is always visible. All import actions occur in the Main region, which is the editor's main emphasis. Every editor serves a particular purpose, resulting in discrepancies in their primary focus and the availability of extra features.

Header

Usually seen at the top or bottom of an area, a header is a tiny horizontal strip. The header of any editor provides a handy location to put menus and tools that are used often. Whatever editor you're using, as well as the object and mode you choose, will determine the layout of the menus and buttons.

Context Menu

When you right-click on a header, a context menu will appear, giving you plenty of options:

- **Show Header**: Toggle the display of the header on or off. Just click or drag the little arrow that shows up at the top or bottom right of the editor to reveal a concealed header again.
- **Show Tool Settings**: Enables or disables the display of the Tool Settings.
- **Show Menus:** The "Show Menus" option lets you switch the menus' collapsed and expanded states.
- **Flip to Bottom/Top:** Choose the position of the header or Tool Settings in the editor: either at the top or bottom.
- **Horizontal/Vertical Split**: With the Horizontal/Vertical Split feature, a professional indicator line is shown, making it easy to choose the area and position where you want to split. To toggle between horizontal and vertical orientation, press the tab key.
- **Toolbar**: The tool bar, which is situated on the left side of the editor area, has several interactive features. Holding down the T key will make the Toolbar visible or invisible.
- **Tool Settings:** An added element of the editor is a horizontal bar at the top or bottom that resembles the header. This section provides access to the many currently selected tool parameters. Replicating the header's context menu capabilities may be moved and hidden.
- **Adjust Last Operation:** The ability to fine-tune an operator after it has been executed is provided by the option to adjust the last operation. If you've inserted a cube, for example, you can change its size using this space.
- **Sidebar**: The Sidebar, located on the right side of the editor area, houses Panels that provide settings for objects within the editor and the editor itself. Pressing N will toggle the visibility of the Sidebar.
- **Footer**: Certain editors feature a bar, positioned either at the top or bottom of the editor area, which provides information regarding the active tool or operator.

Scrolling

Using the middle mouse button, you can drag a section to scroll it horizontally and vertically. You can also use the mouse wheel to scroll the region while hovering over it if it doesn't have a zoom level. Some scrollbars add additional control points for adjusting the region's vertical or horizontal range in specific places, like animation timelines. As shown in the image below, the special scrollbars will add widgets to the ends:

You can use this to show more or less detail within the available screen area by expanding or condensing the range. To easily change the displayed range, just drag one of the dots. Using **Ctrl-MMB**, you can simply drag the editor to change the range's horizontal and vertical dimensions.

Modifying the Dimensions and Hiding

Similar to how you would resize an Area, you can resize a region by moving its border. To hide a region, simply reduce its size until it becomes invisible. An undisclosed area reveals a small arrow symbol.

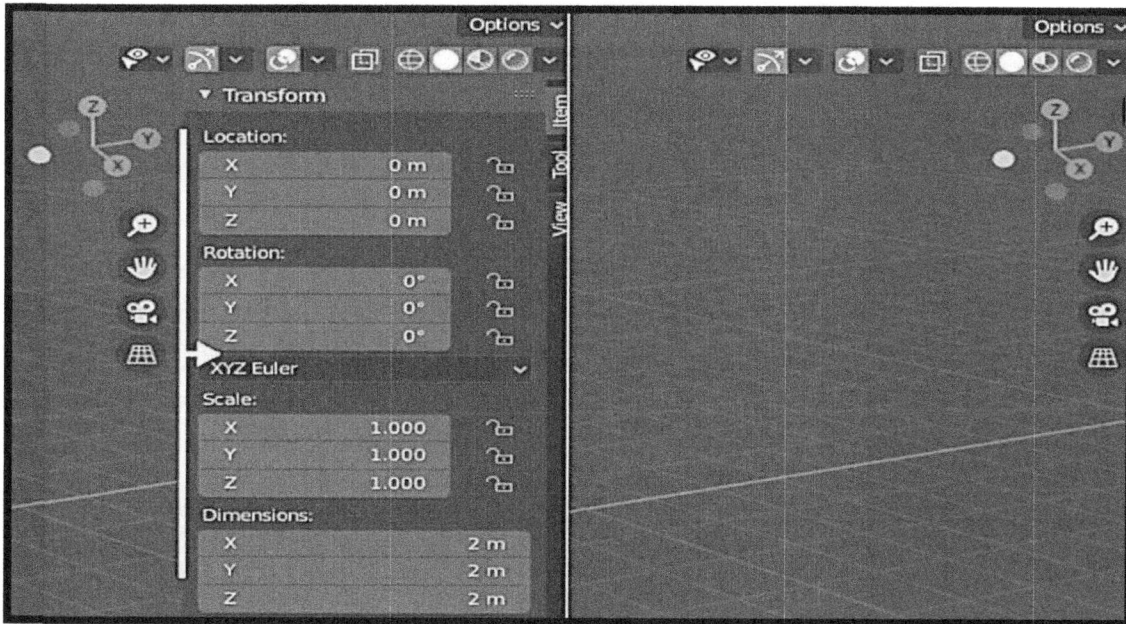

Scaling

You can resize certain parts of the screen, such as the Toolbar, by dragging them with **Ctrl-MMB** or by hovering the mouse over them and using **NumpadPlus** and **NumpadMinus**. To return the scale to its original defaults, press the **Home button**.

Asset Shelf

Search

Just put your search criteria into the search bar by hovering your mouse over the Asset Shelf and pressing Ctrl-F. The poses will be sorted according to your input.

Tabs

Catalogs can be displayed as separate tabs. Every tab will display only its content and the content of its sub-elements. It becomes effortless to narrow down to a specific group of assets.

Display Options

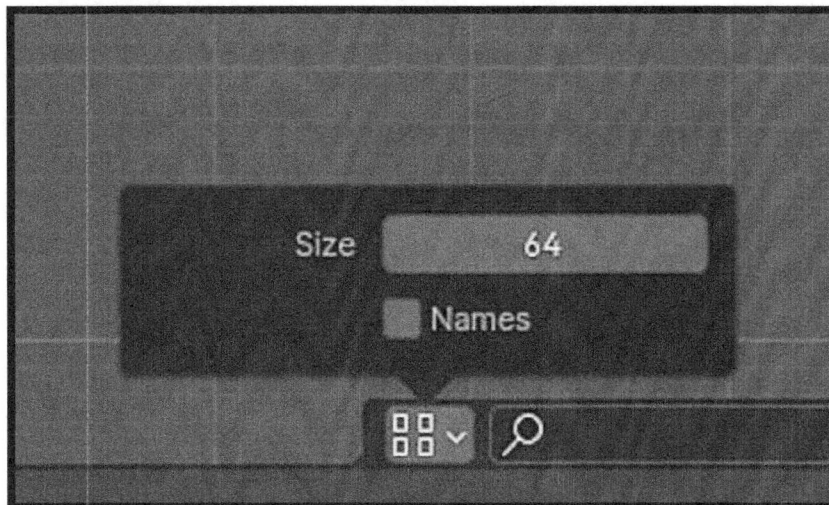

Utilizing the size attribute, one can modify the dimensions of the shelf's contents. Selecting the "**Names**" option will cause the shelf to show the asset names. Showcasing an item's name when you hover over it is another option. The typical feature of the shelf is its ability to hold one row of objects at a set height. Just drag the element's top edge to make it bigger and add extra rows.

Areas

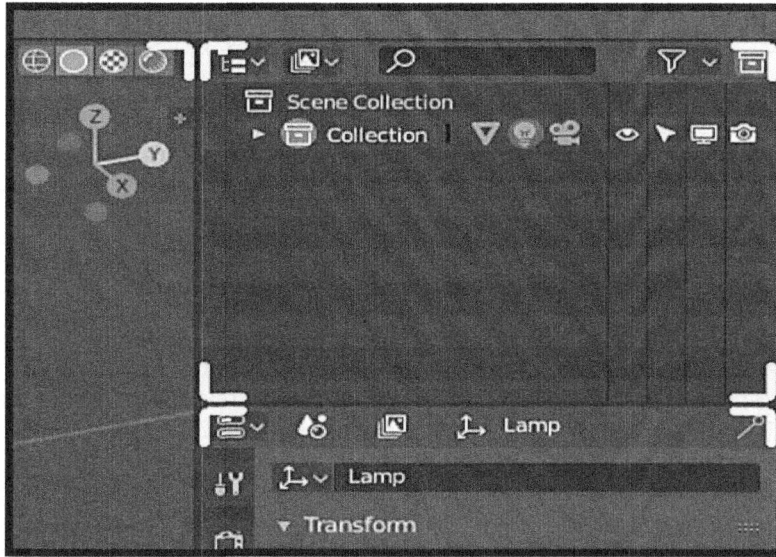

Areas are the rectangular sections that make up the Blender window. The 3D Viewport and the Outliner are examples of areas that give editors screen real estate. There is a distinct set of capabilities offered by each editor. Certain activities, including modeling and animation, are better suited to their own designated workspaces.

NOTE: Some keyboard shortcuts, such as saving with Ctrl-S, influence the whole Blender program. But most shortcuts change based on whatever editor the mouse is currently on.

Adjusting the Size

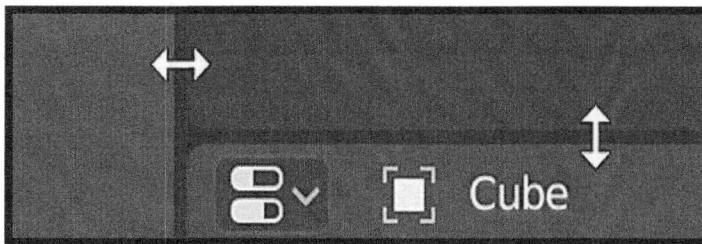

You can adjust the size of an area by dragging its edges with the left mouse button. When you move your mouse pointer across the boundary between two regions, you'll see the cursor change into a double-headed arrow. Next, move forward by clicking and dragging.

Splitting

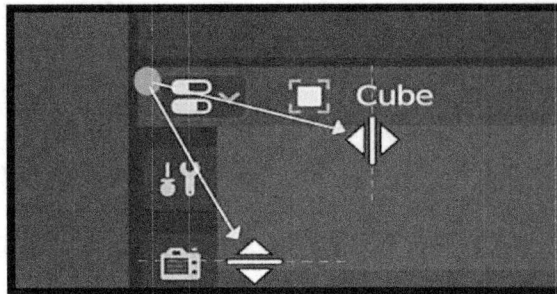

New territory will be created as a consequence of splitting an existing one. A cross (+) sign will appear when the mouse pointer is placed in a corner of the area. Here we can see that the left mouse button can be used to unite or divide the region. It will divide the area in half when you drag it from any corner to the middle. To define the split direction, drag the slider horizontally or vertically.

Joining

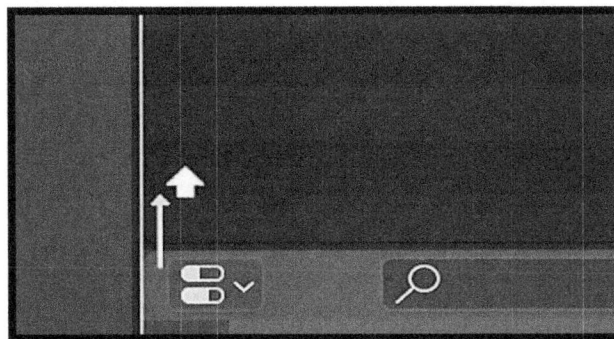

The two areas can be easily joined by dragging from one corner to the other. A black overlay indicates the area that will be evacuated. By dragging your mouse pointer over an area, you can select it to close. To complete the joining, let go of the left mouse button. When you right-click or press the Esc key before releasing the mouse button, the action will be stopped.

Area Options

When you right-click on the border, you will get access to the Area Options.

- **Horizontal/Vertical Split**: You may quickly choose the region and position for splitting with the help of a helpful indicator line when you use the horizontal/vertical split feature. To toggle between horizontal and vertical orientation, press the tab key.
- **Join Areas:** Displays the overlay for the join direction.
- **Swap Areas**: Exchanges this area with the neighboring one.

Duplicate Area into New Window

- Go to the View menu and select the option to duplicate the area into a new window.
- Create a new floating window by selecting **View**, then **Area**, and finally **Duplicate Area** into a new **Window**.
- The new window is functional and fits in with the current Blender instance without any problems. This can be useful in some situations, such as when using numerous displays.
- You may also make a new window by holding down the **Shift key** while left-clicking on a corner of the current area and dragging it slightly to the left or right.

Toggle Maximize Area

- Select **View > Area > Maximize Area**.
- **Shortcut (Ctrl-Spacebar):** By pressing the shortcut key combination of Ctrl and Spacebar, you can expand the area to encompass the entire window, preserving the visibility of the top bar and Status Bar. To restore the default size, you can either press the Back to Previous button on the top bar or press the keyboard shortcut again.

Toggle Fullscreen Area

- View the options in the "**View**" and "**Area**" menus. Enable **Fullscreen Area**.
- If you want to hide the editor's top bar, status bar, and other secondary sections, presses **Ctrl-Alt-Spacebar**. This will extend the area to fill the entire window. Use the shortcut key again, or click the icon in the Area's upper right corner (it becomes visible when you hover over it) to return to the default size.

Tabs and Panels

Tabs

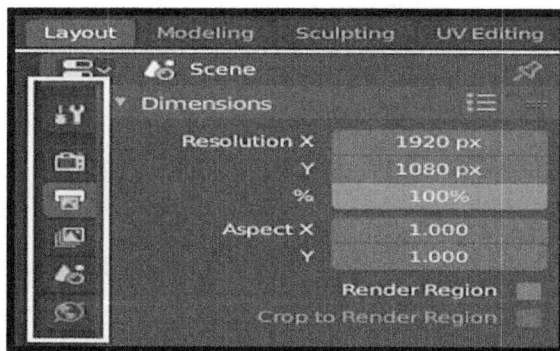

A horizontal tab appears as a header on the top bar. The Vertical Tab header displays the tab icons in the Properties. To handle portions that overlap in the user interface, tabs are frequently utilized. At any given time, only one Tab is visible. A tab header, which can be oriented either horizontally or vertically, contains the tabs.

Cycling/Switching

The Ctrl-Wheel shortcut makes switching between vertical tabs a breeze, so you can multitask with ease. The option to switch between tabs using keyboard shortcuts or by clicking and dragging the mouse over the tab header icons is another improvement.

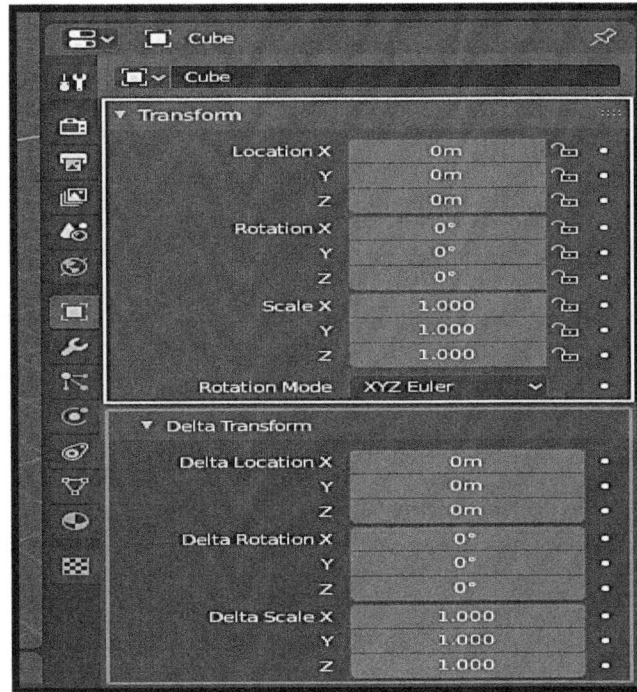

There is a panel that stands out with a yellow color, while a subpanel catches attention with a bold red hue. A panel is the smallest organizational unit in the user interface. The panel header displays the title of the panel. It is consistently noticeable. Additionally, certain panels may also incorporate subpanels.

Collapsing and Expanding

A panel can be expanded or collapsed to show or hide its contents. A panel can be expanded by clicking on the down arrow ▼ in the panel header and collapsed by clicking on the right arrow (>).

- The panel header can be expanded or collapsed by using the left mouse button **(LMB).**
- Clicking the **A key** will expand or collapse the panel that's beneath the mouse.
- You can easily collapse all panels and expand a collapsed one by pressing **Ctrl-LMB** on the header.
- By pressing **Ctrl-LMB** on the header of an expanded panel, you can easily expand or collapse all subpanels.
- One can expand or collapse numerous headers simultaneously by dragging them with the left mouse button **(LMB).**

Pinning

Having many panels open in separate tabs can be useful at times. Having access to a camera's settings even when other objects are selected is one good example. Adding the ability to pin panels is one way to fix this problem. You can see a pinned panel regardless of the tab you choose. Just click the pin icon in the header of a panel to make it stay put. With a simple right-click on the panel header and selection of "**Pin**," or by pressing **Shift** and left-clicking, you can quickly pin panels without a pin icon. Please be aware that not all panels may be able to have their edges pinned. Unfortunately, the Properties editor does not have it, but you can find it in the Sidebar.

Presets

- **Selector**: This is an exhaustive catalog of all the presets that are now accessible. A selection will be prioritized above the properties that are currently present.
- **Add +:** The current set of properties can be extended to incorporate more presets, making it easier to save and utilize in the future. A window will open up where you can enter a name. The name can be selected from a drop-down menu after entry, and other configuration options can be accessed in some cases.
- **Remove -:** Removes the selected preset.

Importing and Exporting Files

Importing Files

Blender allows users to import data from several programs and file formats, allowing them to bring in 3D models, textures, animations, or even full scenes.

1. **Supported Import Formats**

Blender supports many common formats, including:

- **OBJ (.obj):** A universal 3D model format widely used in other software.
- **FBX (.fbx):** Popular for game assets, animation, and working with engines like Unity or Unreal.
- **GLTF/GLB (.gltf/.glb):** Modern 3D format optimized for web and AR/VR.
- **STL (.stl):** Commonly used for 3D printing.
- **Collada (.dae):** Great for exchanging data between 3D applications.
- **Image Formats:** PNG, JPEG, HDRI, etc., for textures and backgrounds.

2. **How to Import Files**

The steps to import a file into Blender are as follows:

- Get Blender going by opening a project or creating a new one.
- Choose **File > Import** from the menu in the upper left.
- File formats such as OBJ, FBX, STL, and more will be displayed in a drop-down menu.
- Select the file type that you wish to import.
- A file browser is launched. Choose the file on your computer, then click the **Import** button.
- The 3D viewport will display your file, but you may have to move or resize it to get it to look right.

3. **Adjusting Imported Files**
- **Scale and Position:** Often, imported files may be too large, too small, or misaligned. Use the transform tools (Move, Scale, Rotate) to adjust.
- **Check Materials and Textures:** Some file types, such as FBX and GLTF, include materials and textures. Verify their proper application in the **Shader Editor** or the **Material Properties** tab.

Exporting Files

Your Blender works can be exported in a variety of formats that are compatible with other programs or platforms.

1. **Supported Export Formats**

Blender can save files in these formats (and more):

- **BLEND (.blend):** Blender's native format. Use this to save your project with all settings, models, and animations intact.
- **OBJ (.obj):** Ideal for exporting simple 3D models.
- **FBX (.fbx):** Great for exporting complex models with animations and materials.
- **GLTF/GLB (.gltf/.glb):** Useful for AR/VR and web-based applications.
- **STL (.stl):** Perfect for 3D printing.

- **Video Formats:** You can render animations into video formats like MP4, AVI, or MOV.

2. **How to Export Files**
- Once your model, scene, or animation is ready, go to **File > Export.**
- Format options (e.g., FBX, OBJ, GLTF, etc.) are available in the dropdown.
- A file browser is launched. After deciding where to save it, you may give the file a name.
- The export window's format-specific parameters are located on the right side. Take this case in point:

  - **For FBX:** Choose whether to include animations, scale the model, or export specific objects.

- For OBJ: Decide if you want to include materials and UV mapping.

- Adjust the settings as needed and click **Export**.

Import/Export Tips

1. **File Scale Issues:** If objects appear tiny or huge in other programs, adjust the scale settings during export (especially for FBX and OBJ files). Blender uses meters by default, so check the scale compatibility with the target software.
2. **Check the Origin Point:** The object's origin (pivot point) determines how it aligns with other software. Use **Object > Set Origin** to adjust it if needed.
3. **Apply Transformations:** Before exporting, apply all transformations (scale, rotation, location) by pressing **Ctrl+A** > **All Transforms**.
4. **Textures and Materials:** When exporting formats like OBJ or FBX, ensure textures are packed or saved in the same directory. Otherwise, the receiving program might not find them.
5. **Animation Exports:** For animations, formats like FBX or GLTF are preferred because they support bones, rigs, and keyframes.

CHAPTER 3
LIGHTING AND RENDERING

Lighting is a crucial part of making a scene in Blender that is visually appealing and captivating. Lighting has a crucial role in setting the scene's ambiance and highlighting objects' depth and finer features. Using Blender, this tutorial will walk you through the basics of lighting a scene, including the many available lights, how to build up a simple lighting rig, and how to alter the lighting to achieve the proper mood.

Types of Lights in Blender

The four main kinds of lights in Blender are point, sun, spot, and area lights. You can use any kind of light for any kind of lighting since each kind of light has its special qualities.

Point Light

One kind of light source that shines light in all directions is the point light. It helps to simulate low lighting, like candles or tiny lights, and casts faint shadows.

Sun Light

Sun Light refers to a concentrated beam of light that is bright like the sun. Its ability to cast precise shadows makes it ideal for usage in architectural designs and outdoor settings.

Spot Light

An example of a directed light source is the spotlight, which produces a cone of light. It works wonders for creating striking lighting effects and bringing attention to certain parts of the image.

Area Light

An area lamp is a rectangular light source that evenly distributes light in all directions. It works well for simulating large light sources like streetlights or windows.

Setting Up a Basic Lighting Rig

After settling on a lighting type, the next step is to put the setup in place. A lighting setup consists of strategically arranged lights that illuminate your room. **Using Blender's built-in tools, you can quickly fashion a lighting system:**

1. Navigate to the "**Layout**" workspace in the 3D viewport.
2. To choose the type of light you wish to use, click the "**Add**" option in the upper right corner.
3. Move the light source to the desired spot in the 3D viewer.
4. Make the desired brightness adjustment and choose the light source to modify the "**Strength**" value in the "**Object Data Properties**" field.

5. To add another light source, repeat steps 2-4.

Adjusting the Lighting to Create the Desired Mood

Once you have a basic lighting setup in place, you can start adjusting the lights to make your scene come to life.

If you want to get the desired result, follow the following guidelines:

1. Match the scene's color temperature to the mood of the scene. Cooler temperatures are more appropriate for clean, clinical settings, while warmer ones are more conducive to a relaxing, at-home vibe.
2. You can add depth and emotion to your scene by manipulating shadows. To imply calmness, use softer shadows; to imply worry, use sharper shadows.
3. Try out several lighting configurations until you find the sweet spot for highlights and shadows.
4. The amount of light that diffuses from the source is controlled by light falloff. A more lifelike lighting effect could be achieved by doing this.
5. Consider employing volumetric lighting if you wish to add haze or fog to your image.

Adding Lights to Your Scene

To adjust the lighting in your scene, follow these steps (remember that Shift+A will open the option to add more objects to the scene):

1. Pick a light for the scene, or make one if it doesn't exist.
2. To fill in the shadows, make a copy of the light and move it to the other side of the screen.
3. To avoid total darkness in the shaded area, you can play around with the lights by making the one on the right brighter and more dramatic, and the one on the left more subdued and of a different hue. This will operate as a fill light.

Understanding a Basic Three-point Lighting Setup

One of the most popular approaches is the "three-point lighting" method. Be careful to read the description carefully, because it employs three distinct sets of lights, as the name suggests. This common studio configuration serves as the foundation for almost all other lighting arrangements and is ideal for conducting interviews.

The Key Light

The first step in making a three-point lighting composition is to center your subject and focus the camera on it. We will then switch on the main light, sometimes called the key light. When lighting a scene, the "key light" often has the greatest impact. It is the source of the brightest highlights and darkest shadows in your composition. Usually, you want to position this light somewhat to the left or right of your camera, and higher than your photo graphs subject. In this way, you can lessen the likelihood that your friends will hand you a flashlight under your chin as they tell you horror stories around the campfire and increase the likelihood that the shadows will fall naturally.

The Fill Light

After deciding where your main light will be, the fill light should be placed. The fill light's job is to illuminate the shadowy parts of your subject. The key light is useful for casting shadows, but it casts such deep black shadows that they will hide your subject in low light. Not what you were going for unless you were going for a dramatic lighting effect—which isn't happening here. Fill lights are often weaker than key lights, but you want them to have a broader and more diffuse throw than the key light. Their toss is the smallest possible space radius that they can enter. In contrast to the narrow beam of a flashlight, the light from fluorescent lights—common in office buildings—is rather wide. Because it will cut down on the amount of highlight and balance out the shadows this light creates, a broad throw is what you want for your fill light. In most cases, it's best to avoid having your fill and key shading and highlights conflict. The standard placement for a fill light is across the lens from the main light and at or slightly below eye level with the subject. On top of that, try to keep the fill light approximately parallel to the floor. Finding the right area to put your fill light is easy if you follow this method. Consider a straight line that begins at the photographer's main light source and finishes at the subject. Then, spin the line through 90 degrees using your subject as a pivot point. A line indicating the exact spot of the fill will show up when you do this.

The Backlight

The backlight, also called the rim light, is the last light of a three-point lighting arrangement. This light source illuminates the subject from behind, casting a thin shadow around their profile while they are photographed. To help your subject stand out from the background, that little bit of light is the charming finishing touch that often separates a decent lighting arrangement from a very fantastic one. Alternatively, it helps to differentiate between an adequate and a subpar lighting setup. Turning the backlight so it faces away from the key light is a preference of some. This strategy is well-executed, but it could lead to the rim effect drowning out the key's highlights. While holding it perpendicular to the camera is another viable option, it runs the risk of inadvertently blinding the viewers if the subject moves. One other approach is to switch the orientation of the backlight such that it faces in the opposite direction of the fill. Using this method can produce a nice halo effect that draws attention to the key, but it could also come across as inauthentic in some contexts. You can see that there are pros and cons to every possible lighting setup. The only object on which the vast majority of people can agree is the idea that the lighting should usually be directed toward the subject. Finally, the best thing to do is to play around with your backlight to find out what works best. Nothing else you can do will suffice. Here we see how various settings of the backlight affect a basic Suzanne scene.

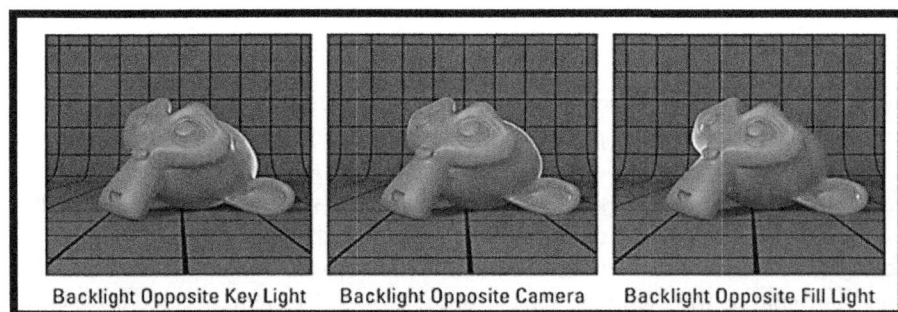

Backlight Opposite Key Light   Backlight Opposite Camera   Backlight Opposite Fill Light

Using a backlight that is not as strong as your main light for power and throw might help things look more natural. Since the highlights are on the other side of your subject, you have some leeway in selecting the throw. To make your subjects look scary, shoot them from a lower angle. This lighting strategy is known as **"basic three-point lighting,"** and it works well in both computer graphics and the so-called "real world." Turning off or reducing the power of the fill and back lights will result in more dramatic shadows. If you're going for a mysterious or romantic effect, position your key behind your subject.

Working with Three-point Lighting in Blender

When photographing a single object, the three-point lighting method can be extremely helpful. It is common practice to use this lighting system when photographing portraits since it simulates a professional studio lighting setup. You need at least three point lights in your scene for it to be considered finished. After that, you may highlight an object in your scene by adding three separate area lights and directing each one to that spot. On the other hand, with only one click in Blender, users can automatically generate three-point lights directed at a single object. The Tri- lighting function will need to be turned on for this. Here you can locate Blender's add-on in the options.

1. Select the options **"Edit,"** **"Preference,"** and **"Add-ons."**

2. Search the internet for **"Tri-lighting."**

3. To save your options, make sure **"Tri-lighting"** is enabled.

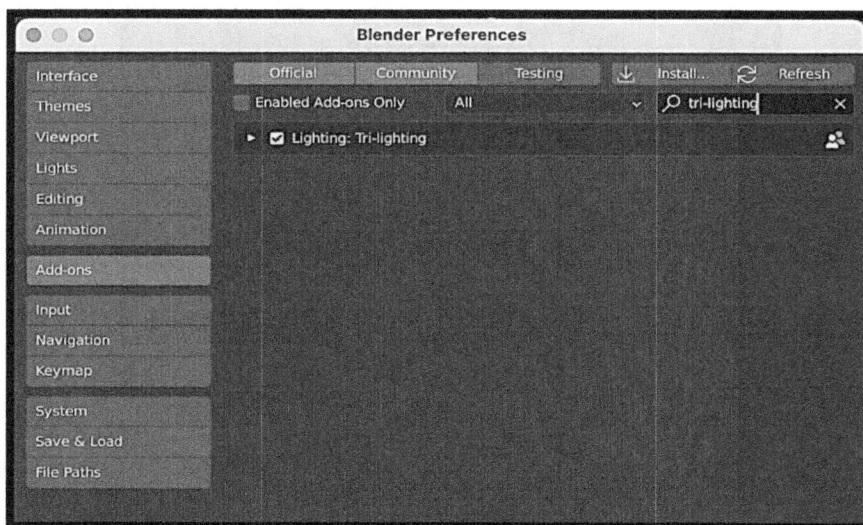

You can now easily add a set of three-point lights with the click of a button.

1. Make sure it's the active object (active objects have an orange outline) and choose which area of the scene you want the lights to highlight and focus on.

2. To access Lights, press Shift and A. Then, select 3 Point Lights.

The object in question will be lighted from three separate angles by use of strategically placed lights.

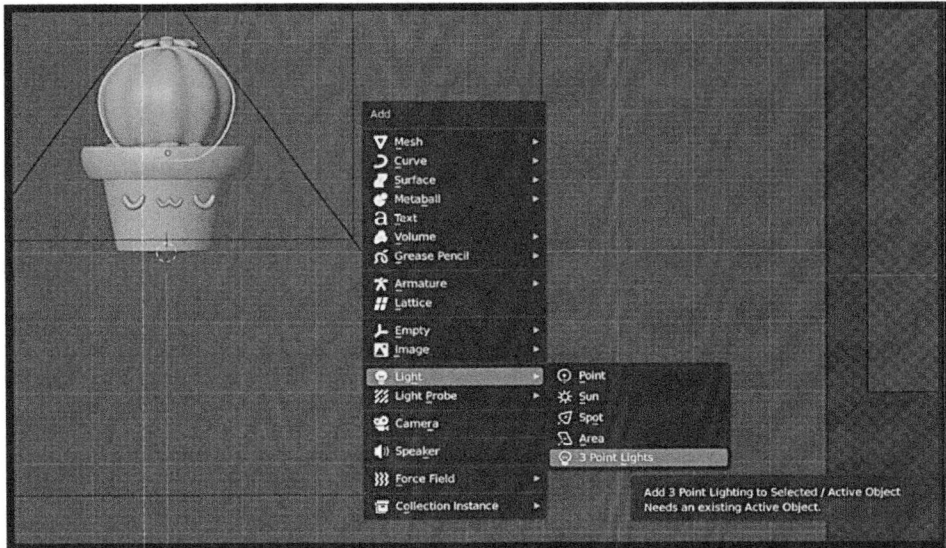

3. Scale all of the lights and position them so they're close to the object you're working with.

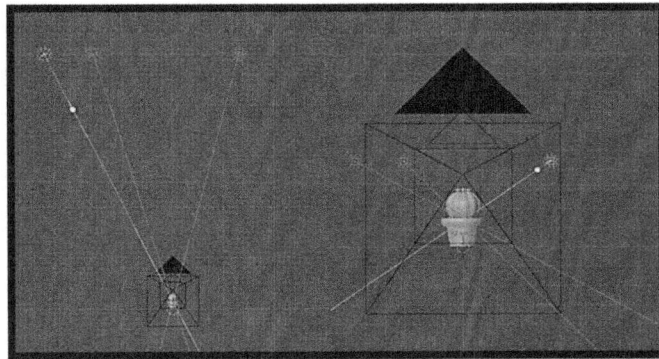

4. You can now adjust the intensity of the lights and try out various scenes.

Using Look Dev to Set Up Lighting

Look Dev stands for "**look development**," an important step in making realistic 3D scenes. If you want a certain effect, you have to build a scene and try out different lighting, materials, and textures to see what works. Look Dev is a great tool for setting up the lighting in Blender. Artists can use this tool to produce the ideal lighting for their projects. Looking into using Look Dev could help alleviate some of the stress associated with the challenging Blender lighting setting method. By showing them how the scene will look after rendering, artists can fine-tune the lighting settings to get their intended results. If you want to alter the lighting in Blender with Look Dev, you have to do these things:

1. Choose the right render engine

It is necessary to choose the correct render engine before beginning the Look Development process. You can choose between Cycles and Eevee as your primary render engines in Blender. These images might require more time to render, even though Cycle is a ray-tracing engine that makes fantastic, photorealistic graphics. But Eevee is a real-time engine, so it can generate renders quickly, albeit with less realism, due to the way it does its rendering. Eevee is frequently the superior option for Look Dev due to its quicker render times and ability to give real-time feedback. Render engine selection is ultimately up to the artist's specific needs; nonetheless, the specific needs of the artist will transcend all other considerations.

2. Set up the Scene

Scene configuration comes after Render Engine selection. As part of this phase, you will set up the camera, add some objects to the scene, and apply some materials and textures. Before moving forward with lighting setup, it is essential to possess a fundamental comprehension of these components.

3. Add lights

After the scene is finished, you can start thinking about the lighting. Lights in Blender can be of many different kinds, including point, sun, spot, and area illumination. Because different types of light have different characteristics and applications, it is critical to choose the one that is best suited to the task at hand. As an example, although natural light is ideal for exterior scenes with realistic shadows, a point light can be used to produce soft, diffused lighting inside a room.

4. Adjust the lighting

The next step, after placing the lights in the scene, is to adjust their parameters as necessary. Changing the color, brightness, and positioning of the lights is what's needed to achieve this effect. The shadows cast by the lighting must be taken into account and how they impact the image's overall image quality.

5. Use Look Dev to preview the lighting

Look Dev is a must-have for seeing the lighting changes in progress. When artists can preview how the scene's lighting will appear before they begin to create it, they can make any required alterations. Artists can observe the instant impact of adjusting the lighting settings in the Look Dev mode, thanks to the scene's real-time creation.

6. Fine-tune the lighting

Using Look Dev, artists can tweak the lighting until they get the look they want. In addition to adjusting the colors and intensities of the lights, this also involves moving them about and changing their angles of placement. To find the lighting setup that works best with the subject matter of the scene, it's important to try out many options.

7. **Add post-processing effects**

When artists have achieved the desired lighting effect, they can further improve the final product by applying post-processing techniques. This includes effects like lens flares, bloom, and color grading, all of which can add to the image's authenticity.

Setting up the World

As you prepare your scene for rendering, lighting is only one component of the equation that you will be dealing with. The tone of your scene is another important consideration. Take this moment: are you indoors or out? What time did the sun rise and set? In what precise way does the sky look? Are clouds looming over the horizon? The appearance of the backdrop piques my interest. When planning the layout of your image, make sure to keep the aforementioned factors in mind. Every time you want to define your environment for rendering, in Cycles or Eevee, you should go to the Properties editor and click on the World tab.

Changing the Sky to Something Other Than Dull Gray

No matter if you're using Eevee or Cycles for rendering, you can easily alter that color. In the World Properties box, you can change the surface's color by clicking on the color swatch. If the 3D Viewport is either in the Render or Look Dev viewport shading, changing the color of the world has an interesting side effect that can substantially change how your scene appears. Once you've saved your changes, setting blue as the global color will make the whole scene look blue, particularly the shadows. Cycles and Eevee attribute this to their belief that the World's hue represents an additional light source. Put the Strength value to 0 if you would like the World color to not affect the game. When taken as a whole, though, World Properties' potential seems limited. This is because these controls are pretty much your only option when it comes to simplicity. Eevee and Cycles view the universe as nothing more than material. Consequently, the Shader Editor will be your primary tool for personalization. Working in the Shading workspace is the most effective method of visualizing what I'm describing. You can find a large Shader Edit at the very bottom of this workspace. Instead of using the preset Shader Edit that modifies the materials of objects, you can easily adjust this option to change the World material. You can modify your scene's World material by selecting the appropriate shader type from the drop-down menu located in the Shader Editor's header. The World's materials will be modifiable for you. Imagine for a moment that you want to create a World material using Cycles that isn't much more complex than a solid color. Sure thing! To add a Sky Texture node, go to the Add menu, select Texture, and then choose Sky Texture. Find the Color output socket of the Background shader node in the Shader Editor and attach it to the node's Color input socket. Finally, a sky materializes before your very eyes. Even better, you can finish your scene even when sunlight isn't present. Would you be interested in making a picture of the surface texture of your environment? Look Dev's viewport shading setting contains some incredibly beautiful photos in its World material. If you uncheck the "Scene World" checkbox in the Viewport Shading rollout, Blender will provide you with a selection of eight "chrome balls" to use in place of the Scene World material. These shiny chrome balls are reflections of the photographs that were utilized to create the atmosphere of your environment. High dynamic range pictures, or HDRIs, provide the impression that your scene's lighting is derived from real-world lighting conditions. This is accomplished by illuminating a specific, high-quality image.

Understanding Ambient Occlusion

The Ambient Occlusion shader is in charge of determining the amount of occlusion on the hemisphere above the shading point. With procedural texturing, you can target certain corners with weathering effects, for instance. Using this shader can greatly reduce Cycles' rendering speed and comes at a high price. If rendering time is an issue, you can speed things up by using the Pointiness feature of the Geometry node or by baking Ambient Occlusion. In the Properties editor's Render tab, locate the Ambient Occlusion panel, and then, with a left click, enable AO in Eevee. After you enable Ambient Occlusion in Blender, the modifications you make there will be immediately applied. Within this panel, you will find all of Eevee's controls for adjusting the AO of your scene.

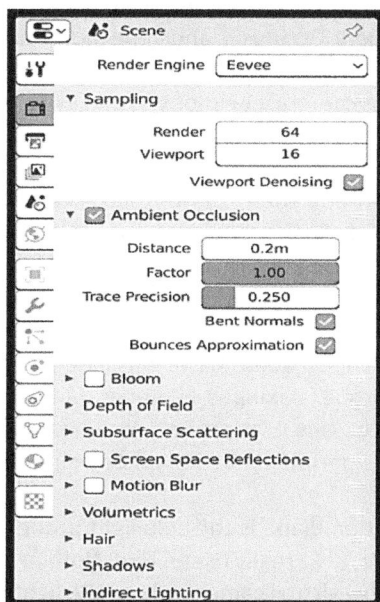

The majority of the parameters in the Ambient Occlusion panel are rather straightforward. A rundown of the possible AO adjustments is as follows:

- **Distance:** By examining how close other geometry is to a feature (such as a crack, wrinkle, or wedge), Eevee decides whether the feature needs the additional shading that AO offers to mimic those beautiful AO shadows. The goal here is to create an effect similar to those stunning AO shadows. By adjusting the value of the Distance parameter, you can observe whether the AO effect is generated by an adjacent piece of geometry. Increasing the value will make the image look less realistic, but it will also cast more shadows.
- **Factor:** The magnitude of the factor represents the overall strength of the AO effect. The effect of the distance you choose is amplified by this factor. While it's generally recommended to leave this at 1.0, you may want to play around with other values to find what works best for your scene. Remember that 1.0 is the soft limit. Inputting amounts greater than 1.0 will require manual intervention.

- **Trace Precision:** Raising this number will make AO shadows more accurate, but it will significantly lengthen the rendering time and can make your scene noisier.
- **Bent Normals:** For bent normals, it's usually best to leave this box selected. When calculating AO shadows, only the direction with the least degree of occlusion is taken into account. Why bother going to the trouble of computing invisible shadows if it's not required?
- **Bounces Approximation:** One useful piece of fakery is the "Bounces Approximation" checkbox, which reduces the shadowing effect on lighter objects. For the most part, you won't need to disable the option that refers to "bounced approximation" (which is like shiny plaster).

Working with Light Probes in Eevee

Screen space effects make up the bulk of Eevee's renderer capabilities. By examining only the subjects that the camera can see, effects like ambient occlusion and reflections can be produced. Off-camera objects, such as a shadow cast by a tree or a person standing behind the camera, will not be affected by a screen space effect since they are outside the camera's field of vision. Eevee can use the additional sampling data provided by light probes to account for objects that are invisible to the camera. Light probes add functionality. The three types of light probes that Eevee offers can be accessed by selecting "Add" from the menu that appears in the 3D Viewport and then "Light Probe." **Two of the probes are intended to study reflections, and one is intended to study indirect lighting, which is similar to global illumination:**

- **Reflection Cube Map:** One useful tool for making reflections of various objects is the Reflection Cube Map light probe. Once you've enabled screen space reflections in the Render Properties, it can serve as a backup for when you need them. In the Render Properties panel, you can locate the Reflection Cube Map light probe. Baking is essential, but even surfaces with intricate curves or features can turn out decently. This light probe's map has a spherical (or box-shaped) shape, and as it approaches the sphere's periphery, its influence begins to diminish in an area known as the falloff zone.
- **Reflection Plane:** The Reflection Plane is the sole light probe that Blender provides to Eevee that can be utilized dynamically. So, it's a really useful tool. Nothing is required of you in terms of baking. To put it simply, Eevee sets up a virtual camera where the light probe is and uses the data it collects to figure out how to get from an object's surface to its reflection. There are a few additional stages to this method, though. Due to its flat design, the light probe we have is most effective when used on mirrors or mirrored windows.
- **Irradiance Volume:** This light probe allows you to create indirect lighting effects like global illumination. You can think of baking the Irradiance Volume as baking the Reflection Cube Map; both are necessary for their respective uses. Screen space effects can be included as a backup to fill in the gaps. By inserting an Irradiance Volume light probe, a container is formed with an internal grid of sampling locations. Both the box and the grid hold the sample points and the zone of effect of the irradiance volume, respectively.

Any of the light probes can be used in the same way:

1. Add the light probe to your scene by selecting [your preferred light probe] under **Add > Light Probe.**

2. The light probe can be rotated and moved into position using Blender's transform tools.

3. To fine-tune the influence region of your light probe, use the controls under Object Data Properties.

A very helpful tool for studying the effect of the light probe's influence area decreasing with increasing distance into space is the Falloff number. The X, Y, and Z resolution parameters need to be watched carefully when dealing with an Irradiance Volume. A greater value for these parameters indicates that more time will elapse before action is conducted.

4. If you're utilizing a Reflection Cube Map or an Irradiance Volume, bake your indirect lighting before moving forward.

Baking from Your Light Probes

Since light probes have the advantage of precomputed lighting, they are frequently used by render engines in video games. Light probes are commonly used in the Rendering of video games. A technique known as baking is used to store the result of the calculation in a lightweight cache. You can skip the baking step if your experiment is limited to using a Reflection Plane light probe. Data for the Reflection Plane is created on the fly according to needs. The Reflection Cube Maps and the Irradiance Volumes, on the other hand, will need to be baked before they can be used. Under the Render Parameters menu, expand the Indirect Lighting panel to bake the indirect lighting captured by your light probes. **Below is a list of the most critical configurations on this panel:**

- **Auto Bake:** If you want your light probe changes to be immediately reflected in your light cache, you can enable "Auto Bake" by selecting the "Auto Bake" checkbox. While it's helpful when putting up light probes, it could slow down your productivity if you leave it on for later steps. When putting up light probes, it is quite useful.
- **Diffuse Bounces:** Similar to cycles, your light cache will be more accurate the more bounces you have. The baking time will be slightly longer, which is another drawback.
- **Cubemap Size:** A shadow map and a cube map are two names for the same complex texture shape. To alter the size of the cube map, you can utilize this variable similarly. An uneven or low-resolution appearance in your indirect lighting or reflections can be fixed by increasing this quantity. It is advised to raise this number to the power of two (512px, 1024px, 2048px, etc.) to maximize the use of the RAM that is accessible.
- **Diffuse Occlusion:** The irradiance volumes determine the amount of light that is produced in your scene. Light leaking into interior scenes is a real possibility, as is the case with the majority of Eevee objects that emit light. Every irradiance sample furthermore maintains a shadow map to forestall these leaks. The magnitude of these shadow maps is dictated by the Diffuse Occlusion setting. With the bigger diameters, the baking time will be longer, but the frequency of leaks should be reduced.

You can start baking as soon as you're satisfied with the settings you've chosen. To start baking, press one of the two buttons on the Indirect Lighting panel's top row:

- **Bake Indirect Lighting:** You will want to select the Bake Indirect Light option if your scene features an Irradiance Volume light probe or a combination of Irradiance Volumes and Reflection Cube Map probes. The indirect lighting will still need to be baked. By selecting this option, Blender will bake the light cache automatically.

- **Bake Cubemap Only:** If your scene does not contain any irradiance volumes, then you can utilize the "Bake Cubemap Only" button. If you haven't added any irradiance volumes, you can only select this option. Because it doesn't have to take into consideration all of the bouncing light in your scene, this option usually results in a final bake that is finished a bit faster.

Understanding the Limitations of Light Probes

Limitations of Light Probes in Blender

1. Limited accuracy

A major issue with Blender is the accuracy of its light probes, which can be rather off. Light probes can capture and save data about the lighting, but they aren't as accurate as methods like ray tracing or global illumination. The reason behind this is that light probes can only capture data from a single spot in the environment, which doesn't take the space's shape and lighting into consideration. When contrasted with the surrounding area, the lighting on moving objects could look flat or uneven.

2. Limited range

In addition to its other drawbacks, Blender's light probes have a limited range. Light probes can only capture light from the immediate area's lighting. So, if a moving object gets too far away from the light probe closest to it, the lighting data it provides will no longer be correct. The lighting quality and realism of dynamic objects that move too far away from the nearest light probe may noticeably decrease when this happens.

3. Limited control

Light probes are one of Blender's many annoying features. Instead of allowing the user to manually adjust the lighting, data is collected autonomously by the light probes. Consequently, it could be difficult to achieve the desired lighting effects, particularly in intricate scenes including several light sources and different lighting situations. This can make it quite hard to get the lighting effects you want in complex scenes. Although light probes can have their color and intensity adjusted, this does not give you nearly as much control as other lighting systems, such as environment maps or light sources. The colors and intensities of the light probes can be adjusted.

4. Limited compatibility

Lastly, keep in mind that not all game engines or platforms support light probes. Light probes are compatible with Blender; however they may not be fully or partially supported by other game engines and platforms. Thus, it can be challenging to use light probes successfully inside a project, especially when developing for many platforms or engines.

How to Overcome the Limitations of Light Probes in Blender

There are workarounds for Blender's light probes that make them more useful in certain situations. But you have to stay within these boundaries. Take a look at these guidelines:

1. **Combine light probes with other lighting methods**

When working with light probes, it is recommended to combine them with other lighting techniques such as ray tracing or global illumination to address their limited accuracy and range. Using the real-time lighting modifications enabled by light probes, you can contribute to the creation of more realistic lighting on dynamic objects by doing so.

2. **Use light probes strategically**

Due to their restricted control, light probes must be used in scenes with meticulous preparation. Light probes need to be placed in regions where dynamic objects are expected to move, and their brightness and hue need to be modified to match the surroundings lighting. This way, one can make the lighting on moving objects more accurate and constant while still having control over the scene's overall lighting.

3. **Test compatibility**

Before being employed in a project, light probes need to be validated on the planned platforms and engines to ensure compatibility. This will aid in ensuring that the light probes function as intended.

CHAPTER 4
MODELING IN BLENDER 4.4

These days, numerous industries rely on 3D modeling, including construction and film animation. Even if 3D modeling is becoming a more popular option in many various fields, Stratview Research forecasted that the 3D modeling market will rise by more than 15% by 2028. Blender is a popular 3D modeling program that offers a lot of functionality in a user-friendly package. 3D modeling, in which specialized software is used to create a representation of an object or scene in three dimensions, is among Blender's most common uses. The models capture the appearance and shape of real objects and then digitally replicate them. Even though 3D artists are the ones who typically employ 3D modeling, other types of professionals can also reap the benefits of this technology due to its versatility. Blender is a modeling tool that architects, product designers, and interior artists can use to create 3D models. These models will allow them to see their ideas become a reality. Additionally, Blender can help scientists make complex ideas more understandable by adding features to their data visualization models. To better understand the effects of potential medical treatments, doctors utilize Blender to create three-dimensional models of the human body.

Animation and Visual Effects (VFX) Development

Blender's powerful modeling features enable artists to create people and objects for films and videos that appear real and are made of complicated materials. Additionally, it includes a physics engine and particle system that can realistically render smoke, fire, and other special effects. Blender provides capabilities for mixing and editing videos right out of the box, which is a major import. You can do a lot of "post-processing" in Blender, such as combining 3D objects and video, changing colors, and so on, to make your visual effects look professional. Additionally, it features sophisticated tools for merging photos and applying effects such as light, depth of field, and motion blur. With this capability, you can add 3D elements to live photos for use in VFX mixing.

Sculpting and 3D Printing

With Blender, you can also design and construct 3D objects. To create objects that appear realistic and detailed, you can use its shaping tool to alter the 3D model's shape and form with great precision. You can use the program's many brushes and tools to express yourself, and it even allows you to work with dynamic structures. By adjusting the mesh's size dynamically, this method streamlines your workflow. Mesh is a 3D graph design that consists of lines and points that are connected. The surface of an object is depicted by it. The mesh can be manipulated to create various shapes, and its resolution can be adjusted to get the desired level of intricacy. Mesh is the term used in 3D modeling software to describe the shape of an object. To bring a picture to life, it can be animated, sculpted, and given textures. One of Blender's many 3D printing capabilities is the ability to facilitate the creation of support structures. You can also print out your creations in three dimensions using the program's integration with several 3D printers. Blender also has an export option for 3D models that can be utilized with 3D printing software and hardware.

For what reasons would you want to model in 3D using Blender?

Because of its versatile feature set, Blender finds application in many creative disciplines. Blender is a great tool for creating 3D models for the reasons listed below:

- **Free and open-source.** Because its source code is open source and accessible to everyone, Blender can be customized to suit your needs and is available for free download and use. Students, hobbyists, and small businesses are among the many groups that can benefit from its accessibility. Blender is cross-platform, meaning it can be used on Windows, Mac, and Linux computers.
- **High-quality features.** Only in more costly applications can you find the extensive modeling, painting, lighting, and animation tools available in Blender. With its many features, you can create highly detailed and photorealistic 3D models.
- **Active community and many tutorials and resources.** Online, you'll find a big and friendly community of Blender users who are always willing to lend a hand and share what they know. This means that you can get a lot of information if you want to learn how to utilize the software.
- **Non-destructive modeling.** Because Blender's modeling tools are non-destructive, you can make changes to your models without permanently altering their underlying shape. This, in turn, allows for greater leeway and adaptability throughout the modeling process.
- **Extensive add-ons and scripting capabilities.** You can write scripts in Python and run them in Blender. You can create duplicates of models, manage repetitive tasks, or even build your tools with scripts.

Mesh Modeling Basics

Creating and Editing Meshes

Starting a New Scene

The "primitive" cube shape that is pre-installed in the scene will be sufficient for this project; no further objects are required. Make a "new" file by going to the menu in the top left corner and selecting "**File >> New**" if you can't see the object. Blender will prompt you to "**Erase All**," which is the preferred choice. Following that, a fresh scene will load, including a cube as its center and light and camera objects on either side.

Switching to "Perspective" mode

Allow me to begin. To observe the mesh correctly while it is being created, we must first switch to "**Perspective Mod**e." Access this in the 3D Work Zone's "View" menu by selecting "**View >> Perspective**." Remember that you can toggle between "Perspective Mode" and "Orthographic" (or "flat") mode using the keyboard shortcut "NumPad 5".

Design Note: Hit "C" to "re-center" the scene if you can't keep your eyes on the on-screen object. Doing so should refocus the view camera on the screen's center object.

It's vital to note that you can move around the workspace using it as a member. For instance, by pressing MMB and dragging the screen, you can view the mesh from a side view. Use the MMB and scroll keys to get a closer look. With NumPad 5, you can access the "Perspective Mode" key to view the model accurately as it is being created. The correct viewpoint is now available, allowing you to perceive the object's shape.

'Edit' Mode and Editing the Mesh Object.

The bulk of mesh editing happens in "Edit Mode." You can then use the many tools and actions that are available to you to cut, shape, and alter the mesh to create an object with the desired general structure. The mesh object must be selected before we can access edit mode. Blender will automatically transition between edit modes depending on the last mesh selected if there are multiple in a scene. To access this menu, just right-click (RMB) on the box object in the Work Zone area and then hit the "TAB" key—the leftmost key on your keyboard, just above "Caps Lock."

Design Note: Once an object is picked, it will appear unchanged. Holding down RMB on other objects will show you what should happen when you choose one. A light pinkish hue should be achieved throughout the object's shape. If you want to select or deselect all objects at once, you can use the "A" key.

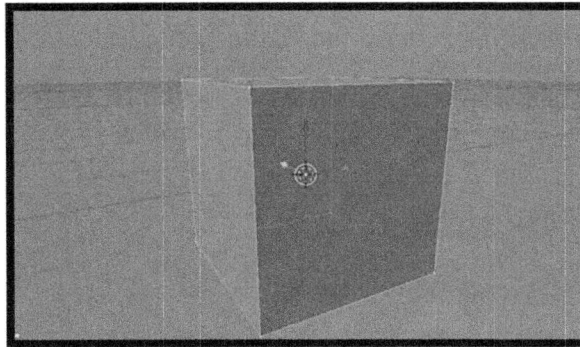

By pressing "**TAB**" and then choosing the object with "**RMB**," you can enter edit mode. To see the mesh better, use **MMB** scroll. When you enter **EDIT** mode, you may have also noticed that the buttons on the Tool Bar have changed. This mode unlocks a new set of tools that you can use to modify the shape.

'Loop Cuts' and Dividing the Mesh

A "Loop Cut" is an important tool for the majority of modeling tasks because we are now in Edit mode. A model can be edited in many ways; however, the most fundamental is to cut a "ring" or "loop" around it in a specific manner. A "loop" is just a half-cut section of an object, as a design note shows. Another option is to imagine a black marking pen being used to draw a line around your waist. There would be just one "loop" that "cuts" around your body, taking into account all of your dips, curves, and overall shape. In mesh terms, a "Loop Cut" is functionally equivalent. When the object is in Edit mode (TAB), click and hold on the mesh. Hit Ctrl+R thereafter. As you move the pink line around the model, it will indicate the precise area to be cut.

Design Note: The pink line will follow the path of the edge nearest to the mouse as you drag it over the mesh. It always lets you know that the cut will be made along that edge or direction when it does this.

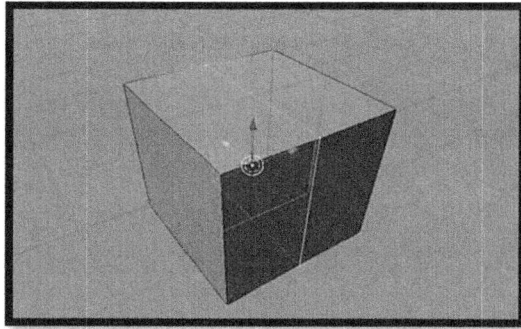

The pink line that appears when you press "Ctrl+R" indicates the mesh area where the loop will be cut. You can "set" the cut by clicking the LMB key. To indicate that the cut will be in the path of the new line, the line will turn yellow. Keep pressing the "Ctrl" key while you drag the mouse. The loop cut line indicator has been "snapped" to the grid and will now "snap" at regular intervals while it moves. The addition of mesh cuts at regular, measured intervals becomes much easier with this. While holding down Ctrl, drag the cursor to the object's center. To do this, look for the numbers in the lower left corner of the 3D workspace; they will guide you. At the display of "0.000," hit the LMB key. Soon after this, the cut will be "set," and the next step can be taken. If you haven't already, you should add two cuts down the middle line of each path. The majority of the chair's construction consists of these cuts. **Design Note**: If you accidentally cut anywhere in Blender, you can undo your action by pressing Ctrl+Z. In addition to using RMB+Shift to multi-select, you can "subdivide" an edge to cut it by selecting it using the two pink dots on either end of the button, which is located in the "Mesh Tools" panel on the toolbar.

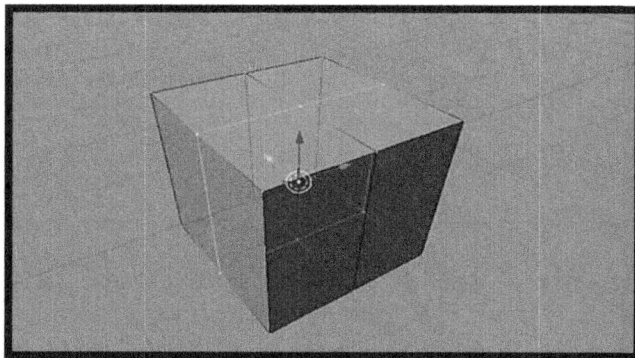

With two presses of the RMB button—one to "set" the desired location for the cut and another to "fix" it— you can create a loop cut. A new loop encircling the mesh will be generated by this.

Adding More Loop Cuts to the Mesh

To "extrude" other shapes out of the mesh, such as the back and legs to create the shape of a chair, we must first make a few more cuts in the mesh. Include more loop cuts, as demonstrated earlier. To keep the tool on the grid as it advances, remind the member to hold down the Ctrl key while making each cut. Additionally, make note of the numbers that are displayed in the lower-left corner of the work area. Here, the distance was shown to be "0.6000," so schedule each cut for when that figure is reached (don't fret if you make a mistake the first time). The final product ought to resemble this image. The chair will be constructed in a general shape like this.

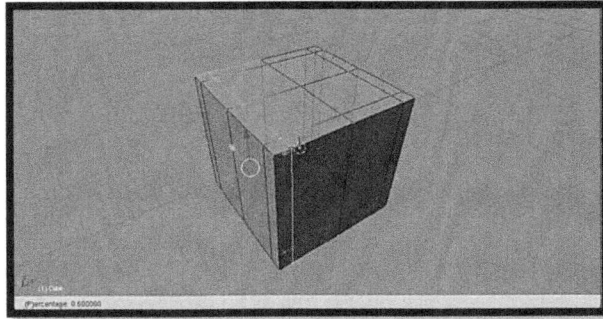

With two presses of the RMB button—one to "set" the desired location for the cut and another to "fix" it—you can create a loop cut. A new loop encircling the mesh will be generated by this.

Change 'select' Type and Back-face Culling.

At this point, we must change to an alternative "selection" mode. They are "Vertex," "Edge," and "Face." At the moment, we're in "Vertex" mode, but we should be in "Face" mode. To access the "**Select Mode**" window, hit "**Ctrl+TAB**." From there, choose "Faces" from the menu. The viewport's representation of the mesh object updates as a result of this action. Near the middle of each surface, black spots take the place of the pink dots (called vertexes) that have disappeared. "Faces" or "quadratic polygons" (often spelled "poly," "tris," or just "quads") are the names here.

Design Note: When you press **Ctrl+TAB**, make sure the mouse is over the 3D work area.

You should get a screen similar to the one below as soon as you switch modes.

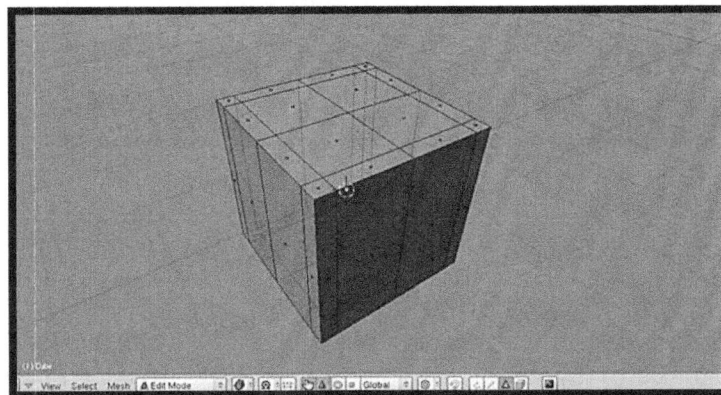

49

With two presses of the RMB button—one to "set" the desired location for the cut and another to "fix" it—you can create a loop cut. A new loop encircling the mesh will be generated by this. We can see the mesh's reverse side at the moment. For future ease of selection and work, we must disable that. We risk repeatedly selecting unwanted faces if we don't. Located beneath the work area and to the right of the menu area are two sets of buttons. Take a look at the set of four buttons that reads "dots," "lines," and "triangles," in that order. To observe the object's transformation into a mesh, click the "box" button. Thanks to our newly enabled "back face culling" (Blender: "occlusion"), the back faces should vanish. Ideally, the mesh would resemble the image provided below. Now we can continue.

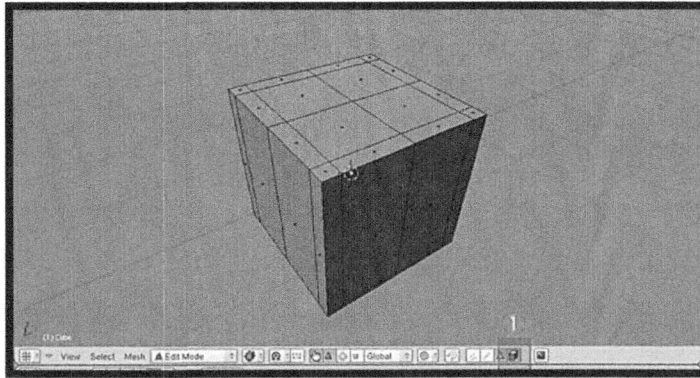

1) It shows the button that says "Occlude Background Geometry." Turn this on so we can pick faces without thinking about picking the wrong ones.

Selecting Faces and Extruding

Blender often uses the right mouse button for item and object selection. To pick multiple objects simultaneously, press and hold the "Shift" key. The next step is to select a few faces, which will later be shaped to form the back of the chair. In case you can't see it already, reposition the mesh such that you can see its top. One edge of the mesh has a row of faces that may be clicked with the RMB key while holding down the SHIFT key. **This will look like the image below.**

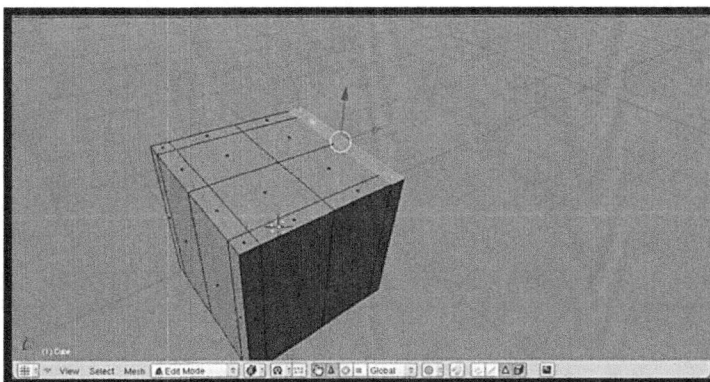

Once that is done, use the MMB to navigate to a higher level, away from the mesh. There must be room for us to lift those faces skyward. Press "E" to activate the "Extrude" function on the selected faces (refer to the image below) after releasing the "Shift" key. If you press "E" on the faces, they will "jump" out of the mesh because they are "active" objects. For the time being, you can "release" them by pressing and holding RMB; they will return to their original position. Our goal is to become accustomed to the idea that the default angle for automatically extruding faces is not always necessary. So far, they've taken the correct approach, but we'd like to exert a bit more influence. **Design Note**: faces are pushed out along a "face normal," which is the way that the hexagon is facing.

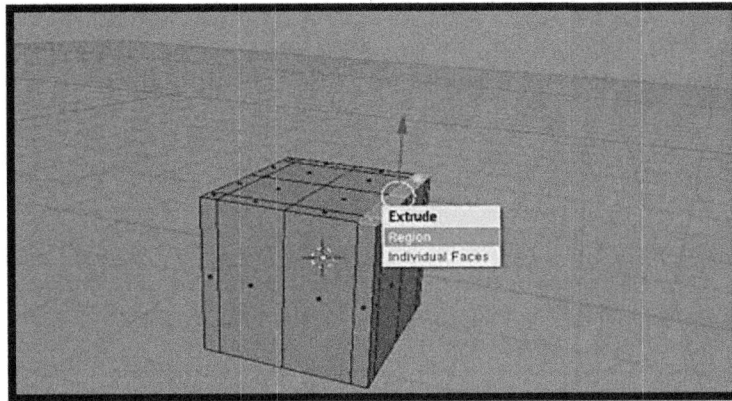

Below is an example of something that should always be visible: an object with red, green, and blue arrowheads. The selected face will have additional black dots produced around its perimeter; pay attention to these. Click the blue handle of the device to spin (MMB), zoom out (MMB scroll), and then click the LMB button to create room. Before dragging it, use Ctrl to have it snap to the grid. Then, raise it by two or three "steps" (snap points); the objects you've chosen will "jump" to the nearest snap point according to the travel direction. As soon as you release the device, the faces will "set" to their new height and position, creating the chair's back.

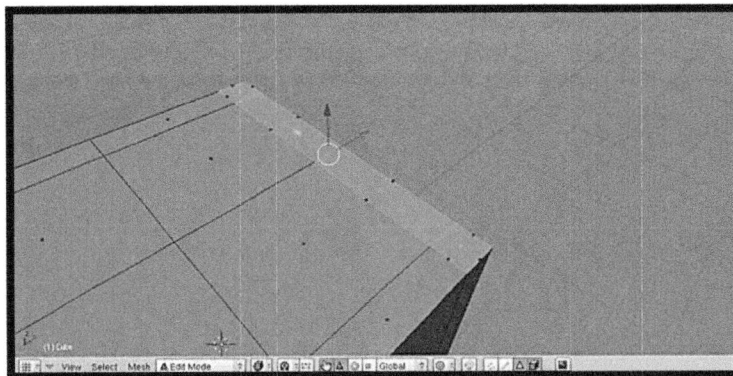

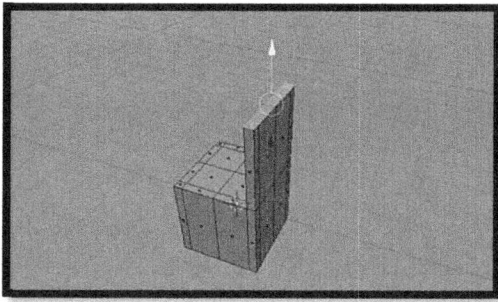

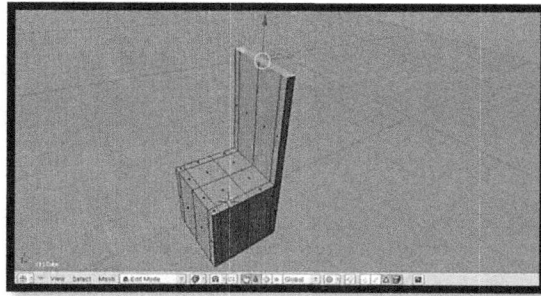

Border Select – Selecting a Group or Number of Faces in One Go

Creating the base of the chair is the following stage. "Border Select" will be utilized to simultaneously choose multiple faces. To view the mesh's bottom, rotate and reposition the scene till you can, as shown below.

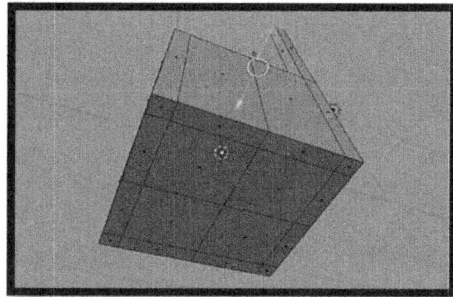

Before we can do anything else, we must deselect the faces that were originally utilized to create the chair's back. As a shortcut, you can use the "A" key to switch between "Select/Deselect All" modes. Pressing "A" will pick or deselect all faces or objects, depending on the "mode" you're in. This removes all faces from the selection, allowing you to perform border selection without worrying about other faces "interfering." A "brush" edge or an "area" edge can be selected when the tool is turned on. To move on to the next phase, press the "B" key twice: once to select the "area" and again to select the "brush." The cursor will transform from a lengthy "crosshair" to a "circle," and we want the "brush" (circle).

Design Note: RMB deactivates the tool.

The "brush" Border pick tool is useful for selecting faces within the brush's boundaries; alternatively, you can "paint" the faces you wish to pick by hovering the mouse over them while holding down the LMB button (the Shift key isn't necessary). To delete any faces you might have selected by mistake, use MMB. As a last step, select all of the faces and then press RMB to disable the tool. Ideally, you'd get something similar to the image down below.

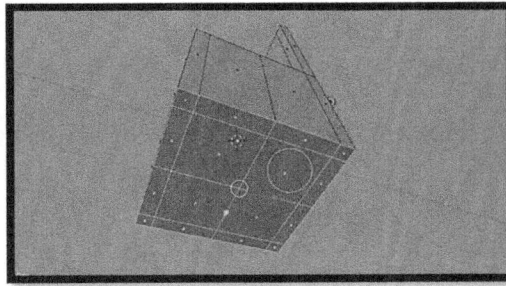

For the chair's "seat," these selected faces must now be raised. Just as you did before selecting the bottom faces, flip the scene so that you can see the mesh from below.

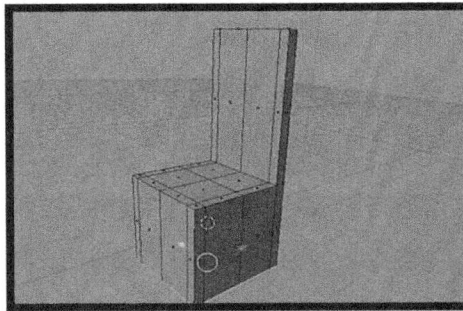

Because the "grid snap" steps are too big, this next bit will likely lead to the next one.

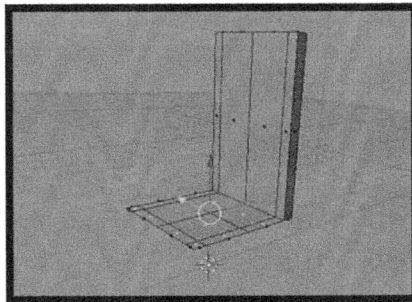

After pressing the blue arrowhead before bringing it up, press **Ctrl+Shift** and drag the mouse up. Keep an eye on the numbers on the left side of the work zones menu area; release when they say "1.6000" or a similar amount; you should see that the movement still snaps to the grid but with smaller steps. While it still clamps to the grid, you have more control over the movement by using **Ctrl+Shift+LMB** drag. By the end, you ought to have something similar to this. The seat for the chair is finally complete.

Design Note: If you don't leave enough space, you may need to do this again. To complete the smaller grid snaps, the mouse needs more room to maneuver.

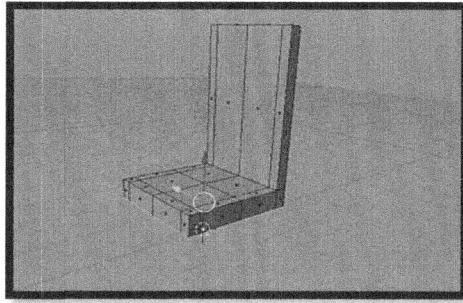

Extruding Individual Faces

To finish, make the chair's legs protrude once more using the "extrude" tool. We must now identify specific faces. To deselect all faces that have been selected before, rotate the object so that you are staring at the base of the mesh again and hit "A." After that, select the four corners by pressing **RMB+Shift**. You ought to be able to see this now.

Design Note: **RMB+Shift** can also be used to reject specific faces that are already chosen.

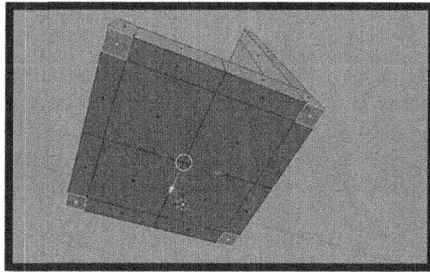

Zoom out to make room and then rotate the scene so you can view the chair from above again. For this extrusion, we'll use a little new method. On this occasion, press "E" to extrude the faces instead of "RMB" to halt the process. Rather, keep it in the "active" state and hit the "Z" key once. By pressing "Z," you've fixed the axis along which the faces will move—in this instance, "up-down" (the "Z" axis)—and the line that appears when you initially extrude the faces changes from pink to pale blue.

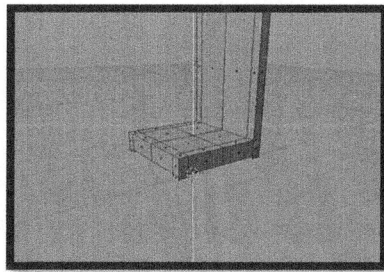

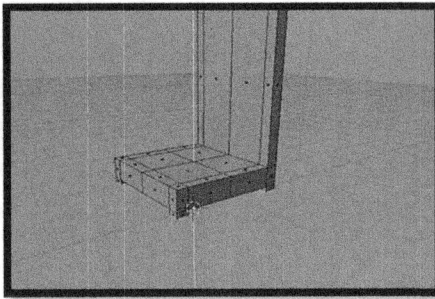

Next, lower the faces by two "steps" (snap points), then remember to hit "Ctrl" to capture motions. Find "2.0000" in the lower-left corner of the workspace once more. You should end up with a result similar to the one below after completing this. Amazing work! The chair's basic mesh frame is now finished.

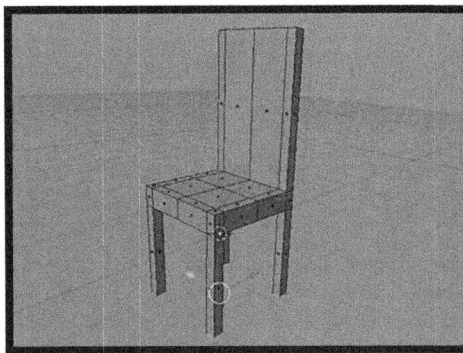

Toggle "Object" Mode

You should have the fundamental chair shape completed after the legs are extruded. Pressing the "TAB" key again will take you back to the "Object" mode. At this point, your workspace ought to resemble the image below.

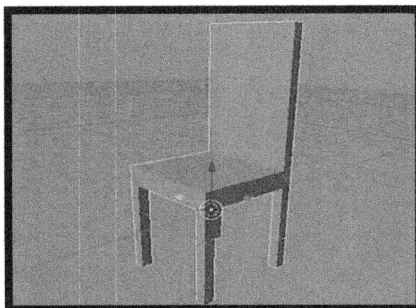

Using Modifiers

One feature of Blender that helps to break up the regularity of the process is Modifiers. Modifiers are quite helpful tools that can save you a lot of time and frustration, even though their name isn't particularly captivating. The computer is then given the task of adding smoothing edges or making your model symmetrical, among other things, to do this. The fact that they inflict no harm is one of the many benefits of modifiers. If you want to modify an object, you can add or remove modifiers at any time. So long as you refrain from applying the update to the object itself, it will not modify it permanently. A return to the original format is an option that you will always have. The modifications tab of the Properties editor is where you will gain access to your mesh's numerous mods. You can view a list of the available mods by clicking the Add Modification icon with your left mouse button. In the image below, you can observe the Modifier Properties together with a compilation of all the many methods for altering a shape.

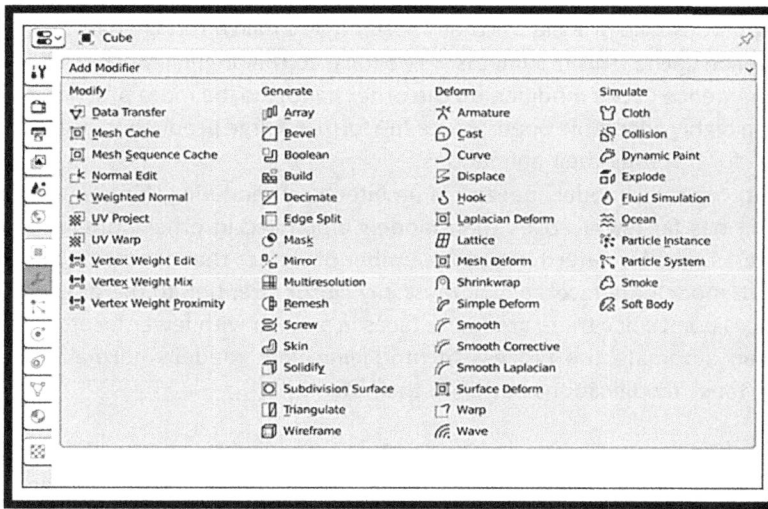

Understanding Modifier Types

In Blender, you can make use of a vast array of diverse tools. Certain objects, such as curves, could only require a subset of the available modifiers. Furthermore, Grease Pencil objects are unique in that they have their own set of modifiers. The majority of modifiers can be found here because handling shape data is Blender's primary responsibility.

Below, we will examine each modifier briefly;

Modify Modifiers

The first column's factors are disorganized; they contain modifications that don't have a proper home in the rest of the table. They all affect points or the data associated with them, which is the main thing these modifiers have in common. Don't stress too much if the UV Project modifier is the only one you can't see yourself using right away. Complex scenes, such as those created by a more seasoned Blenderhead, are the most common use case for these modifiers. **While most things adhere to this principle, the UV Project filter does not. Here are some of the words that appear in this column:**

- **Data Transfer:** When working on large-scale projects, it is common for multiple individuals or models to work on separate but comparable versions of a mesh. This is especially true when it comes to data such as vertex groups, UV maps, or vertex colors. Vertex groups can be utilized as a means of transmission of this data. Points with the same hue make up Vertex Groups. Vertex colors can also be shared between vertex groups. You could find that moving such data across models simplifies things. Donating your time to complete tasks that have previously been completed is unnecessary. You will be able to save this amount of time since the Data Transfer modifier is present.
- **Mesh Cache:** All of your mesh's shape will be updated with new data from a mesh cache file if you make this change. Before going on to lighting and rendering, it is usual practice in large animated films to "bake" completed character motion into the vertex data. This is done before the modeling and lighting phases. The process becomes easier if you follow this change.
- **Mesh Sequence Cache**: This modifier is very similar to the original Mesh Cache in how it operates. The Mesh Sequence Cache modifier, on the other hand, maybe more practical because of its usage of Alembic, a highly adaptable open-source file format. Large production organizations often utilize this file type for finalizing their animations.
- **Normal Edit**: Typically, models utilized in architectural rendering, film animation, or video game development has far fewer edges than models employed in other domains. The reason is: that several systems exist for determining the number of shapes that constitute a point. To conceal the fact that your models are faceted, you must pay closer attention to the direction that the normals on those faces point since there are fewer faces in a mesh with fewer facets. With the Normal Edit tool, you can automate the process of modifying your model's normals and then seamlessly incorporate those modifications back into the model.

Tip: Remember to check the Auto Smooth box in the Normals tab of the Object Data Properties if you wish to utilize the Normal Edit or Weighted Normal modifiers. You can locate this in the Object Data Properties.

- **Weighted Normal**: The Weighted Normal modifier offers a set of controls that are comparable to those of the Normal Edit modifier. But instead of blending back in the mesh normals, this modifier erases them.
- **UV Project**: You can compare the UV Project modifier to a movie or a slide show. View it from that perspective. Although it allows you more freedom, it creates an image that resembles an object-mapped texture.
- **UV Warp**: One such modifier is the UV Warp. Similar to how the UV Project modifier alters your shape's UV values, this one does the same. In contrast, you may rig and warp your UV coordinates for motion using the UV Warp tool, which is quite similar to rigging your mesh's vertex data. Here we can see the difference between the two for ourselves.
- **Vertex Weight Edit, Mix, and Proximity**: As their names imply, these three modifications alter the vertex weights. In a mesh, a vertex can belong to multiple vertex groups. Every vertex can have a weight, which can be any integer from 0 to 1. The strength of a vertex's connection to a given group is indicated by this number. With these changes, you may now adjust the vertex weights with more precision. (When you need to create intricate animation sets, they are invaluable.)

Generate Modifiers

Those are the most popular tools among Blender modelers. You can find them in the library's Generate group of mods. You can add geometry to your model by following this set of steps. Sometimes, they might even eliminate geometry. Because they are modifiers, you can build complex models out of simple base objects by stacking them on top of one another. The factors in that stack of modifiers can have their values changed! **Here you can find a wide variety of inputs. An overview of each of them follows in this sequence:**

Array: Arranging elements in an array is all about making duplicates of your base shape and positioning them precisely according to an offset value. One of my favorite modifiers is called "Array."

Bevel: Nothing in the actual world has perfectly crisp edges or sides. No matter how small, you can always round them. You can make your object look more lifelike by using the Bevel modification. You can adjust a variety of parameters using this modifier and the Bevel tool together. **In contrast to the destructive Bevel tool, this modifier has no effect.**

- **Boolean**: By using the Boolean modifier, it is possible to combine two separate models. To work with several meshes at once, you can simply add, remove, or link them. Sometimes, this transformation can result in unsightly building designs.
- **Build:** With this simple change, you can see how the mesh's different faces are made over time. Reversing the effect is also an option. This will make your mesh slowly disappear over time, one face at a time.
- **Decide:** There will be times when you need to cut back on the amount of geometry in your model, so be prepared to make a decision. In the 3D computer graphing sector known as video games, for instance, where each object is subject to stringent geometry budgets, your model could find application. Using the determining feature, you might perhaps begin to reduce the shape of your model.
- **Edge Split:** While you're constructing, you can select if a face in your mesh will be shown as flat or smooth. You should aim for a smooth appearance most of the time. Just so we're clear, this will result in a loss of information along the model's sharp edges. If you're trying to cut down on the number of points in your model, you can remedy this problem by adding a Bevel modification, but this can result in too much geometry. Using the Edge Split modifier, you can maintain clean edges even when you add a lot of shapes.
- **Mask:** In your model, you can hide specific vertices using the Mask change. This is done by looking at their link to an armature bone or their membership in a vertex group. If you want to hide some edges, you can choose which ones and how.
- **Mirror:** This adjustment will reproduce the geometry in your base mesh and flip it in at least one direction perpendicular to your object. Doing so is useful when painting something that occurs symmetrically in nature.
- **Multiresolution**: Using the same reasoning as the Subdivision Surface Modifier, your shape can be divided into several sizes when you use this modification. One key distinction is the ability to reuse Multiresolution. Another is the fact that you can modify the points at each level of subdivision you create using Sculpt mode. Furthermore, shapes can be rendered with Multiresolution.
- **Remesh**: Some meshes simply cannot have their geometry stored, in which case you may need to remesh the mesh. When dealing with Booleans or heavy modeling, this is an example of such a situation. Utilize the Remesh modifier to acquire a mesh that boasts an improved initial point and

a less complex topology. To get more detailed sculpting, you can acquire appropriately dispersed masks.

- **Screw**: Create many copies of your mesh's shape and rotate them around one of its local directions using the Screw modification. You can use this adjustment to create awesome effects. Spiral shapes, such as springs and screws, can be created using this method. You can also create an object from a basic profile, similar to how Blender's Spin tool works. You can use this to make an object out of a simple description.

- **Skin**: Using the Skin modifier, you can "skin" your shape's points and edges, causing additional modeling to be created around them according to the radius you select in Edit mode. Similar to, but distinct from, raising the Bevel number on a curved object. Using the tools provided by this module, you can easily create basic models from which you can further shape and distribute organic objects, such as vines and plants. Plus, this tool has the potential to generate a mesh model object. Incorporating the proper vertex weights into the armature object will provide shape modification and movement.

- **Solidify**: To demonstrate that 3D shapes can have as thin a profile as the user likes, they can use the Solidify tool. Therefore, if you attempt to view them from specific angles, you will be completely blinded. This is completely unlike the way the actual world operates. In meatspace, there is a very thin layer that covers everything. Using the Solidify tool, you can easily and quickly add extra thickness to each mesh.

- **Subdivision Surface**: One of the most popular and helpful tools in Blender is the Subdivision Surface. To sum up, by dividing each face and edge into smaller parts, the Subdivision Surface modification will increase the number of points in your model. This quality will allow your mesh to have more intricate details and fewer sharp edges. Also, it's great for plant and animal models, which are biological.

- **Triangulate**: All models must have triangle-shaped faces according to certain gaming systems (the programming "behind the hood of a video game"). One term for this orientation is the "triangulate" pattern. Using quads and ngons is not allowed. You won't have to rush into choosing a shape; this adjustment will show you what your model would look like with all faces set to triangles.

- **Wireframe**: Like the Skin modifier, the Wireframe modifier can generate shapes along any lines in your model. But this change's goal and the rules themselves are distinct. You can build renderable wireframes of your mesh using this tweak, which is great for showing your coworkers the configuration. You should not use this modification to produce a base mesh as a starting point; it is designed to be used to make a base mesh.

Deform Modifiers

The word "deform" does not imply anything bad when applied to digital pictures. In the context of digital photographs, "deformed" signifies the manipulation of an object's constituent pieces. The vertices, edges, and faces that comprise your mesh define its shape. The term for this in the context of three-dimensional computer graphics is "sub-components." You should be able to deduce from this that the Deform factors alter the placement of preexisting geometry in your mesh. No changes will add or remove shape, unlike the Generate adjustments. They can only change the arrangement of that shape in response to external restrictions or regulations. Although these adjustments can be applied to models, they are commonly utilized to construct animation rigs. **You can read in detail about each Deform modifier in the list below:**

- **Armature**: When first working with motion rigs, the Armature modifier is where you should focus your efforts. This is so because it enables the creation of armatures. After you apply this modification, a skeleton object will be attached to your mesh. The skeleton's bones can also alter the shape of the mesh to which they're attached.

- **Cast**: One of three fundamental shapes can be specified using the Cast modifier for your mesh: a cube, a sphere, or a cylinder. Put simply, it facilitates the creation of complex shapes.

- **Curve**: The Curve modifier is similar to the Armature modifier in many ways, but it does not alter the mesh's shape by manipulating an armature object's bones. The mesh is used as a curve object instead. Like a cartoon fish, this will be useful if your object's shape changes organically. Any alteration to the shape will cause it to organically bend.

- **Displace**: If you have a grayscale image, sometimes known as a height map, where lighter pixels represent high points and darker pixels represent low points, you can use the Displace tool to relocate specific vertices relative to their original locations. Pixels with lighter shades represent higher levels in the image, whereas pixels with darker shades represent lower levels. You can easily add terrain or rough textures to your model using this method.

- **Hook**: With this adjustment, you can link your mesh to an external object at one or more places (the "hook"). By combining it with other words, its meanings can be transformed. You can use the hooks to compress or expand some of your plastic. Beyond that, they facilitate the handling of curved objects.

- **Laplacian Deform**: This method can effectively change the shape of armatures and hooks, but it has the potential to "fuzz out" the features in your model or bend it too much, resulting in the loss of volume from your base mesh. This can happen because the model could be subject to Laplacian distortion. A computer-based technique is provided by the Laplacian Deform modifier, which helps solve that problem faster than lattices or the Mesh Deform modifier.

- **Lattice**: This Blender object type is composed of a network of interconnected control points arranged in a grid-like pattern. You can alter a mesh's shape in numerous ways by applying a Lattice modifier and then using one of these lattice objects. Using lattices effectively in animated character animation can provide the impression that the characters are being compressed and stretched.

- **Mesh Deform**: This tool allows you to alter the shape of a normal mesh like how a grid can be altered. Here are some examples of what the Mesh Deform tool can do to help clarify things. We need to have a far more in-depth conversation on the advantages and cons, though.

- **Shrinkwrap**: This modifier will allow you to fuse the borders of your current mesh with another mesh's surface. As a result, it will appear as though you covered the other mesh with shrink wrap. Take this modification as an example: if you're aiming to create a cartoonish film with the old-fashioned effect of a water hose bursting, you can achieve your goal. On top of that, while retoposing a sculpture; some modelers employ this factor as a starting point.

- **Simple Deform**: You can stretch, twist, bend, or curve your mesh about its local Z-axis when you make this change. Reducing the thickness of your mesh is another available option.

- **Smooth**: Sometimes you need a model with fewer sharp edges and wrinkles.

- **Smooth Corrective**: The name of this smooth modification is altered so that it can be more easily associated with other smooth modifiers. Most people will refer to it as the Corrective Smooth modifier instead of "Smooth Corrective." Because the character's armature or grid could undergo bizarre shape changes, the Corrective Smooth adjustment is a lifesaver when working with rigs. A portion of its roughness can be immediately remedied using the Corrective Smooth modifier. It aids in the realism of character rig deformations by suggesting the presence of fat or muscle on a character. This objective can be accomplished by making the figure appear to have more mass.

- **Smooth Laplacian**: The words "smooth Laplacian" are defined slightly differently than in our language. The Corrective Smooth adjustment is similar to this in that respect. The modifier menu just refers to it as "Smooth Laplacian" so it can be placed alongside other smooth modifiers. While the Laplacian Smooth modification accomplishes smoothing in a different way than the Smooth modifier, it nonetheless accomplishes the same primary goals. The Smooth Laplacian modifier is typically more time-consuming to apply than its Smooth counterpart. Nevertheless, this modifier frequently produces more aesthetically pleasing outcomes on meshes that utilize more intricate shapes. Cleanup of 3D-scanned or Remesh-modified meshes could be accomplished with the help of the Smooth Laplacian modifier.

- **Surface Deform**: An element of the Mesh Deform modifier is the Surface Deform, which you can think of as an extension of it. Since the Surface Deform modifier is surface-only, it is most effective with empty meshes. In contrast, a well-contained mesh is ideal for use with the Mesh Deform modifier. Surface Deform just modifies the mesh's surface, which is the key distinction between the two. This mode change is commonly employed in scenes when a simulation of cloth is being made on a plane and subsequently extended to a more complex mesh, such as chainmail.

- **Warp**: By stretching the points of your mesh from the origins of two objects, you can warp it. To accomplish this, you can utilize the size, position, and rotation of any two reference objects. Any two reference objects can take advantage of this capability.

Consider this modification as a means to acquire proportional editing without explicitly selecting any vertices if you are already proficient in that area.

- **Wave**: To simulate dropping a pebble into calm water, use the Wave modifier on a heavily fractured plane. Any model can be modified using the Wave adjustment; a split plane is not necessary. Be mindful that the wave effect will not be seen if your shape has very few edges. Your entire mesh will appear to be climbing and descending at the same time throughout the procedure.

Simulate Modifiers

You can locate the Simulate modifications in the last column of the Modifiers table. The Properties editor's Modifier tab is rarely used to add any of these modifications. Except for Ocean and Explode, there are no major exceptions to this norm. You can add a particle system or a physics simulation to your model using the Physics and Particle tabs of the Properties editor, respectively. These will be added without delay. Alternatively, you can manually add them in the Mesh tab of the Properties editor.

The Mirror Modifier

You can make it seem like you reflected the modifications you make to a mesh on one side of a center point on the other side by using the Mirror Modifier. To the scene, add a UV Sphere in the Top Orthographic View. In Edit Mode, use the Tab key to deselect the Vertices. Using the B key (Box pick) and dragging a box will allow you to select half of the vertices on the Sphere. To remove the selected Vertices, simply press the X key. **Tip:** Ensure that the Toggle X-Ray is on in the 3D Viewport Editor Header before attempting to pull the square.

Clicking the Modifier buttons in the Properties Editor while in Object Mode and selecting the half sphere will add a Mirror Modifier.

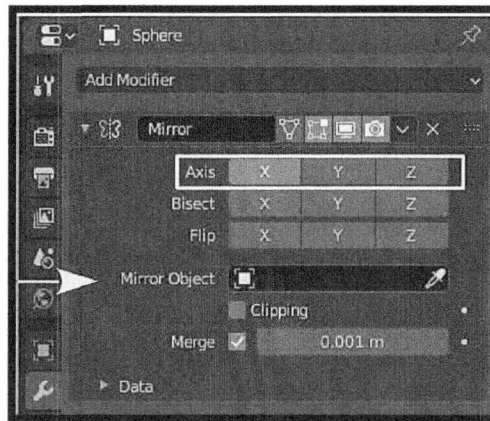

The 3D View Editor will re-add the cut UV sphere. Upon entering Edit Mode, you will observe that the sphere is only partially filled up.

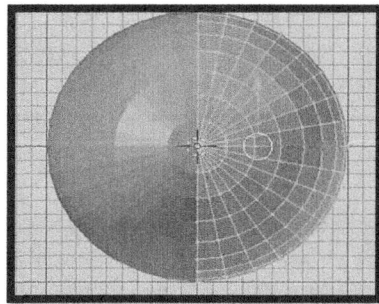

By selecting and translating a single vertex, you can observe that the opposite side's mesh is mirrored. You can make vertices on the reflected side by applying the modifier (Apply in the Modifier Panel). In the center of the Mirror Modifier panel, you will discover Mirror Object. The mirror will be centered on the new object you add to the scene instead of the previous one if you type its name into the Mirror Object Bar after adding it to the scene.

Smoothing Things Out with the Subdivision Surface Modifier

Thanks to the Subdivision Surface Modification, you can divide the surface of an object into smaller slices. Vertices, Edges, and Faces are added in this manner. Doing so will make the Object's surface appear softer and more rounded. A more realistic level of modeling is now achievable as a result of the modifications.

1. Following the "Add" button, select "Mesh" and "Monkey."

2. Use the "Shadow Smooth" option in the "Object" menu to get a picture of the smooth monkey.

As things stand, Suzanne is believed to be quite ordinary. She still appears blocky, but she no longer resembles the one she had when she was first implanted.

3. Go to Modifier Properties, select Add Modifier, and then select Subdivision Surface to add a Subdivision Surface modifier to the monkey. For added convenience, you can also use the shortcut Ctrl+1.

Suzanne, that is! Despite her often ridiculous size, for an instant she seems much more organic and natural. By adjusting the Subdivision Surface and increasing the View number, you can observe Suzanne's potential improvement. However, I believe it would be wise for you to refrain from going absolutely bonkers. Adding more than three portions could further slowdown a machine that is already operating too slowly.

4. Upon entering Edit mode, you will observe that the original mesh is serving as the control cage for the split mesh.

The mesh within the cage immediately adapts to new components as they are added or removed.

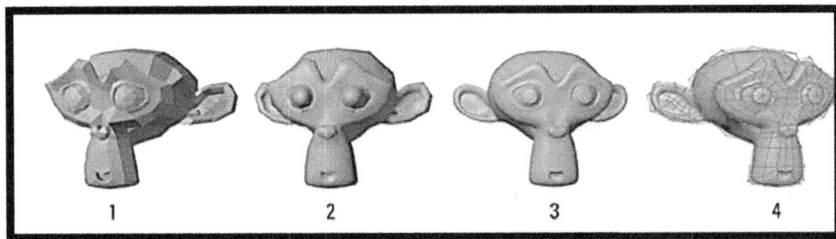

The Subdivision Surface modification is potent, but it comes with limited options when it comes to the stack of mods that can be employed. Below is an example of what the Modifier Properties window looks like when you choose the Subdivision Surface modifier block. The first available option is a selection between the Catmull-Clark and Simple subdivisions. As you might expect, it is configured to split and smooth your mesh when set to the first option. This alternate method is more akin to the Smooth tool while you're in Edit mode. In contrast to this method, the Catmull-Clark method will produce results devoid of biological smoothness. On the contrary, it will boost your model scores. Still, it's helpful to have the Simple subdivision method as an option because it can be useful in some instances.

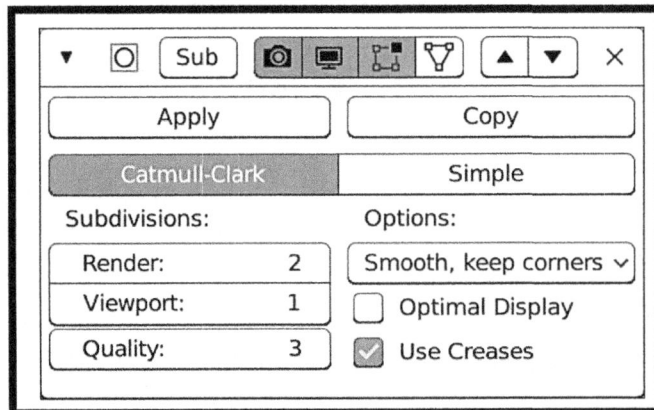

Using the Power of Arrays

The Array modifier in Blender has a ton of cool features that you can use in all sorts of cool ways. You can train a computer to be lazy by giving it as many monotonous, repetitive jobs as possible to do. Utilizing the Array modifier, one can construct a brick wall, a chain-link fence, or even stairs. However, it can also be used to create unique tentacles, rows of dancing robots, and stunning abstract movements! The Array modifier's strength lies in its handling of offsets, also known as the distances that copies are instructed to be from one another. **You can utilize all three of the offset types provided by the Array modifier simultaneously by selecting the necessary options:**

- **Constant Offset**: This offset maintains a constant distance between two objects in an array that are duplicated. If you set the value under this checkbox to -5 meters, all of the duplicates will be moved 5 meters away from X. What occurs when the offsets for the Y- and Z-axes are modified? Their actions are identical.
- **Related Offset:** This factor, which acts like a multiplier, is determined by the object's width, height, and depth. Use it as a multiplier in your calculations. For instance, regardless of the size of the duplicated object, if you set the Z number to 1.0, all of the array's objects will be stacked directly on top of each other. Even without an array, this is still required. This kind of offset is initially utilized when you first apply the Array modifier.
- **Object Offset:** I love the Object Offset the most because of all the ways you can manipulate it. It determines the offset depending on how far away the object is from the mesh you add to the Array by using the Object field to locate the object you want to add (I prefer to utilize Empties for this reason). Having said that, this is merely the beginning! Not only does this offset consider the object's location, but it also takes its rotation and size into account. If you have a space one meter away from your object that is twice as large and rotated by 15 degrees on the Y-axis, then make two copies of it, each with an additional rotation of 15 degrees. Constructing a circular staircase is now second nature to you. Just by animating the offset object, you can create a staircase animation where the stairs can collapse into each other to hide themselves.

Furthermore, you can modify the number of copies made by the Array modifier using the Fit Type drop-down option located at the top of the block. By default, the Fit Type is set to Fixed Count. To specify the precise number of copies, use the Count Field underneath it. Beyond Fixed Count, more Fit Type options are available. These three are for you:

- **Fixed Count**: If you wish to generate exactly 1,000 copies, you can choose the "Fixed Count" option.

You can only modify the Fixed Count number by clicking the mouse once, and Blender refers to the maximum allowable value of 1,000 as a "soft maximum." But you can type in numbers much larger than 1,000 if you click in that spot. Blender will make use of the value you entered.

- **Fit Length:** Choose the appropriate number of copies of objects to match the space you've chosen with the "Fit Length" option. The measurement is not in whole units, so please keep that in mind. An object's local coordinate system is used when an array of that object is made. As you can see in the 3D Viewport's Sidebar (N), the length you select is multiplied by the object's size.
- **Fit Curve:** If you want to use an existing curve object, you can enter its name in the Object data block box that is located below this option. Doing so causes Blender to calculate the length of the

slope and utilize that value as the length to fill in regions with duplicate objects. You can create a crude metal chain using this option and a Curve modifier.

Sculpting Tools and Techniques

Sculpting Tools

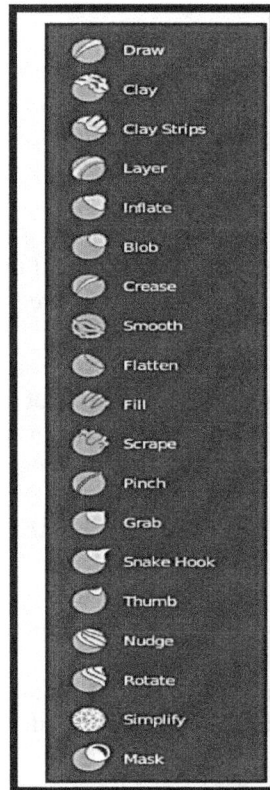

Draw (X)

Changes the location of points within a brush stroke by adjusting their average normal.

Clay (C)

Similar to the Draw brush, but with options to alter the working plane. Its operation is quite similar to that of the combined Flatten and Draw brushes.

Clay Strips

Similar to the Clay brush, but with a cube instead of a sphere for the brush's effect area.

Layer (L)

The displacement layer height can't be unlimited with this brush, unlike Draw. As a result, it appears as though a consistent layer is being drawn. A single brushstroke passes through the entire thing, rather than drawing on top of it. By releasing the mouse button halfway through an action, you can initiate a new stroke that will paint over the previous one and reset the level.

Persistent

You can keep shaping on the same layer even when you move between strokes if you enable this.

Set Persistent Base

If you want to add another layer, you can clear the base by pressing this button.

Inflate/Deflate (I)

Similar to Draw, but with the points expanding in the direction of their normals in Inflate mode.

Blob

You can shape the mesh into a spherical by pushing it inward or outward, and then adjust the settings to pinch the corners to your liking.

Crease Shift-C

This instrument produces sharp ridges or depressions by drawing the mesh taut and pressing the edges together.

Smooth (S)

As its name implies, this function smooths out the positions of the edges to remove irregularities in the mesh that are within the brush's reach.

Flatten/Contrast (Shift-T)

The Flatten brush often establishes an "area plane" at the average height above or below the brush points when used. From then on, the points are drawn in this direction. To apply contrast, just raise or lower the brush tips, keeping them at a distance from the brush surface.

Fill/Deepen

It's quite similar to the Flatten brush, except that it just raises points that are below the brush plane. Contrast the Fill brush with Deepen. In a downhill motion, it shifts points below the plane.

Scrape/Peaks

Similar to the Scrape brush, the Flatten brush shifts points above the plane downwards. Contrasting with the Scrape brush, To Peak forces points above the plane to rise and fall off the plane.

Pinch/Magnify (P)

The point is drawn towards the center of the brush. In contrast, magnify shifts the brush's tips away from the center, making the image appear larger.

Grab (G)

Turn a set of points on their heads. When dragged across the model, Grab stays in the same spot the whole time, unlike other brushes. With a single press of the mouse button, Grab selects multiple locations at random and repositions them so they track your mouse pointer. Grab can utilize other Sculpt Mode options like texturing and symmetry, but moving a group of vertices in Edit Mode with Proportional Editing selected yields the same result.

Snake Hook (K)

Using the motion of the brush creates serpentine shapes by drawing points in tandem.

Pinch

With a pinch value higher than 0.5, you can still make shapes with the Snake Hook brush, even though its volume decreases as you move it.

Rake

The component that allows the mesh to follow the pointer's movement and rotation.

Thumb

The Nudge brush and this one are similar in that they both flatten the mesh in the brush area and move it in the direction of the stroke.

Nudge

The movement of the tips mimics that of a brushstroke.

Rotate

In the same manner as the pointer, rotate the brush points. When the angle is zero, you can spin around the center to create a whirling effect without any drag.

Simplify

No matter how you select the Collapse Short Edges option, this brush will collapse the edges that are determined by the size of the detail. In the absence of a dynamic shape, this brush serves no purpose. You can locate it in the Brush Sculpt Tool option.

Mask (M)

You can select which areas of the mesh will remain unpainted by painting their vertex colors. Grayscale displays mask numerals. The effect of shaping will be less noticeable in darker, blocked-off areas. The options in the Mask menu can be perused as well.

Mask Tool

Mask brush has two settings:

Draw

Using a mask.

Smooth Shift

When you press Shift while the mask brush is selected, the mask smoothing mode will change.

Annotate

Write annotating by hand.

Annotate Line

Make an edit with a straight line.

Annotate Polygon

Note: Draw a circle.

Annotate Eraser

Get rid of any previously made notes.

Setting Up Your Sculpting Workspace

You can switch to Sculpt mode from any other 3D Viewport simply by clicking the Mode option in the title. Pressing Ctrl and Tab simultaneously will significantly accelerate your journey. If you're using the standard file that comes up when you select File > New > General, you can also access the Sculpting section on the third tab from the left side of the window. Clicking that tab will immediately switch Blender to create mode, where the 3D Viewport is configured to remain out of the way while you work. Applying this will allow you to commence your project without delay. Even though most 3D modelers won't begin with a cube, it's good to know that Sculpt mode is always an option. Most artists prefer to begin with a denser mesh since it requires more geometry changes to get the desired level of detail. In the past, sculpting required breaking up and smoothing out a cube, but now there is a better and faster way to get started. The "Sculpting" option is accessible via the "New" submenu of the "File" menu on the main menu. The only workspace tabs that appear at the top of the Blender window as soon as you start modeling are modeling and shading. You can start a new General work session using the same layouts for both of these categories. One major difference is that in Sculpt mode, you are not initially presented with a cube as your 3D Viewport primitive. Rather, you are given a high-poly sphere to work with from the get-go.

Sculpting a Mesh Object

While holding down the left mouse button and dragging the brush pointer around the 3D Viewport, you can use any of the tools on the Toolbar. You can get a lot more done with this brush method of editing on a drawing pad. The majority of tools in the 3D Viewport include a "brush cursor" that accompanies your mouse movement. When you bring the brush pointer near the object you're molding, it adapts to its surface. By keeping an eye on the brush cursor in this way, you can easily keep track of the orientation of your modeling tool, which is very important when sculpting. Symmetry along the local X-axis of your create object is enabled for all tools in the default create environment. Because a tiny dot on the opposite side of your mesh follows the position of the brush cursor as you move it over your mesh, you can tell its working. You can swiftly alter the radius by pressing F, regardless of whether you're using a different tool or if it has a brush cursor. Once you press that button, the brush cursor will stop moving and instead face you. Then, by dragging the mouse pointer in and out of the brush's center, you can adjust the tip size. You can also alter the visual strength of your brush by pressing Shift+F. In this scene, you can strengthen your brush by bringing your mouse cursor closer to the center of the handle.

Advanced Modeling Techniques

Retopology

Retopology is a crucial stage in Blender's import process for optimizing models for speed and animation. Using a suite of retopology tools and advice, users can simplify complex high-poly designs into clean, usable models that are prepared for production. Blender retopology improves the aesthetics of your models by placing a new topology on top of an existing shape. It strengthens the distribution of polygons, which enhances the performance of both rendering and motion. To create top-notch 3D content, this stage is essential. To get the topology appropriate for animation, retopology can be somewhat challenging. In many cases, the solution lies in carefully monitoring the polygon count and edge flow to overcome this obstacle. If you want to study Blender retopology and create models that look amazing and function well for animation, it's necessary to understand these issues. One can retopologize using Blender's numerous tools and approaches. **A high-level overview of Blender's retopologizing process is as follows:**

- Retopologize your high-poly model by adding a new mesh object to Blender after you've loaded it.
- Use the "Add Vertex" or "Add Edge" tools (Ctrl+Left Mouse Button shortcut) to add a new vertex or edge to the retopology mesh while you're in edit mode.

- For the high-poly mesh, use the snapping tools to add more edges or points to the surface. Select the appropriate snap type (such as "Face") after clicking the magnet icon in the 3D viewer's header. Then, you can begin snapping.
- Create a basic shape that resembles the high-poly mesh by adding points and lines.
- To enhance the topology, you can add details and adjust the edge flow to match the high-poly mesh's shape once you have the fundamental shape. To create new edges, use the "Loop Cut" tool (Ctrl+R shortcut). To reposition existing edges, use the "Slide Edge" tool (G twice to open it in shortcut mode).
- If you want to create a mesh for mirrored retopology, you can avoid wasting time and effort making a separate mesh for the other side of the model by using the "Mirror Modifier."
- To add the mirror modifier and join any points that meet, use the "Merge Vertices" tool (keyboard shortcut: Alt+M).
- To ensure the retopology mesh adheres precisely to the original mesh's shape, you can use the "Shrinkwrap Modifier" to apply it to the high-poly mesh's surface.

Using Booleans

In many cases, the Boolean modifier is an excellent tool for solving modeling difficulties. After you've chosen an object, head to the modifier stack in the properties panel to apply the Boolean modifier. Choose "add modifier" and then search for "Boolean." The Boolean modifier typically requires two items to function properly. An object that needs to be finished and a task. You can choose these on the screen that shows the modifiers. Now that we know what Blender is, let's find out more about it.

What is a Boolean Modifier?

Blender provides a tool called a Boolean modifier that allows us to apply Boolean functions to our 3D models. To be a Boolean, two objects must overlap, and the result will change depending on the dot. You have three options when it comes to binary operators.

- Difference
- Union
- Intersect

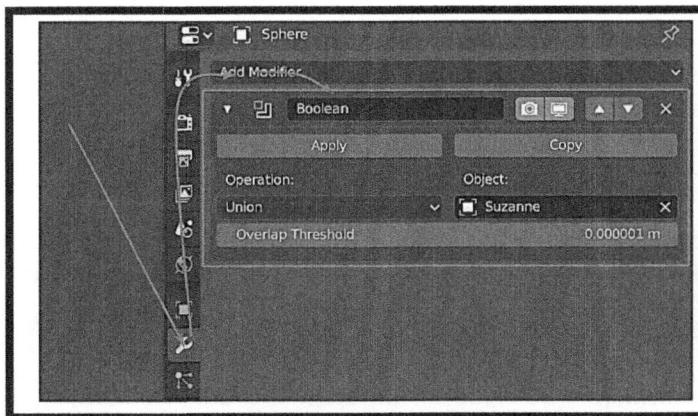

We eliminate the shared volume between objects whenever we act on one of them. Like "cutting" or "carving" into an object according to its shape, this also applies here. A union procedure will attempt to combine the two objects by looking for spots where they meet. If you combine the volumes, you get something like a single object. To remove all but the space that is occupied by two objects, the intersect procedure will use them.

How to Enable the Boolean Modifier in Blender

A Boolean is used as a modifier in Blender. If you're in the settings panel, you can access the modifier stack by clicking the wrench tab. If you would like to delve more into the modifier stack, you can see my beginner's guide here: Select "Boolean" from the list of modifiers, then select "add modifier." The red name of the modifier will be highlighted.

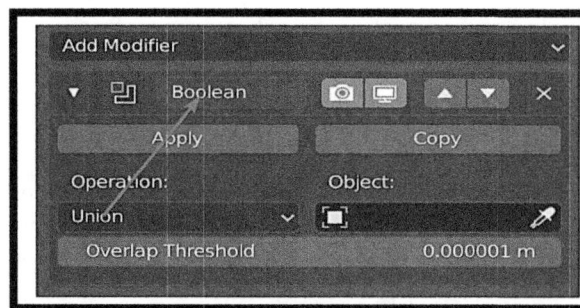

So far, the modifier has done nothing. It's blocked. We require knowledge about the other object we wish to utilize to complete the binary action. To activate the modifier, look for the eyedropper icon adjacent to the object slot and click on it. Once you're in the 3D viewer or outliner, select the object you wish to edit.

How to Cut a Shape Out of another Shape in a Blender

The most common use case for Booleans in Blender is cutting off shapes from other shapes. Here are the simple steps:

- Be sure you're in Object mode.
- Pick out the object you want to cut.
- In the properties box, go to the modifier tab and add a Boolean modifier.
- Make sure Definition is chosen for the process.
- Press the eyedropper button in the interface for Boolean modifiers.
- Apply pressure to the object you want to cut.

There can be no impact until the objects make physical contact with one another. The object you decide to cut will stay intact, so keep that in mind. Changes will only affect objects that have the Boolean modifier.

Blender Boolean Is Not Cutting

The object we used to cut will still be in the cutout region after a different action, so it can be difficult to perceive the difference at first. Pick the object and hit H to make it disappear. Later on, you can open all objects again by pressing Alt+H. Additionally, the object options can be accessed through the settings panel. The small yellow symbol is that. If you want to configure the Display as wire or limit, you can do so here. You can still see the result, even though Blender will only display the object as an outline or bounding box to indicate its presence.

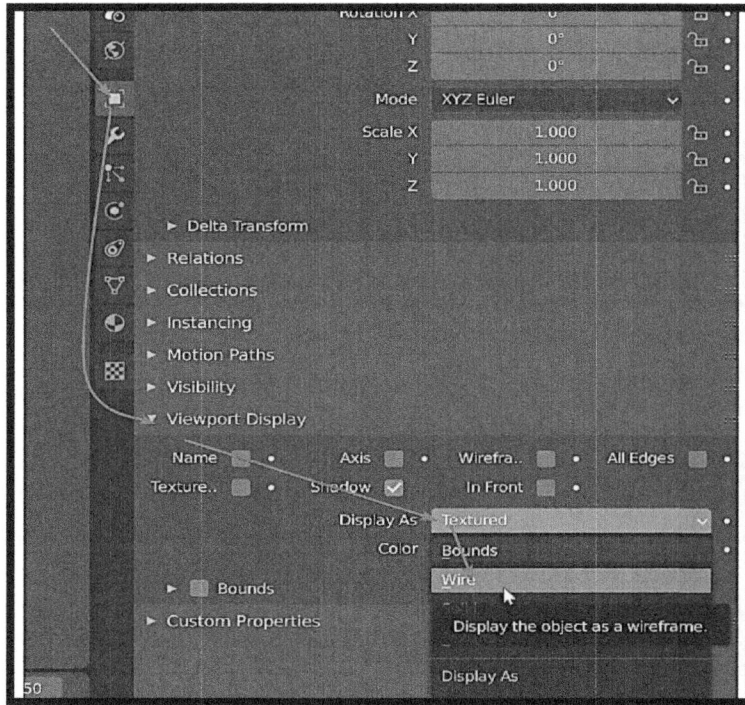

It is typical to have to troubleshoot Booleans, particularly for newcomers whose structure isn't always perfect. When it comes to this, Blender's Boolean method is quite particular.

Boolean Union Multiple Objects

Another common scenario is when we wish to merge multiple objects into one larger one. To make a single object out of multiple Boolean modifiers, we can stack them. Make careful to add all of the modifiers to the same object as long as the overlapping section isn't merging with the original. **Here are the simple steps:**

- Be sure you're in object mode.
- The object that will house the modifier stack is something you must select.
- Add a real modifier to the stack.
- Change the course of action to merge.
- Press the eyedropper after clicking the object you wish to use the boolean modifier on.
- The last three steps must be repeated for every object that you wish to union.
- You can prevent the viewport from becoming distorted due to overlapping geometry by hiding any objects without a modifier stack.

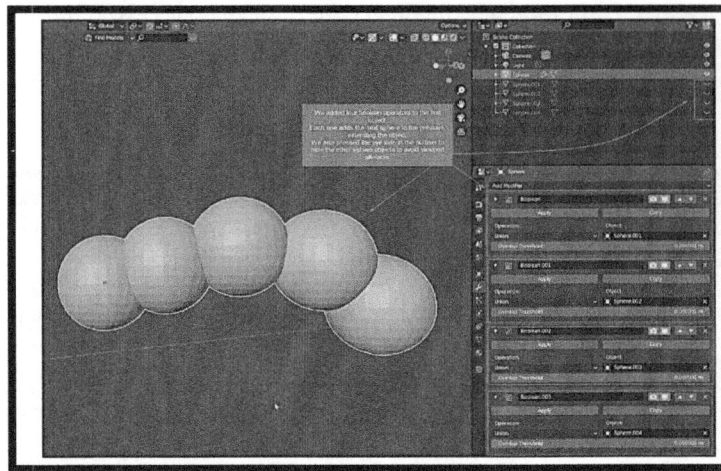

To continue editing the raw shape in edit mode after objects have been combined, press "Apply" on all modifiers.

Boolean Intersect

My least common function is intersecting. However, there are instances when I do still find it helpful. It can be used to make broader shapes and to restrict the amount of space an object can occupy. The way you normally think about difference is backward. Our goal is to have the majority of our objects participate in a cross-process as much as possible. By using an overlap, we can also add shape to an object. We will not go over the same procedures again. All is well with the Boolean operator now. However, the contents of the object we select for the Boolean modifier will be retained after applying the cross method. For example, if we wish to retain an object in a specific region of our scene, this can be rather useful. Avoiding places that cannot be printed is important when we are modeling for possible use in 3D printing. We may wish to partially shape our object in a different scenario. In this scenario, we might have an inverted shape in mind that we'd like to accommodate the object.

Blender Boolean Modifier Failed to Set Value

Try again once you see the warning "failed to set value" in the information bar at the bottom of Blender's screen when you attempt to use the eyedropper tool. Simply put, you are attempting to access an object that already has the Boolean modifier applied to it. It is possible to have two models that represent the same object in this scenario. By using the tab key, you can enter the editing mode. Next, select a single face, edge, or point of the mesh to utilize, just as you would with the Boolean modifier. To select all connected shapes, press CTRL+L. You can make this mesh its object by pressing P and then choosing "selection." Once you're in object mode, you can use the eyedropper tool again.

How Do I Troubleshoot Boolean Modifier Problems?

If a Boolean indicates that they do not wish to cooperate, we can take certain measures. Typically, I have a procedure that I follow when this occurs. Making ensuring the mesh won't let water in is the first step. Later versions of Blender allow you to switch the modifier settings from fast to accurate, so you can adjust the

73

pace as you choose. We can try a lot of different approaches to see if the quick fix works. Press Ctrl+A and then select a scale from the menu to confirm that you have applied scale. Now Blender will use the object's current size as its starting point. Next, see if you can eliminate the duplicates. In 2.80 and later versions, you can find this function in the "merge menu"; to access it, press Alt+M (or simply M) and select "by distance." When the edges are superimposed or very near to one another, they will connect. As a result, zero-area faces are handled and any holes in the mesh are filled. A count of the vertices that Blender deleted will be displayed. If you're not sure about that figure, you may always go back and alter the level in the operator settings (found in the lower left corner). Try to determine the reason behind any unusual behavior displayed by one of these processes. A more significant issue is likely occurring. Verifying that all of the normals are identical is the next step. Pressing Shift+N when in edit mode allows us to select everything. To make the normals face forward the majority of the time, Blender will recalculate them. If you're still not satisfied with the reliability of your normals, you can enable the normal direction view for faces. In edit mode, go to the overlay menu and select the face symbol to locate the normal area. Next, enlarge the picture till you can make out facial lines. It will be easier to tell which way each regular face is if you look at this. Be careful that they are all facing forward. Apply these three procedures on the target object as well as the base object. After you're done, your objects can be processed using a Boolean function.

Even if both objects still don't fit, there are still steps to take. The object can be shifted just a little so that the intersections of the objects seem nicer. Stay away from lines that move very closely together and from intersections that are quite tiny. Blender will have to determine how to connect the two objects if one has millions of polygons and the other only a handful. This can be challenging. Boolean operations work well when the densities of the shapes are close to one another. You can separate a piece by entering into object mode, picking one element (face, vertex, or edge) in the object you wish to separate, and then push "P" to separate by the Boolean modifier. It is recommended to add a new Boolean modifier to the underlying mesh and set this divided portion as its target. Finding loose shapes can now be done. Isolated edges, faces, or points can be the source of the problem. In such a case, you can choose the object whose properties you wish to modify, then use the keyboard shortcut CTRL+L to choose "linked." To invert the selection, press CTRL+I. It will now be chosen if there is any more geometry that is circulating. Cut out the extraneous parts of your object. When all other options have been exhausted, try experimenting with the Boolean modifier. By doing so, the cause of the modifier's malfunction may become apparent. Additionally, we may discover that addressing the issue takes more time than actually correcting the problem. Then, save time and fix the problem.

Hard Surface Modeling

Cars, armor, tools, and other inanimate objects with smooth surfaces can be described in this way. The effectiveness of this method for creating weapons, robots, defense mechanisms, machinery, and structures makes it a popular choice in science fiction and shooter video games.

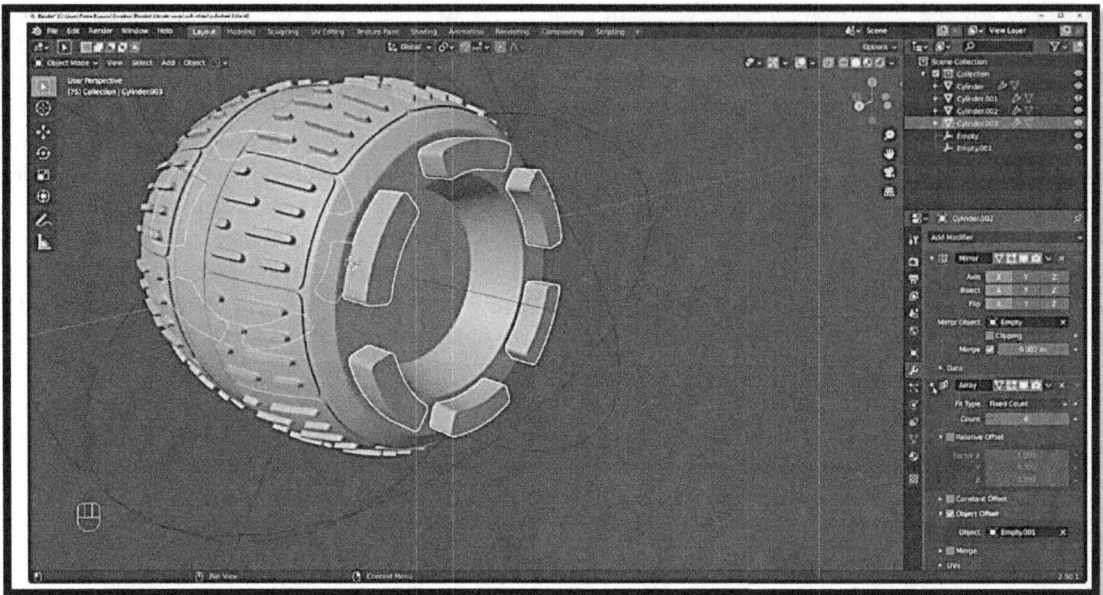

The precise definition of hard-surface modeling is a point of contention among some. Most individuals utilize their own "hard surface" models as there isn't yet a precise definition of what one is. Contrarily, when simulating hard surfaces, it's best to use a geometric mesh that is smooth and devoid of fine details, as opposed to when simulating living things, such as animals.

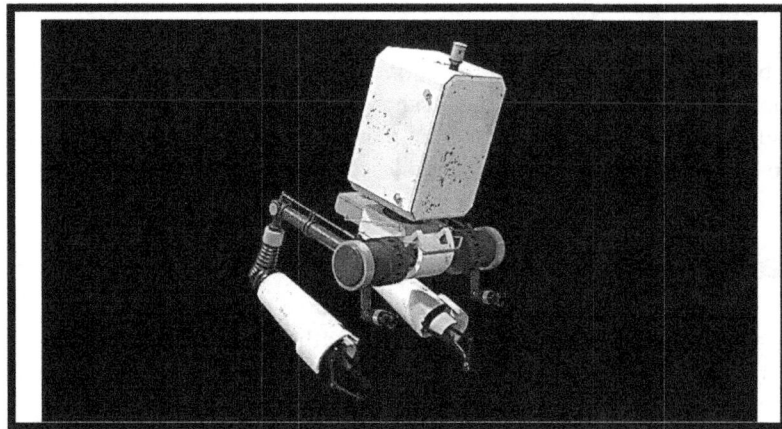

Biological bodies are designed to move and flow, in contrast to stiff structures that don't change shape and are typically modeled using hard surfaces. Wheels, which are rubber and can be bent, would nonetheless be represented as hard surfaces in an automobile model. The reason behind this is that even after being drawn, they maintain a flawless surface. Clean, contrasting colors and simple settings are usual for rendering hard-surface models. However, this serves the artist's purposes and has no practical justification.

Hard-Surface vs. Organic Models

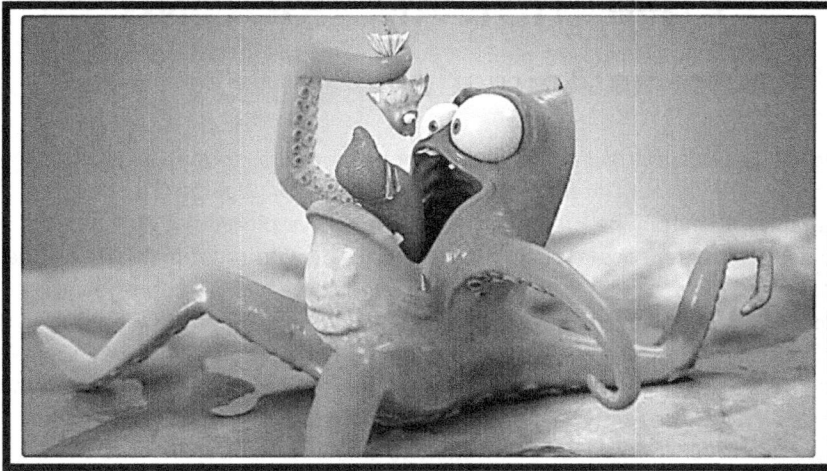

Hard surface modeling is used to create objects with smooth surfaces, sharp edges, and well-defined lines. This kind of modeling is commonly used for man-made objects such as vehicles, homes, robots, and equipment. Hard surface modeling makes use of a variety of tools, including Boolean operations, which create complicated shapes by joining or cutting them, and modifiers such as Bevel, which rounds edges, and Array, which replicates portions. Lines and snaps are precision tools that are utilized to ensure the shapes are accurate. On the flip side, organic modeling is all about creating objects that mimic the appearance of real-life entities or organic structures through the usage of organic, organic shapes. You can apply this method to plants, animals, and even humans. Organic modeling employs the sculpting process. To achieve high levels of detail and seamless transitions between them, artists meticulously shape and polish meshes. Subdivision surfaces can also be used to create rounded, smooth shapes. When you use proportional editing, you can create smooth transitions by changing points with a falloff. However, retopology is fantastic for motion and adding features since it creates a tidy and efficient mesh topology over a high-resolution sculpted model. Finally, hard surface modeling is concerned with precision and the creation of objects with distinct, well-defined shapes, whereas organic modeling focuses on the creation of smooth, organic forms. Each method relies on a unique combination of resources and procedures to do its task.

CHAPTER 5
ANIMATION AND RIGGING

Basics of Keyframe Animation

Keyframing in Blender is a skill that every digital artist or animator has to master. By creating keyframes and assigning values at predetermined intervals, you can animate any Blender attribute. Locate the starting frame you want to use for keyframing on the timeline once you've picked the object to animate in Blender. To return the object's characteristics to their original positions, you must first land on the proper frame. Once you're ready to add a keyframe, simply press the I key. A menu will pop up when you keyframe specific attributes like position, rotation, or scale. To animate a place, for example, you would need to highlight it in the Dope Sheet editor and be in the appropriate animation channel at all times. As you go around the timeline, you can change the object's location or condition for the following keyframe. When you're ready to insert the keyframe, press the I key again at this new location. Your keyframes will be represented on the timeline by golden diamonds. If you decide you want to change anything or move them later on, you can always do that. Remember to save frequently so you don't lose any work. **TIP:** The Graph Editor is a great tool for making fine-grained adjustments to the animation's smoothness using keyframe interpolation. You can add dynamic transformations and motions to your projects once you master the basics of keyframing in Blender. Keyframing is a versatile tool for bringing your creative ideas to life, as you'll see as your skills improve. Knowing how to ease and interpolate in animations will be covered in the next lesson, which will be prepared for this one.

Setting and Editing Keyframes

Select an object in the 3D Viewport to start animating. The object can be made active by clicking on it. You can navigate to a certain frame in the **Timeline** by either clicking on its number or by dragging the green pointer. You need to put the first keyframe here. With the left and right arrow keys, you can go frame by frame for detailed animation. The last step is to make the desired adjustment to your object, which could include scaling, rotating, or translating. To access the 3D viewport, click on it. For this edit to be saved as a keyframe, press the "I" key. Keyframe types will be displayed in a menu; select the one that best suits your needs to initiate the transition. A yellow marker will show up on the timeline to identify the location of your keyframe. Now that you've moved to a new frame, you can make your next keyframe by following the same methods. Blender interpolates the frames between keyframes to create a smooth transition.

Playback Animations in the Timeline

To preview your animation, press the Play button on the Timeline or use the shortcut Alt + A. Track the object's progress as you drag it between the keyframes you've specified. You can use this visual feedback to assess and enhance your animations. The Spacebar will take you to the Timeline, where you can observe your animation. You can change the speed and duration by changing the keyframes. To become an accomplished Blender keyframe animator, practice makes perfect.

Master Keyframe Animation: Navigating Your Tools

Learn the ins and outs of the Blender animation timeline if you're an animator who wants to save time without sacrificing quality. Your animation's progress can be seen on the timeline, which functions similarly to an animated storyboard. Keyframes are the building blocks of your projects, and with their guidance, you can manage their sequence and schedule. Use the Shift + Up Arrow and Shift + Down Arrow shortcuts to move between keyframes, or use the Right Arrow and Left Arrow to move one frame at a time, to make the most of the timeline. With the G command, you can accurately grab and modify keyframes. In this manner, you can modify the action's timing without affecting the keyframe's properties. Simply right-clicking on a keyframe and selecting "Interpolation Mode, member," you can manage the animation's progression from one frame to the next. You can change the pace and slowing of your animation by utilizing the Bezier or Linear options. When you master Blender's animation timeline, you'll be able to create smooth, lifelike animations with ease. Once animators have mastered these fundamental skills, their creativity can soar. Now that we've gone over the fundamentals, let's look at how to use modifiers and constraints to add realism and complexity to your animation.

Animating Objects with Blender Advanced Keyframe Tips

As your skills in Blender grow, exploring intricate keyframing will broaden your animation possibilities. This advanced Blender keyframing course will help you refine your animation workflow. Mastering the Graph Editor is essential for working with keyframes and interpolation. Investigating F-curves will teach you how to control motion with pinpoint accuracy. If you use the Graph Editor's Bezier handles, you can make the transitions less abrupt. Animations created using this method will seem more animated and realistic. A character's facial expressions or other complex deformations can be easily achieved with the help of shape keys. You can assign keyframes to make these shape keys come to life. This method enhances detail without overwhelming the timeline by avoiding the usage of an excessive amount of bone keyframes. Look into nonlinear animation (NLA) as a method for combining and layering. You can effortlessly make complicated sequences by superimposing gestures with the NLA Editor. This capability is crucial for animated character complexes. When combined with modifiers and constraints, keyframes allow for the creation of dynamic effects. Make use of keyframes to tweak details and limitations to automate motions. These capabilities work together to simplify the process of animating complicated setups and how they interact with their environment. Make an effort to understand drivers so you can exert indirect control on animations. The drivers save time by automatically correlating attributes and linking them so that one can activate another. They are particularly effective while handling multiple objects simultaneously or doing repetitive tasks. Experiment with various motion trajectories at will. They provide visual feedback on the trajectory of an object before the final depiction. Having this visual aid at your disposal is invaluable for refining your scene's finer aspects. You will master **advanced keyframing in Blender** if you refer to these methodologies. Keyframes are constantly subject to fine-tuning, and it's important to remember that digital animation is non-destructive, thus adjustment is always an option.

Rigging and Weight Painting

When animating biological models in Blender, weight painting is a must. It specifies the parameters within which the mesh of a model can be modified concerning the bones of the rig. To create genuine movement, animators must master a well-executed weight paint. Blender makes stringing weights considerably easier with a customized painting guide. This guidebook provides a crucial method for exact weight distribution. This is essential if you aim for a realistic appearance in your 3D animations.

Setting Up Initial Rigging Compatibility

Beginning with these steps will get you up and running with rigging compatibility and weight blending:

- Make your mesh and armature selections.
- Use the shortcut **Ctrl + P** to parent them with automatic weights.

We start with these weights because of this straightforward link. You can turn them up or down to get better deformations.

Testing and Refining the Rig

Once the binding is complete, you can test and adjust the rig as follows:

1. Watch for any abnormal deformation when you pose the rig. This highlights the areas that need work in the weight mixing to provide the best possible rigging compatibility.
2. **Follow these steps to make the weight painting better:**
   - In pose mode, choose the troublesome bones.
   - Use the Weight Paint tool to switch to Weight Paint mode.
   - Adjusting the weights until the movement appears natural by painting over the mesh.

You can use Blender to make weight changes less noticeable. Use the Blur brush that is part of the Weight Paint tools. Using smoother gradients results in more realistic motions, improved rigging compatibility, and weight blending.

Ensuring Consistency and Precision

Having stable weight values is crucial. In addition to improving performance, they ensure mesh rigging compatibility. **Here is some guidance to think about:**

- Make use of the Vertex Groups panel to check weights.
- Maintain a balanced distribution of influence by making modifications as needed.

Various weights can be applied using the Subtract and Add brushes. They let you control how much of an effect bones have on your model. Experts rely on precision like this for rigging compatibility and weight mixing.

Finalizing the Rig

The end goal is to have an animated model that is well-rigged. Coordination between each vertex and its corresponding bone is essential when moving. You can help the rigging work together and integrate weights more effectively if you paint the weights accurately. Pose your character to view the weight painting once you're happy with how it appears. If there are any remaining issues, identify them and address them.

Using the Graph Editor

In the graph editor, we may manipulate the object's behavior between two neighboring keyframes, change the response of each associated frame to the next, and add more control over how the animation looks in the viewport by placing points on the graph. When creating 3D animations in Blender, the graph editor isn't always required, but it often has a significant influence on the final result.

What Is the Purpose of the Graph Editor?

While some of Blender's editor types are more fundamental than others, each one is useful for its specific task when animating. There are three distinct types of editors needed to create a 3D animation.

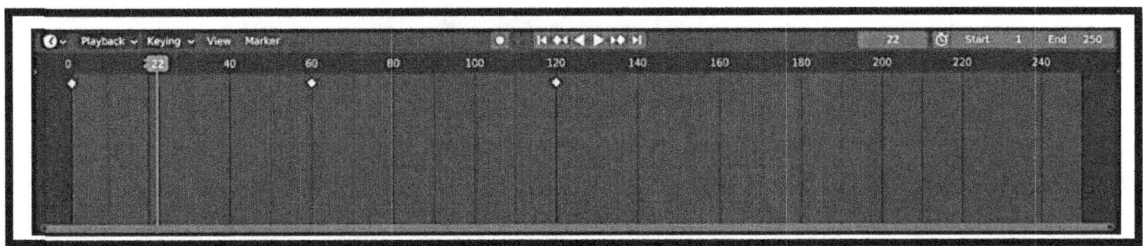

The timeline is where you should begin your work as an animator. You can preview your animation in the viewport with the playback controls before rendering, and you can see the locations of the keyframes you've placed on your selected objects here. This editor is the most important to use because you should always be able to see a preview of your work in progress.

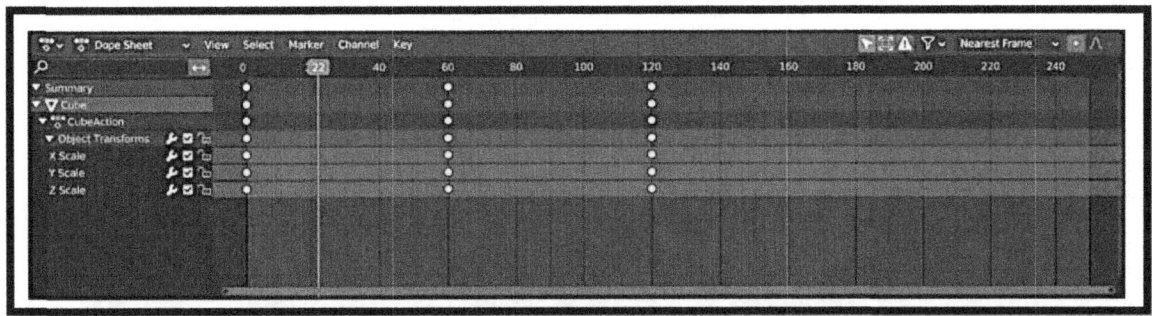

Alternatively, the dope sheet facilitates the positioning and manipulation of the many keyframers we produce. We can control the keyframe structure and tweak specific channels with its help. We have much more control over the layout of the animation with the additional options provided by the channel and key menus.

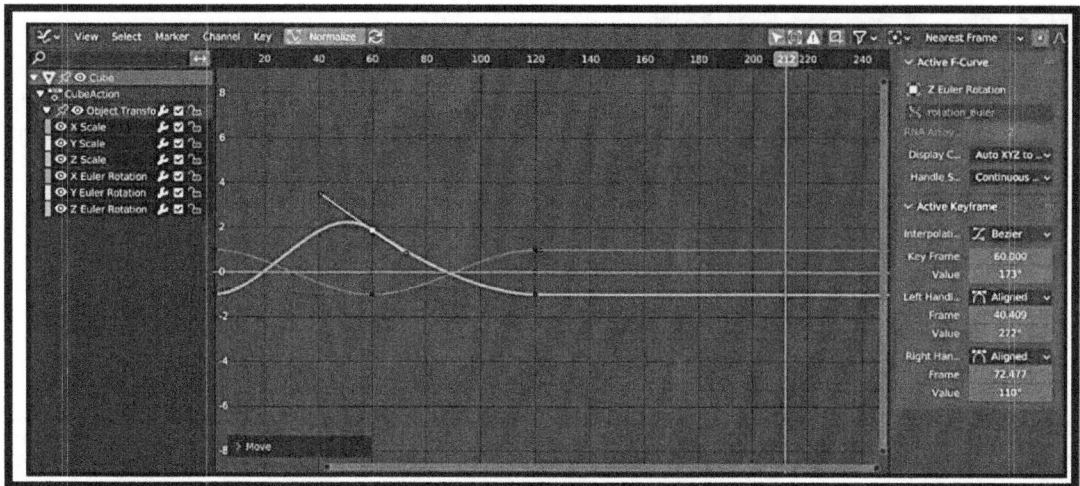

The graph editor gives us a different way to see the relationships between our keyframes graphically. With the graph editor, we can primarily alter their behavior using keyframe handles. Picture this: you can change the animation's general settings in the timeline, tweak the keyframes in the dope sheet, and alter the events that happen between them in the graph editor. Among the many things we can do with the graph editor is speed up the rotational shift as we get closer to the next keyframe or have an object travel farther than it should and then come back.

How to Access the Graph Editor?

The graph editor is an add-on that no animator's workspace presently has. Up to this point, the only tools accessible in the animation workspace are the outliner, properties, two 3D viewports, timeline, and dope sheet. The graph editor is still hidden.

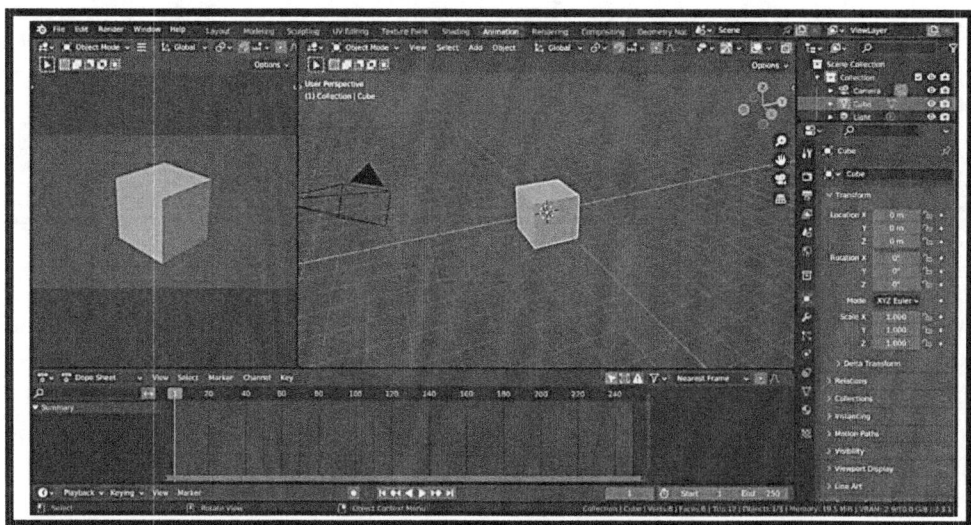

The main reason for this problem is that our workspace is too small to handle the additional editor type. The Graph Edit occupies a lot of space, both horizontally and vertically, thus we should switch out one of the two 3D viewports if we wish to use it.

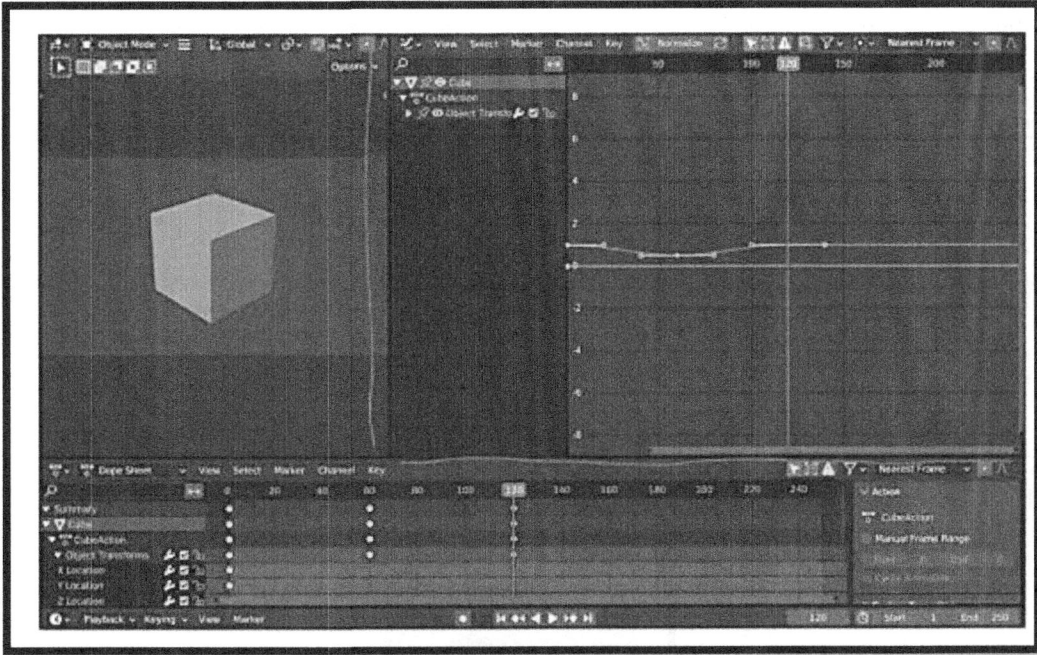

You can use the graph editor in the same way as any other editor by going to the editor type menu and then finding it in the animation category. To change the available space for the editor's user interface, you can either use the hotkey Control + Spacebar or the maximum area option in the view menu.

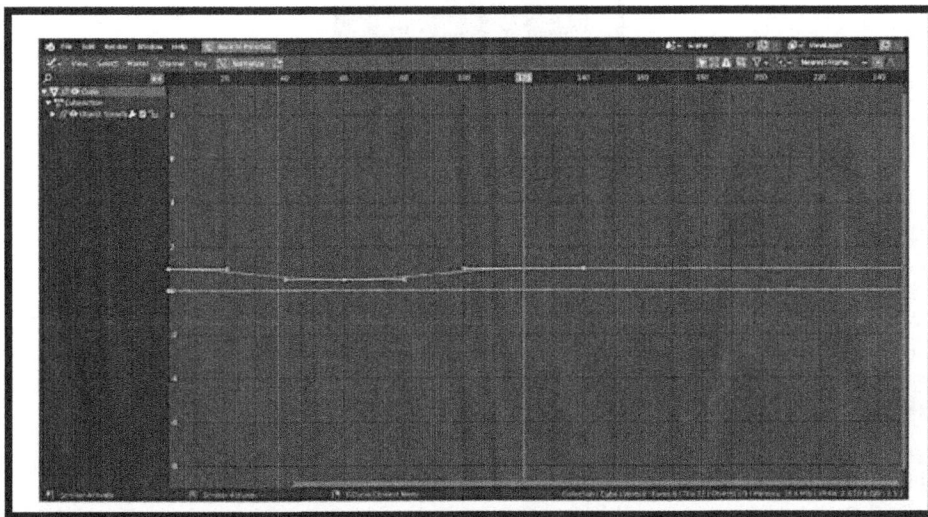

How to Read Your Graph Editor

You won't have any trouble reading either the dough sheets or the timetable. They represent the frames and keyframes placed on top of them. For example, the numbers assigned to our timeline reflect the frames or seconds of our animation. Following the instructions on our schedule or dope sheet is all that is required of us.

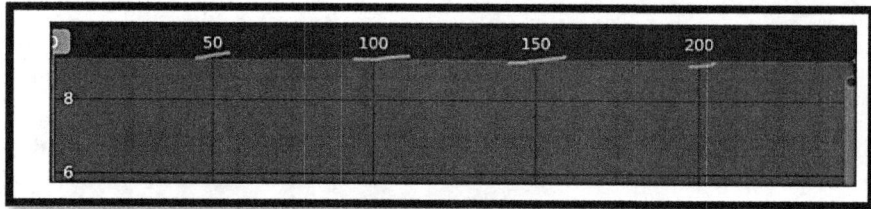

Using the graph editor, though, requires us to read in both vertical and horizontal orientations. Like the timeline, the graph editor's horizontal numbers show the amount of time the animation has been running, in frames or seconds.

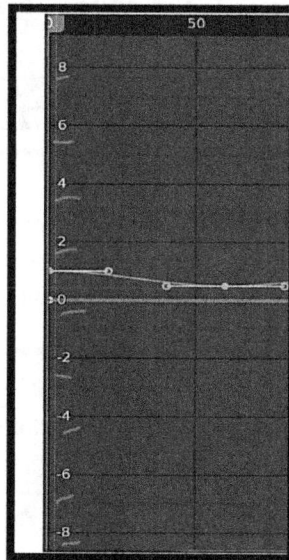

By examining the vertical numbers in the graph editor, you can observe the values that were supplied to the keyframes. We can use the wheel to zoom in and out of our growth editor to get a closer look at all of its keyframes. To move about the graph editor, we can utilize the middle mouse button, just like in the viewport.

Controlling Handles in the Graph Editor

We can easily modify the animation's behavior by moving the keyframe handles in the graph editor. More circular dots with two handles per point have replaced the diamond-shaped ones, according to the editor in question. You can use these handles to specify the transition to or from a keyframe. As a result of their interconnected design, shifting the left handle will have the same effect on the right. How then can we control these handles? One example is reverting to an earlier value after it has passed a keyframe.

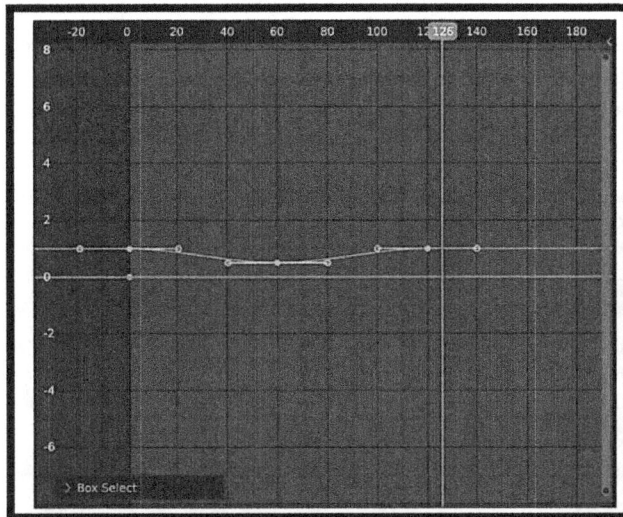

Think about adding three keyframes to the cube's scale. The object's rescaling occurs at the end of the keyframe sequence, the beginning represents the starting point, and the center represents the reduced cube size. The animation will automatically scale to the final number once we reach the third keyframe, but we can modify this scaling using the handles. That handle will likely indicate three channels, one for each axis. Use box select to grab all the handles there, then choose the left one and pull it up.

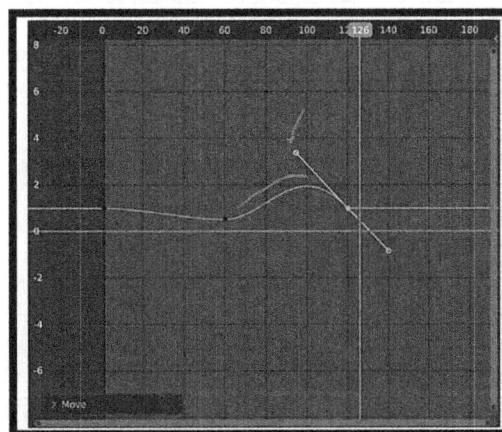

With the appearance of a hill just before the third keyframe, the shape of the line linking the second and third keyframes will alter. The object will scale up to the third keyframe and then down again, so begin playing your animation from the beginning using the timeline's playback settings. I should say it again: it will look like the object has ballooned. Put another way, the third keyframe starts with a scale value of 2, but it goes all the way up to 2.4 and back down again as soon as the handle is raised.

Can You Add Keyframes in the Graph Editor?

The timeline and dope sheets are the greatest ways to see the keyframes you create in Blender. Keyframes can now be seen and selected in a different way in the graph editor. We can even add more keyframes if we so desire. The simplest method for adding a keyframe is to select the frame in the graph editor that you want to do so.

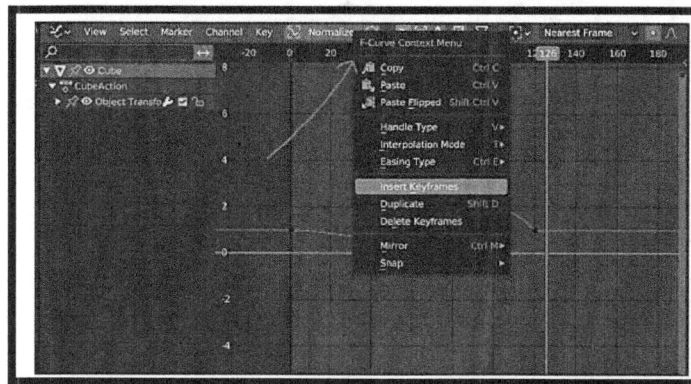

The next step is to access the graph editor's context menu by clicking the right mouse button. In the context menu, you can find the option to insert a keyframe. Then that keyframe will be applied to the channel of your choice. To add the keyframe to several channels, make sure to select all of them.

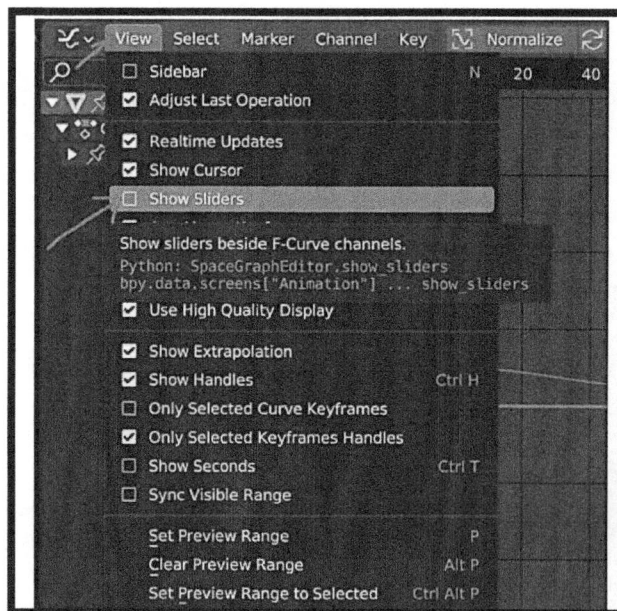

Conversely, you can adjust the visibility of various graph editor items via the view menu. A feature like this is exemplified by the channel-specific slider values. With this enabled, you can change the values of the different channels for the current frame.

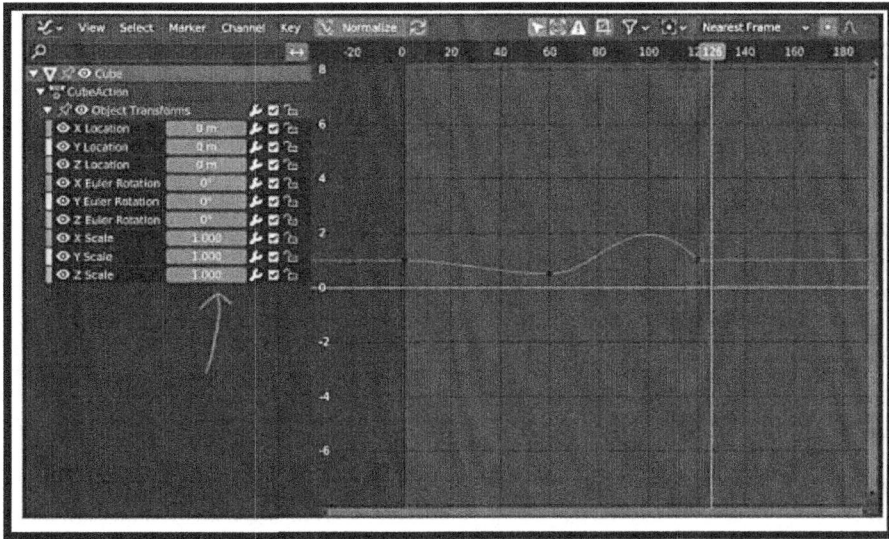

If you modify these values, more keyframes will be appended to the present location. It's better to examine the Graph Editor as a whole to see what you're doing because the tools inside can overlap when seen as the entire display of your user interface.

How to Better View Rotation Values

Although the graph editor clarifies the position and scale values, the rotation becomes more complicated. The values displayed in the graph editor are independent of the keyframed parameter. By adjusting the scale, we can increase its height by 4 or decrease it by 0.5. In the editor, you can see these little figures.

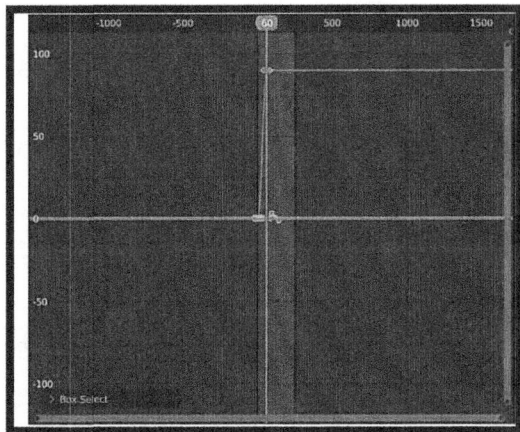

86

But when we talk about rotation, we're talking in degrees, and degrees use much larger integers; for instance, when we want to turn the Z-axis 90 degrees. It gets much more difficult to comprehend the graph editor when we have to zoom out to discover our keyframes. Our present method of visualizing keyframes, the F-Curve, can be readily normalized.

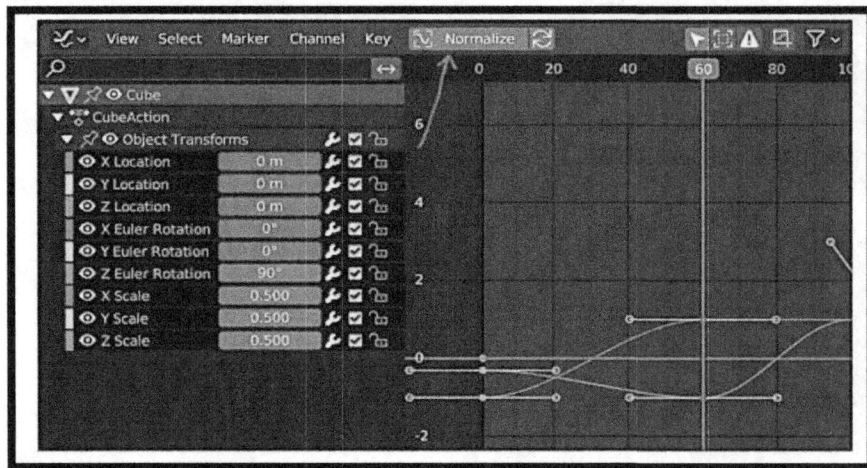

You will find the option to toggle the normalize function in the header bar of the graph editor. Returning the points to a -1 to 1 range will make seeing your keyframes easier. Near the normalize button is a small toggle that you can use to activate automatic normalization. When enabled, any time you modify the graph editor, it will immediately return to the -1 to 1 range.

Non-Linear Animation

We can make bigger and more complex animations with the help of several animation programs because of how easy it is to reuse groups of keyframes. The term most often used to describe them is non-linear editing. A frequent technique involves initializing an action as keyframes once and then looping it using an NLA block, which is comparable to a walk cycle. It may come as a surprise, but animations can be mixed and flipped without hesitation or unexpected consequences. Walking, blinking our eyes, and waving our hands are all examples of gestures that can be combined into one. **The following Blender features, although very complicated at first glance, are quite simple to use:**

- Create an animation using regular keyframes or import one from a provider like Mixamo
- Convert this group into an Action Strip, which Blender refers to as an NLA block.
- Add this Action Strip to an NLA track, repeat it, or mix it with other strips.
- Add transitions between blocks for smooth motion.
- Add tracks to combine animations.

This is how it functions for me. While it may lack precision, it is sufficient for creating impressive animations.

Turning Keyframes into NLA Blocks

Once you've set up your animation, this could be the result. I added a Mix Amo Animation to my FBI Agent character. You can see the keyframes that make my man move down there. The regular **Layout workspace** (the tab at the very top) is where you can find it. My character has been selected, so please be informed. The timelines are sensitive to the current context and only display the keyframes of the selected object.

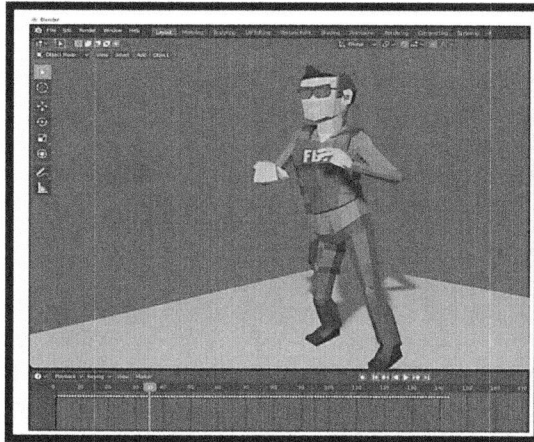

When I need to convert entire sequences like this into NLA Blocks or Action Strips, I use the Animation Workspace. It is prepared using a customized schedule called the Dope Sheet. It differs in how it deals with keyframes compared to the standard timeline, but other than that, it's the same. Making Action Strips for the NLA Timeline is just one of many things it can do.

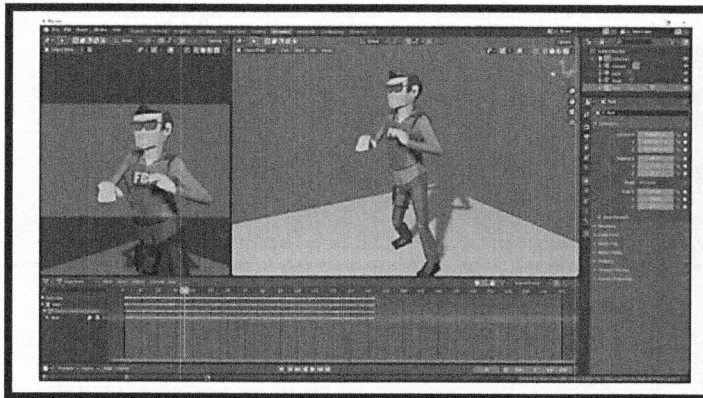

Right now, my desk looks like this while I'm working in Animation mode. Here we can see the Dope Sheet at the very bottom of the screen, the standard viewport on the right, and the active camera on the left. Instead of seeing a single keyframe in the regular timeline, we can study keyframes for specific parameters like position and rotation for each axis. Locate the "**Dope Sheet**" option in the left-hand menu. We can modify the **Action Strip**, which is indicated by the red box in the screenshot.

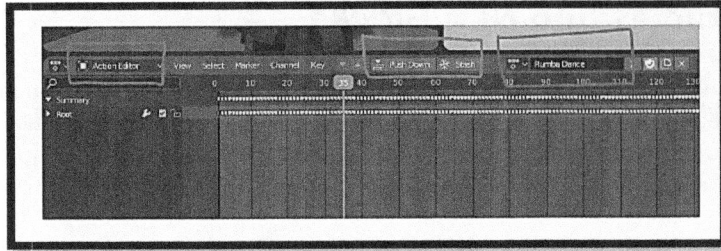

The screenshot shows two new options, Stash and Push Down, in a green box. You can reap the benefits of either one, depending on your needs:

- **Push Down:** An Action Strip will be created from the animation and added to a new NLA Track (more on that later).
- For later usage, **Stash** will convert it to an Action Strip.

There's no need to worry about the intricacies just yet because I will provide a more detailed explanation when we work together with the NLA Editor. Both options are accessible at this time. Before you hastily push any of those buttons, it might be prudent to review the blue box in the image up there. We call it our Action Strip. The button will say "new" if an object does not currently have an Action Strip, so we can build one. You can just modify it to something more attention-grabbing, even though "Action" is the default. Mixamo animations usually have quite long names, thus it's a good idea to rename them now. The Rumba Dance is my favorite. You will not lose this name when you hit Stash or Push Down. I think it's time to push down and watch what happens.

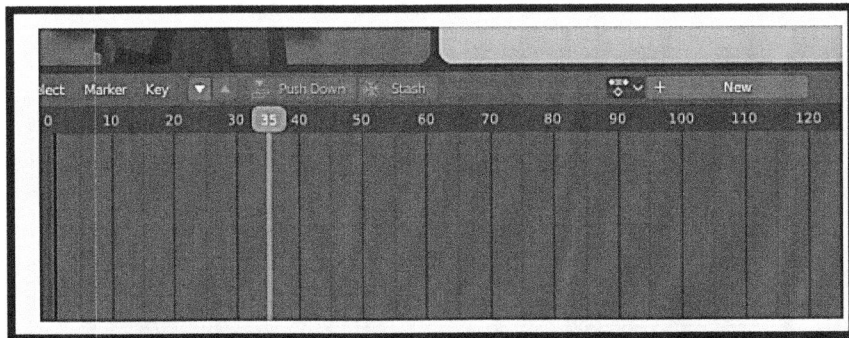

All keyframes have disappeared, so there's no way to tell if our character was selected or not. That's okay; we'll get them back in the following phase.

The Fabled NLA Editor

Change the old Dope Sheet timeline to the NLA Timeline while remaining in the animation workspace. Just find the small icon over on the left and choose Nonlinear Animation to do that.

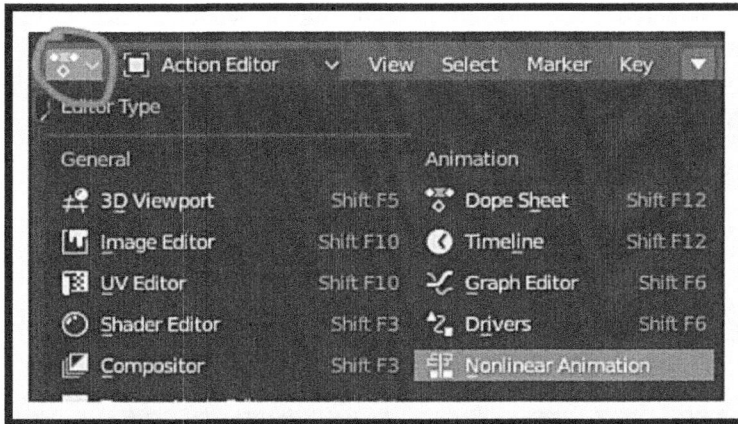

The bottom portion of the interface will then look like this:

On the left side of the screen, you can see three separate strips; one of them, NlaTrack, features an action strip named Rumba Dance. The keyframes we previously utilized are those! Our "push down" approach includes the NLA Track. If "stash" had been used instead, the interface would have looked like this:

Very similar, with the exception that our Action Strips do not include a track for playback. The Action Stash helps you maintain order in your stuff by acting as a closet. Using the Dope Sheet, we can select what's inside and then release it as needed. This comes in handy when you're starting from scratch with your animation and adding blocks to a track.

Transitioning Action Strips

I imported another animation from Mixamo and "pushed it down" in the Dope Sheet, adding it to the one we had just created. From my first one, which is rumba dancing; I would like to effortlessly segue into a cheering gesture. Whenever I go back to my NLA Editor, a visual like this one, with the two tracks superimposed, appears.

Consequently, Blender lowered both actions and created a second non-linear action (NLA) track for me. That's not the vibe I'm aiming for, especially if my FBI agent isn't into simultaneous cheering and dancing. You might use this to add a blink to your animated walk. Perhaps at a later day. With a little room between it and the block ahead of it, I'll grab the Cheering block and slide it onto the first track. Because of this critical gap, Blender can interpolate both operations in a minute.

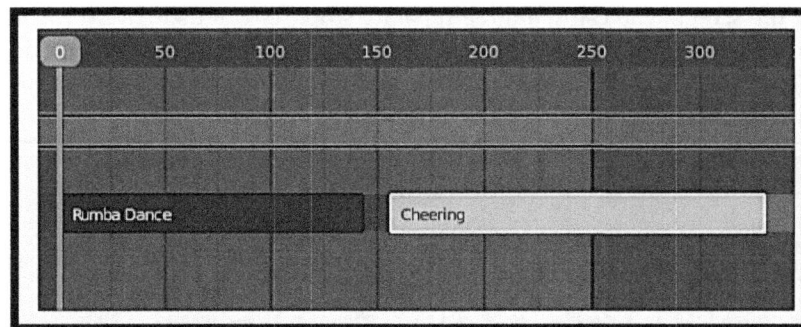

Once I've made my selections for the two Action Strips, I'll either use the Add - Transition menu item or press SHIFT + T to add the transition. In the space between the stripes, a small blue dot will emerge as a consequence of this. A new transition will appear when you move the second strip to the left or right.

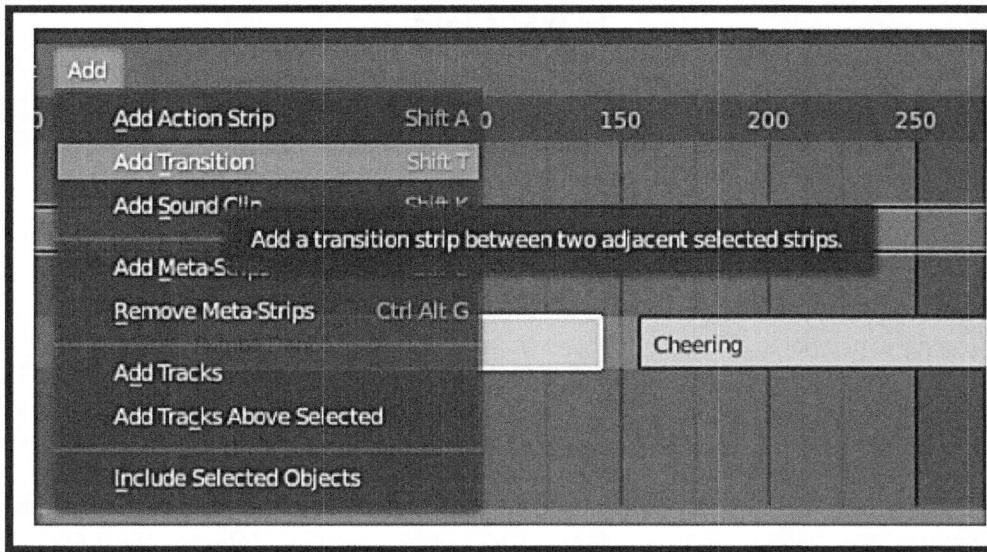

Add
Add Action Strip	Shift A
Add Transition	Shift T
Add Sound Clip	Shift K

Add a transition strip between two adjacent selected strips.

Add Meta-Strip	
Remove Meta-Strips	Ctrl Alt G
Add Tracks	
Add Tracks Above Selected	
Include Selected Objects	

Cheering

When I go back and watch my animation, it smoothly transitions from Rumba Dancing turns to cheering, without any annoying pops. As previously stated, this smartphone is both powerful and packed with features. I think you'd enjoy it!

CHAPTER 6
ASSIGNING MATERIALS

How to Assign Materials

Here are the actions you must take to allocate materials in Blender 4.4:

1. Start by starting Blender and going to the project where your model is saved.
2. To apply a material to an object in Object Mode, just click on it.
3. You should see the Properties Editor over on the right. Pressing the spherical icon will take you to the Material Properties page.
4. If the object is lacking a material, you can add one by selecting the "New" button. Your object will be assigned a default material when you create it.
5. All of the material parameters can now be customized. A couple of common modifications are these:
   - **Base Color:** Click on the color box to modify the base color of the material.
   - **Surface Type:** Select from a variety of shader types such as **"Principled BSDF"** or **"Diffuse BSDF"** to achieve your desired effect.
   - **Roughness and Metallic**: Adjust the sliders to modify the material's shininess and metallic appearance.
6. **Feel free to designate which faces will receive the material:**
   - Switch to **Edit Mode** by pressing the **Tab key**.
   - Choose the faces that you would like to assign a particular material to.
   - Click the "+" button in the Material Properties to add a new material slot.
   - Choose or generate a new material in this slot.
   - Click the "**Assign**" button under the material slot to apply the material to the selected faces.
7. **Use Nodes for Advanced Material Creation:**

You can move to the Shader Editor if you're dealing with complex materials:

   - Either divide your screen into two panels or move one of them to the Shader Editor.
   - You can construct complex materials by adding nodes and connecting them in the Shader Editor. With the help of nodes, you can make fine-grained modifications and make complex material effects.
8. **Use Textures:**
   - Use the Shader Editor to add an "Image Texture" node to your material if you want to add textures to it.
   - A diffuse texture, for example, would need to connect the Base Color input on your shader to the Image Texture node.
   - To load your image file, click on the folder icon on the Image Texture node.
9. **UV Mapping:**
   - For textures to be shown correctly, ensure that your object has the appropriate UV mapping.
   - To unwrap and modify the UV maps as needed, you can access the UV Editor while in Edit Mode. Just choose your object and go from there.

10. **Preview the Material:**
    o To see how your material will look on the object in real time, go to the Material Preview or Rendered view.

Material Properties

Create photorealistic and aesthetically pleasing 3D models with ease using Blender 4.4's many sophisticated tools for managing and customizing material characteristics. Important factors include:

Basic Material Properties

- **Base Color:** The main color of the material.
- **Specular**: Adjusts the strength of the specular reflection for a polished look.
- **Roughness**: This factor influences the roughness or smoothness of the surface, with lower values resulting in a shinier appearance.
- **Metallic**: Indicates the material's composition as either metallic (1.0) or non-metallic (0.0).

Advanced Material Properties

- **Normal Maps:** When making complex surface textures, Normal Maps are a lifesaver since they let you add detail without using extra geometry. Imperfections and folds in the surface can be faithfully reproduced using this function.
- **Displacement Maps:** Using a texture, displacement maps change the surface's physical structure.
- **Subsurface Scattering (SSS):** This method precisely imitates how light scatters as it passes through transparent materials like skin, wax, or marble.
- **Emission:** The ability of the material to emit light makes it perfect for making objects that radiate light.

Shader Nodes

Using Blender's Node Editor and shader nodes, complex materials can be easily created. Here are a few nodes that are used often:

- **Principled BSDF**: A flexible shader, Principled BSDF simplifies the production of complicated materials by merging numerous layers into one node.
- **Image Texture:** Applies an image to the material, enhancing it with intricate textures.
- **Mix Shader**: Blends two shaders using a factor.
- **Bump**: Incorporates bump mapping to replicate intricate surface details.

Developing a Material

- **Create a New Material:** To make a new material, go to the Material tab in the Properties panel. After that, click on "New" to bring up the option to make a new material.
- **Choose a Shader**: When working with different materials, choose the Principled BSDF shader because it provides a variety of controls.

- **Make adjustments to properties:** To get the look you want, you can change the parameters such as the base color, metallic, roughness, and more.
- **Add Texture**: Insert an Image Texture node into the Principled BSDF shader's Base Color input using the Shader Edit command.

Viewport Shading Modes

To see and work with your 3D models successfully in Blender 4.4, viewport shading modes are essential.

The primary shading modes for the viewport are:

1. **Wireframe**:

When dealing with complex models, this function is very helpful because it enables a clear picture of the object's edges.

Shortcut: Z > Wireframe.

2. **Solid**:

Things without textures or complex material features are shown in this display, which focuses on objects with basic shading and lighting.

Ideal for creating models and sculptures.

Shortcut: Z > Solid.

3. **Material Preview (formerly known as Look Dev):**

Using a basic method of lighting and shading, this presentation showcases materials and textures.

Great for quickly changing textures and materials.

Shortcut: Z > Material Preview.

4. **Rendered**:

Showcases the final image or animation's materials, textures, and lighting in their real form, offering a preview of the eventual render.

The selected render engine (such as Eevee or Cycles) is utilized in this mode.

Shortcut: Z > Rendered.

Material Node System

Create complex materials with ease using Blender 4.4's enhanced Material Node System and its intuitive node-based UI. Blender 4.4's Material Node System has the following features and critical details to keep in mind when working with it:

Basics of the Material Node System

1. To access the Shader Editor in Blender, launch the program and look for the "Editor Type" option toward the program's bottom.
2. An extremely flexible shader, the Principled BSDF shader unifies numerous shader types with ease. This provides a firm basis for the production of a wide range of materials.
3. Shaders, textures, and inputs are just a few of the many nodes available in the Add menu, which may be accessed by pressing Shift + A.
4. Inputs and outputs professionally link the nodes. Link nodes together by dragging and dropping their respective output sockets from one node to another.

Common Nodes and Their Applications

1. **Shader Nodes:**

- **Diffuse BSDF**: Basic diffuse shader for matte surfaces.
- **Glossy BSDF:** Reflective surfaces.
- **Mix Shader:** This shader allows for the blending of two different shaders, creating a seamless transition between them.
- **Emission**: Enhances the surface's ability to emit light.

2. **Textures Nodes:**

- **Image Texture:** Uses an image file as a texture.
- **Noise Texture**: Creates procedural noise patterns.
- **Voronoi Texture:** Generates intricate cell-like patterns.

3. **Input Nodes:**

- **Texture Coordinate**: Offers a range of texture coordinates for your convenience.
- **Fresnel**: Calculates the reflectivity for the Fresnel effect.
- **Geometry**: Offers precise geometric information, including position and normal vectors.

4. **Utility Nodes**:

- **Math**: Executes mathematical operations with precision.
- **MixRGB**: Blends two colors using a factor.
- **Color Ramp:** The ColorRamp function remaps values to create a gradient.

Tips for Crafting Materials

1. **Organize your Node Setup:**

- Group relevant nodes together using frames.
- Label function and import nodes so that you can easily keep track of them.
2. **Experiment with Procedural Textures:**
- Noise, Musgrave, and Voronoi are among Blender's procedural textures that may generate intricate patterns in the absence of picture textures.
3. **Adopt a PBR Workflow:**
- The materials' realism is improved by the PBR technique. Make use of maps like Normal, Base Color, Roughness, and Metallic.
4. **Node Groups:**
- By choosing nodes and hitting Ctrl + G, you can make groups of nodes that can be used again. A neat and modular structure for the node tree is encouraged by this.
5. **Preview your Nodes:**
- You can use the Viewer Node to obtain a brief overview of how a node affects your material. To use this function, you must enable the Node Wrangler plugin.

Example: Setting up Materials

A simple material setup utilizing the Principled BSDF shader is shown here:

1. Press Shift + A, then navigate to the **Shader menu** and select **Principled BSDF**.

2. Press Shift + A and navigate to the Texture menu. Select **Image Texture**. Load your texture image.

3. Connect the color output of the Image Texture node to the base color input of the Principled BSDF node.

4. The Principled BSDF is automatically connected to the Material Output by default.

Default Material Node System

Principled BSDF Shader

The default material node system is built around the Principled BSDF shader. This node integrates multiple shading models, making it easy to work with a wide variety of materials.

Important Factors

- **Base Color**: Sets the main color of the material.
- **Subsurface**: The subsurface scattering level can be adjusted to simulate the actual transmission of light through various materials including skin, wax, and jade.
- **Metallic**: Adjusts the material's metallic characteristics from 0 to 1, where 0 signifies non-metallic and 1 is fully metallic.

- **Specular**: Influences the intensity of specular reflections.
- **Roughness**: The roughness slider lets you change the amount of reflection sharpness, thus lower values give you sharper reflections.
- **Anisotropic**: It's great for getting a brushed metal look because it boosts reflections with directionality.
- **Sheen**: The material is given a subtle and exquisite sheen, which enhances its appearance.
- **Clearcoat**: An additional layer is added to the material to make it look more reflective, similar to how clear coatings or varnishes work. This is called a clearcoat.
- **Transmission**: The material's transparency is altered via transmission, which is especially useful for glass or liquids.
- **IOR (Index of Refraction):** The impact of transparent materials on the bending of light is described by the Index of Refraction (IOR).
- **Emission**: Enables the material to emit light.

Extra Nodes

It is common practice to raise materials using the Principled BSDF shader in addition to the following nodes:

- **Texture Nodes:** You can add complex patterns and surface flaws using texture nodes like Image Texture, Noise Texture, and Voronoi Texture.
- **Mapping and Coordinate Nodes:** To control the placement and resizing of textures, nodes such as Texture Coordinate and Mapping are utilized.
- **Mix Shader:** You may create more complex material configurations with the help of the Mix Shader node, which lets you blend between different shaders.
- **Bump and Normal Map Nodes**: By modifying the surface normals, these nodes improve the surface and add complex details.
- **Fresnel and Layer Weight:** To provide more realistic edge reflections and to regulate mix shaders depending on the viewing angle, these nodes can be utilized: Fresnel and Layer Weight.

Node Groups

You can now encapsulate complex node setups into reusable and controllable components with Blender 4.4's support for node groups. This is particularly helpful when creating complex materials that can be easily shared across several projects.

Example: Setting Up Materials

Sharing a simple material node setup example with the Principled BSDF shader:

1. Add the Principled BSDF Shader and connect it to the Material Output node.
2. Link an Image Texture node to the Base Color input of the Principled BSDF shader.
3. Set the desired roughness and metallic values using the sliders provided.

Properties Assignment Components

To efficiently manage and fine-tune the attributes and settings of various project parts, the Properties Assignment Components are important. You can find these components in Blender's standard interface, the Properties Editor.

The primary parts you might deal with are these:

1. **Object Properties**

   - **Transform**: Control the size, location, and orientation of objects by using the transform command.
   - **Visibility**: Control the visibility of objects in both the viewport and the render.
   - **Instancing**: Expertly handle object instancing and duplication.
   - **Viewport Display:** You can personalize how objects appear in the viewport.
2. **Modifier Properties**
   - Modify objects such as Subdivision Surface, Boolean, Mirror, and Array by applying and managing appropriate modifiers.
3. **Material Properties**
   - **Shader**: Configure and assign shaders for materials.
   - **Surface**: Customize surface properties such as base color, roughness, and metallic.
   - **Volume**: Adjust volume shaders and properties with precision.
   - **Displacement**: Manage displacement settings for materials.
4. **Texture Properties**
   - **Type**: Select the texture type, such as image or procedural.
   - **Mapping**: Take control over the way textures are applied to surfaces
   - **Image**: Manage and load image textures with ease.
   - **Influence**: Adjust the impact of textures on material properties.
5. **Particle Properties**
   - **Emission**: To get a professional look, tweak the particle emission settings.
   - **Physics**: Modify particle physics properties such as gravity and forces.
   - **Render**: Oversee the rendering of particles.
6. **Physics Properties**
   - **Rigid Body**: Keep an eye on how objects' rigid body physics are being managed.
   - **Soft Body:** Fine-tune soft body dynamics.
   - **Cloth**: Modify the simulation settings for clothing.
   - **Fluid**: Control the parameters of a fluid simulation effortlessly.
   - **Force Fields:** Use and control force fields with expertise.
7. **Render Properties**
   - **Render Engine:** Choose your preferred rendering engine (such as Cycles or Eevee).
   - **Output:** The resolution and file format of the output can be changed.
   - **Sampling**: Adjust the sampling parameters to improve the quality of the rendering.
   - **Light Paths**: Render by controlling the properties of light paths.
   - **Performance**: Optimal results can be achieved by improving the rendering performance.
8. **World Properties**
   - **Surface**: Configure the surface shader to work with the given surroundings.

- **Volume**: Adjust the volume to match your environment.
- **Ray Visibility**: Control the environment's ray visibility settings.
- **Color Management**: Master the art of managing the world's color settings.
9. **Scene Properties**
- **Units**: Configure units for the scene.
- **Gravity**: Adjust global gravity settings.
- **Rigid Body World**: Take control of the settings for the rigid body world.
- **Manage View Layers**: Take control of view layer properties.
10. **Output Properties**
- **Output Resolution**: Change the final output resolution.
- **Frame Range:** Define the range of frames that will be rendered for the animation.
- **File Format:** Choose the preferred output file format.
- **Metadata**: Handle output file metadata efficiently.

How to use Multiple Material Slots

You may apply different materials to different parts of your mesh using the new option to use multiple material slots in Blender 4.4.

1. Launch Blender and choose to import an existing project or create a new one.
2. You can apply various materials to an object by selecting it.
3. Alternating between Object Mode and Edit Mode is a breeze with the Tab key.
4. The Materials tab, represented by the spherical icon, may be found in the Properties panel on the right. Click on it.
5. For your review, you will find a list of material slots. As a general rule, one is sufficient. To add more material slots, simply click the plus sign. A different material will fit into each slot.
6. At the material slot selection screen, you should see the option to either create a new material or choose an existing one from the dropdown menu.
7. This must be done for each material slot that is needed.
8. If you're in Edit Mode, you can quickly select the vertex, edge, or face of the mesh that you want to materialize.
9. Pick the material slot that you'd like to use.
10. Select the mesh area you want to apply the material to, and then click the Assign button.
11. Proceed with the selection and assignment of additional mesh sections and any other material slots that may be needed.
12. To get back to Object Mode, hit Tab again.
13. Go to the Material Preview mode to make sure the materials are applied correctly. Press Z and then select Material Preview to do this.

Step-by-step guide:

1. Indicate the object you wish to focus on.
2. Press Tab to enter **Edit Mode**.
3. Access the Materials tab located in the Properties panel.
4. Simply click on the + symbol to incorporate a fresh material slot.
5. Choose the faces that you would like to assign a material to.

6. In the Materials tab, choose a material slot and click Assign.
7. Repeat the process for the remaining sections of the mesh.
8. Switch to Object Mode and check in Material Preview mode.

Multiple Data Blocks Assignment

To manage numerous data blocks for objects, you can use the Properties panel, Python scripting, or the Outliner.

Using the Outliner

1. **Choose multiple objects:**

Just press and hold the Shift key while clicking on the objects you want to pick in the Outliner.

On the other hand, you can choose numerous objects in the 3D Viewport by right-clicking on them while holding Shift.

2. **Assigning Datablocks:**

To assign a particular data block, such as materials or modifiers, go to the Properties panel and choose it.

For materials:

Press the spherical icon, which signifies the Material tab.

Click on the desired material once you have selected the objects. All of the objects you've chosen will have the material applied to them.

Using the Properties Panel

1. **Choose multiple objects:**

If you hold down Shift and right-click on numerous objects in the 3D Viewport, you can select them all.

2. **Assigning Datablocks:**

Navigate to the appropriate Properties tab, like Material or Modifier.

For materials:

Choose the **Material tab**.

To choose an existing material or make your own, use the dropdown menu.

All the stated objects will be covered with the selected material.

CHAPTER 7
VISUAL EFFECTS (VFX)

Introduction to Blender's VFX Capabilities

To get the most out of Blender's particle system, you need to familiarize yourself with all of its features. Fancy effects like smoke, fire, or debris can be made via the Particle Properties panel. Here you can customize the particle physics, emission rate, and velocity for a one-of-a-kind visual effects feel. Another important method for Blender visual effects is shader dynamics. You can make materials that react to UV light and have realistic lighting with the Shader Editor. By blending shaders and adding texture using nodes, you can create effects like shimmering magic or energy fields. For anyone looking to add a dark touch to their scenes, Blender's robust simulation features are important. You can activate rigid body dynamics in the Physics Properties if you wish to simulate the chaos that follows an explosion. If you want to see your simulation come to life and see the animation play, press Alt + A, member. Blender has powerful compositing features that you may utilize to make advanced visual effects. The compositor is a useful tool for enhancing the visual quality of animations and ensuring that visual effects blend well with live-action footage. You may achieve that cinematic look by manipulating the color grading, adding lens flares, or blurring certain regions to create the illusion of depth.

Motion Tracking and Stabilization

Using Blender's Motion Tracking is the best option for visual effects tasks like tracking and merging 3D objects with live-action footage. **The following are the entry and exit methods for this one-of-a-kind setting:**

Accessing the Motion Tracking Workspace

1. **Start with a VFX Template:**

Select "File" followed by "New" before going to "VFX." So you can go immediately into motion tracking, this template will run Blender with the default parameters.

Motion Tracking Workspace Overview

Blender will automatically apply the following window layout when you run it with the VFX template:

1. **Workspace Tabs:**

Motion Tracking: This is the default workspace for visual effects when you launch the VFX session.

Compositing: This technique is used to combine tracked video with 3D components.

Rendering: For rendering the final composite.

Masking: A post-tracking masking workspace that is a subset of the motion-tracking workspace.

2. **Right Side Panels:**

Outliner: The hierarchy of objects and data in your scene is displayed via the Outliner.

Properties Editor: In the Properties Editor, you can find the options and details for the objects and modifiers you've chosen.

3. **Bottom Section:**

Timeline: Displays the timeframe relevant to tracking information and animation.

4. **Top Right:**

3D Viewport: Until tracking is set up, the 3D viewport is empty at startup.

5. **Main Workspace Area:**

Movie Clip Editor: The Movie Clip Editor is where you'll mostly find the motion tracking features. This editor is a must-have for working with tracking data and video footage.

Movie Clip Editor in Detail

The Movie Clip Editor is an essential part of motion tracking:

- **Clip Viewing Mode:** The majority of the Motion Tracking interface is devoted to the Clip Viewing Mode. In this mode, you can watch multiple videos simultaneously.
- **Graph Display:** A graph display is located on the bottom panel of the Movie Clip Editor. It offers graphs of tracking data for fine-tuning tracks.
- **Dopesheet Display:** A Dopesheet Display is included in the premium Movie Clip Editor. Gives tracking information in a spreadsheet-style that's easier to work with while adjusting keyframes and tracks.

Differences from the Sequencer

Movie Clip Editor: One option is the "Movie Clip Editor," which lets you cut down to a specific clip. Video file processing and monitoring is its main function.

Sequencer: This tool handles many video sequences and is used for more complex video editing jobs.

Key Tips for Motion Tracking

- **Initial Setup:** Start tracking right away by importing your video clip into the Movie Clip Editor after you've completed the initial setup.
- **Tracking Process:** Make use of the many views and editors to fine-tune your data and tracking points.

- **Review and Adjust:** Use the Graph and Dopesheet displays to make complete modifications to your tracking data.

Adding Markers and Tracking

Thanks to Blender's robust tracking system, you can create markers and have them animate with you as you move around your movie. **In Blender, you can easily add markers and monitor their progress by following these steps:**

1. Simply navigate to "File" > "Import" > "Movie" in Blender to import videos.
2. The "Movie Clip Editor" can be accessed by clicking the camera symbol with a filmstrip in Blender's upper-right corner.
3. Choose the imported clip by dragging and dropping it into the "Movie Clip Editor."
4. Select the "Add Marker" option from the "Movie Clip Edit" menu to add a marker, or use the "M" key on your keyboard. Simply right-clicking on the video will bring up a menu from which you can choose "Add Marker."
5. By clicking and dragging the marker, it can be relocated to any location in the video.
6. You can begin tracking the marker by hitting "Ctrl+T" on your keyboard or by clicking the "Track Markers" button in the "Movie Clip Editor" toolbar. After Blender has evaluated the movement of the marker, it will start to follow its trajectory.
7. Simply repeat steps 4-6 to add other marks to your monitoring list.
8. Select the "Graph Editor" or "Dope Sheet" icon at the bottom of the "Movie Clip Editor" window to see the tracking results. Each tracked marker's evolution can be viewed here.
9. You can utilize the tracked markers to create 3D objects that move with your video by going to the "Object" > "Create" > "Track to Object" option in the 3D Viewport. If you do this, a new object will be created that can follow the tracked marker's path.

Particle Systems and Effects

Particle systems are essential for the generation of strand-based objects like clouds, smoke, fur, and grass, as well as effects like fire, dust, and clouds. When you add a particle system to an object, it will start to produce and discharge particles that can take on a variety of shapes, including character models or movement patterns. An army of troops and a swarm of insects are two examples.

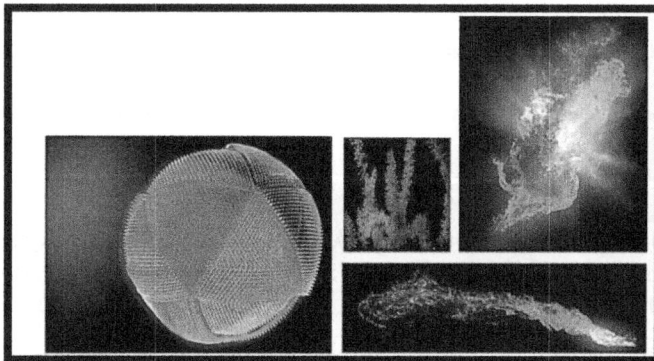

Creating a Basic Particle System

1. Add a Particle Emitter

Arrive at the 3D Viewport. To create a grid mesh, select Add > Mesh > Grid from the menu. Emitting particles will be a breeze with this grid.

2. Add a Particle System

Once you've selected the grid, head over to the Particle Properties panel. You can add a new particle system by clicking the plus sign (+) next to the particles list box. Particle system settings will now be visible. You can press the Spacebar or click the Play button in the Timeline to rewind the animation and see the particles fall from your grid. You receive immediate feedback when you make changes with Blender since the particle system is updated in real-time.

3. Observe the Particle Cache

Explore the Timeline. The data about motion is stored in the particle cache, which can be seen by the red bar located at the bottom. Timeline pointers outside the cached zone may cause playback to be sluggish and inaccurate. We will refresh the cache if there is a major change in Particle Properties.

4. Choose Particle Physics

To customize your particles' physics, head to the Physics section of the Particle Properties menu. Although Newtonian physics is often used, the behavior of bosons provides an intriguing option for more complex interactions.

5. Adjust Particle Velocity

Scroll down to the Velocity section in the Particle Properties menu. Newtonian physics relies heavily on knowing the starting speed. By and large, positive and negative values for face normals go in the same direction. Adjust the parameters to change how Booids' particles engage with their environment.

6. Play Back the Animation

Use the Spacebar or Play button in the Timeline to watch the particles move. Keep the timeline pointer one frame before the Frame Start parameter in the Emission panel to maintain predictable behavior. To pause the current scene and tweak the particle movement, hit the Esc key. Then press the play button again.

7. Reset and Cache

Restarting the animation from the first frame will allow you to cache the particle system from the beginning, even after making considerable changes. You can utilize the Cache panel in the Particle Properties menu to store the cache on your hard drive so that particle motion is preserved when you reopen the project.

Introduction to Physics Simulations

Its integrated physics engine is one of Blender's best features. You can use it to make animated videos and graphics that react to things in the real world. When you use this well, you have a ton of options for producing visually great material. The following are a number of the physics options in Blender that we can go over fast. We will go over the process of adding and modifying rigid body modifiers to objects in Blender so that you can fully understand its physics engine. In Blender, the Physics Properties tab in the Properties Editor is where you'll mostly find controls for the physics engine. You can execute a collection of given models for each object.

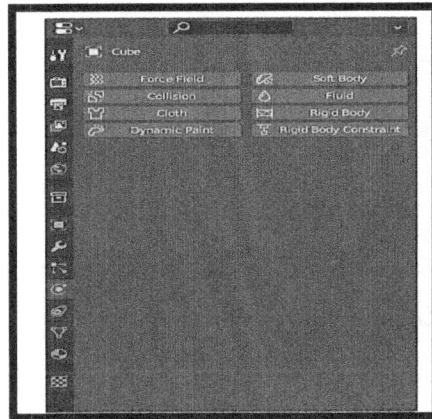

You can find physics, which can be utilized as modifiers, on the right tab as well. The Physics Properties page already contains all the parameters for this Physics; therefore you won't find many uses for it.

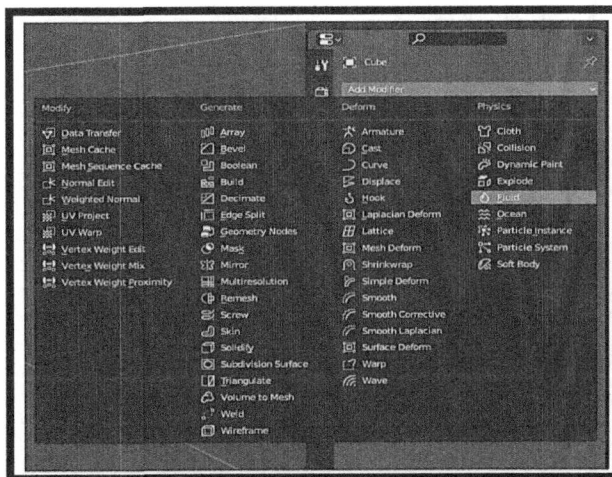

Various models that we can employ were introduced to us. Each one will function differently if used independently.

Rigid Body Physics

Since I preferred to start with the simplest issues, I used a rigid body simulation. Its actions will be controlled by the rules of physics because it is an actual physical object. As we can observe in the video, it falls immediately after application.

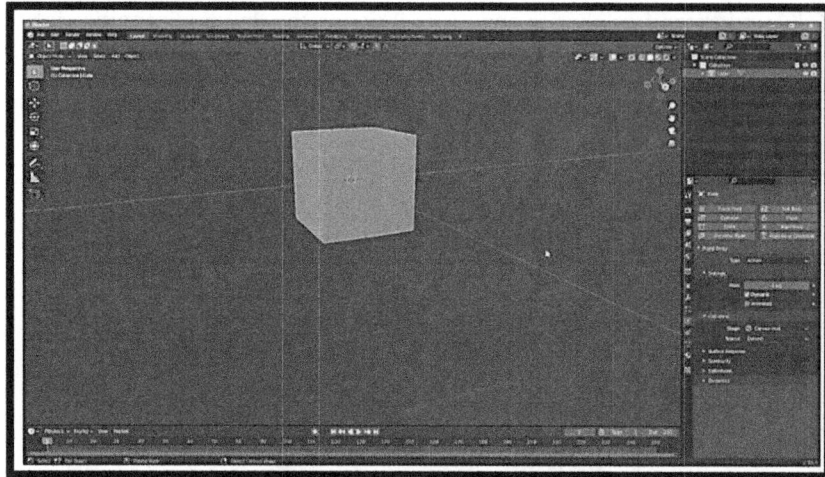

You can't just let it fall into the abyss without adding another hard-body object. You need to go into the object's settings and alter its type from **Active to Passive.**

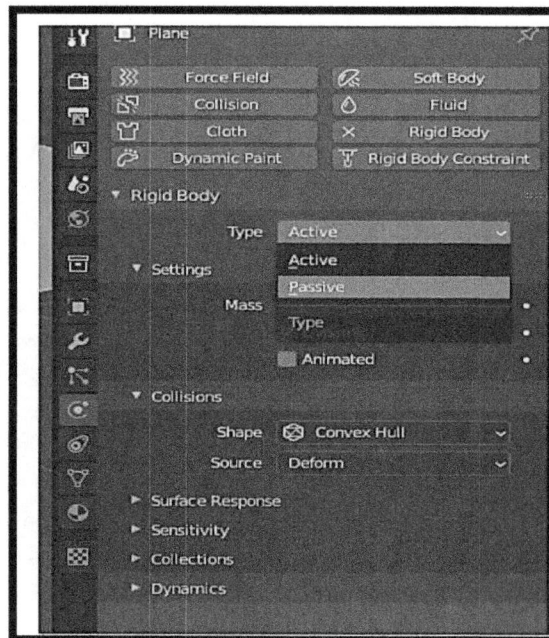

This ensures that the object will remain in place. Use that type on floors, walls, and everything else you can think of. The Passive Rigid Body is now subject to falling, not Cube.

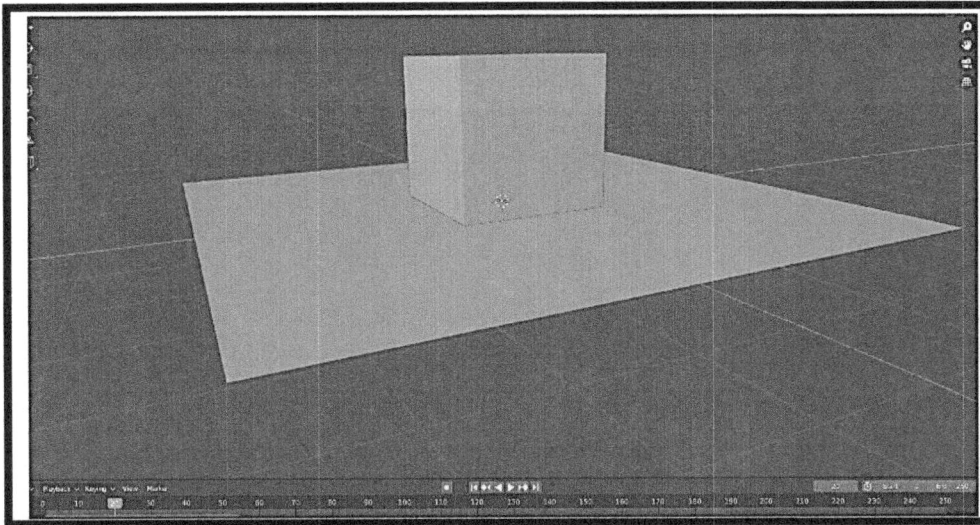

You can change an object's weight under the Physics menu. It may be useful to make it heavier so that it can force smaller ones out. In this area, you can also change the shape of the impact and how it will respond to surface friction and bounce. Miniature scenes like the one below can be created using Rigid Bodies and their settings.

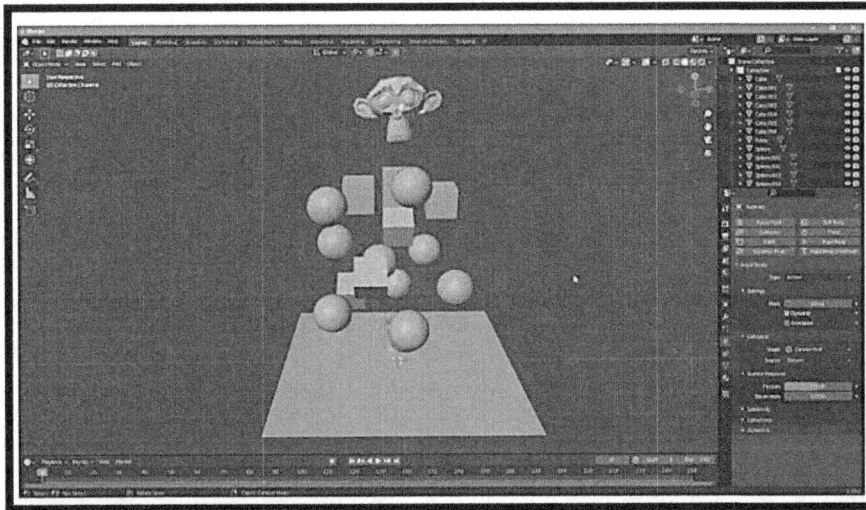

See how the monkey gets out of the way. The heaviness of the monkey object is the sole determinant of this.

Collision Physics

Here is the Physics of Collisions. This one is very simple: you just make the objects you choose smash with each other. Collision is functionally equivalent to a Passive Rigid Body, meaning that all other models, such as Fluid, Cloth, etc., will likewise render with it. Nonetheless, the rigid frame couldn't take advantage of it.

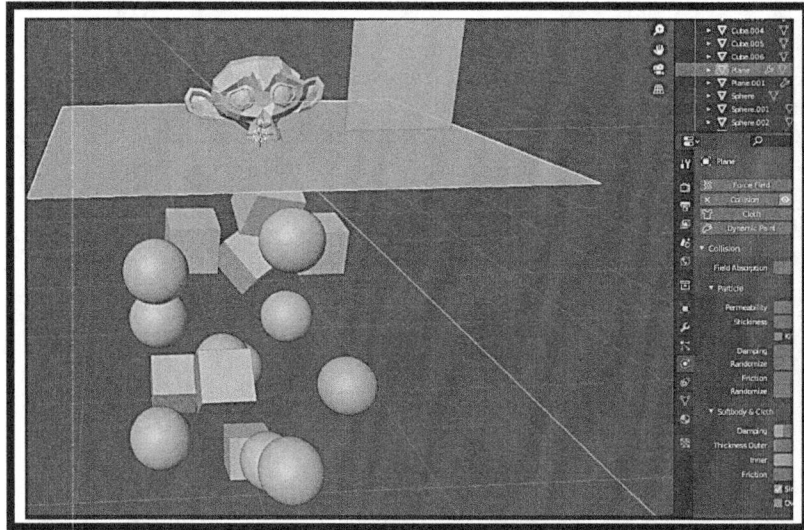

Force Field Physics

The Force Field keeps a constant force around the object you've chosen. To begin with, it acts as a pulling force. I boosted this planar simulation so it would affect my rigid bodies.

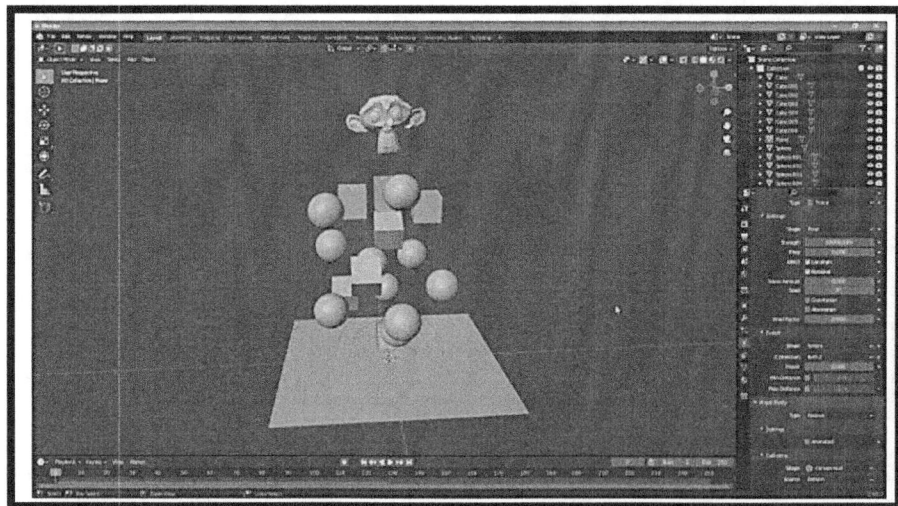

From our vantage point on the plane, we can see how everything is spreading out. The exception is the Suzanne object, which is fairly heavy. You can't drive it because the force field is too strong. An exciting aspect of Force Fields is the multitude of forms that can be utilized. Views of the scene may vary greatly depending on the kind.

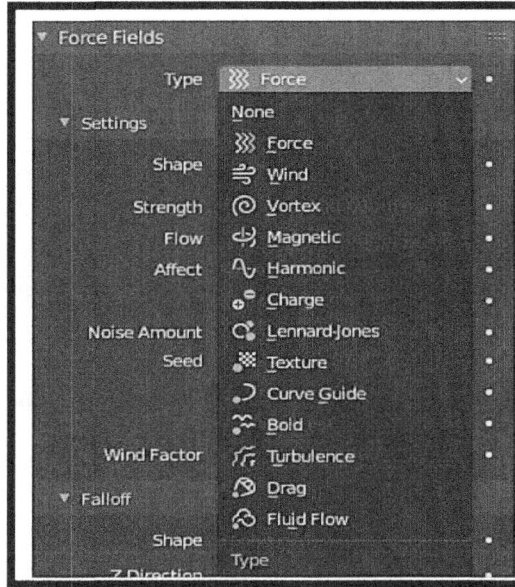

Right now, there are thirteen different kinds. I will not regale you with every one of them. In addition, there is a great deal of variation in both their relative utility and the amount of interest in them. In case you're interested in experimenting with these kinds of Force Fields, feel free to do so. To give you an idea, **Wind Force Field** is pretty much like regular Force One. The main difference is that force acts in all directions relative to the object. The only direction in which wind can be perceived is about an object's direction. We can see that instead of a downward force, it is pushing all the objects upwards in this case.

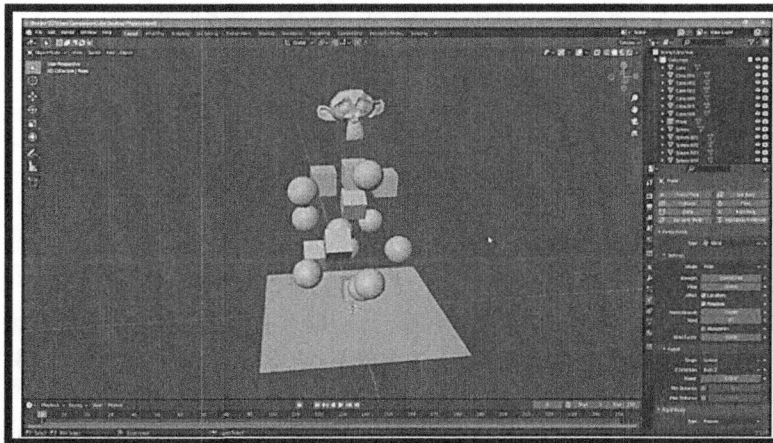

The vortex variety is yet another fantastic one. The first two have little resemblance to the third. It doesn't lift objects; instead, it spins everything in its path into a vortex, which draws away from the object.

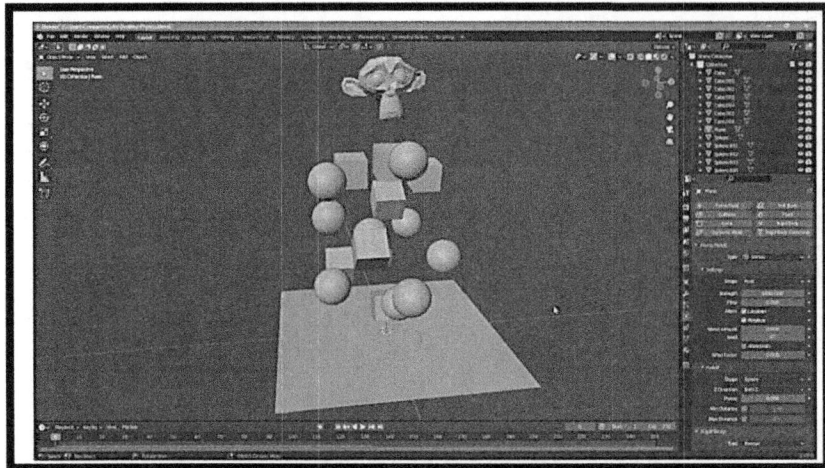

Blender Cloth Physics

Due to cloth physics, objects act as if they were made of fabric. Thus, it would be easily bent or compressed in reaction to gravity, other objects, or the ground. Being a significant and essential part of using physics in Blender, we will go over Blender Cloth Simulation to understand standard Cloth Physics and Blender Cloth Brushes to understand the brushes in the Sculpting menu later on.

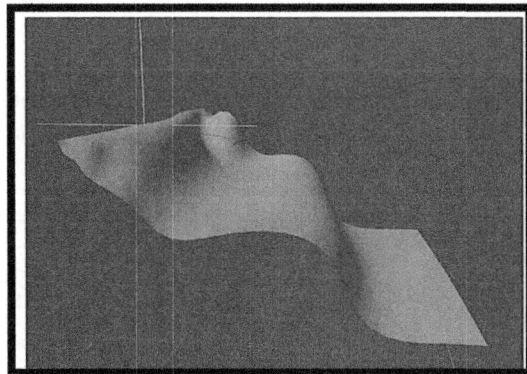

Blender Dynamic Paint Physics

This one is unbelievable. Your everyday objects can become interactive canvases and brushes with Dynamic Paint. These brushes can then have an impact on paintings in some way. The fact that the brush can be printed onto paper is just one example of many. To make it look even more like wet paper, you can also make waves with a brush.

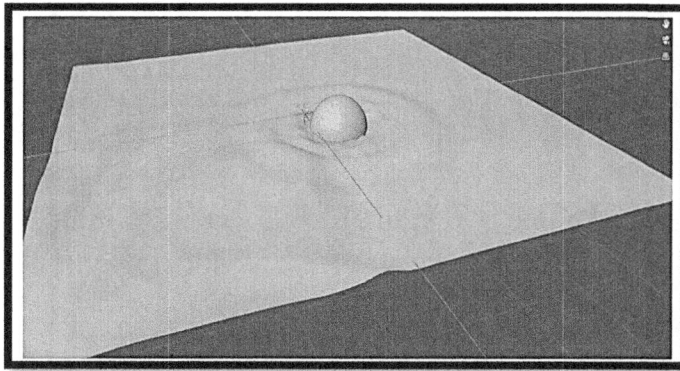

Another option is to use the brush to move shapes around on the canvas or to paint straight onto it. One major issue is that this simulation can be difficult to understand and use at times. However, it can be pretty helpful if you can make it function.

Blender Soft Body Physics

Soft Body is an unusual one. When you add it to an object, you may expect it to act like a Rigid Body but with softer traits. When you try it, though, it's different. Despite the application of gravity, the object does not budge. It starts going up and down without much happening at the same time. This is because Soft Body simulation is not a particularly interesting concept in and of itself. But when it can link things together, it becomes much more interesting. Every improvement, no matter how minor, is better than none at all when an object to hit is included.

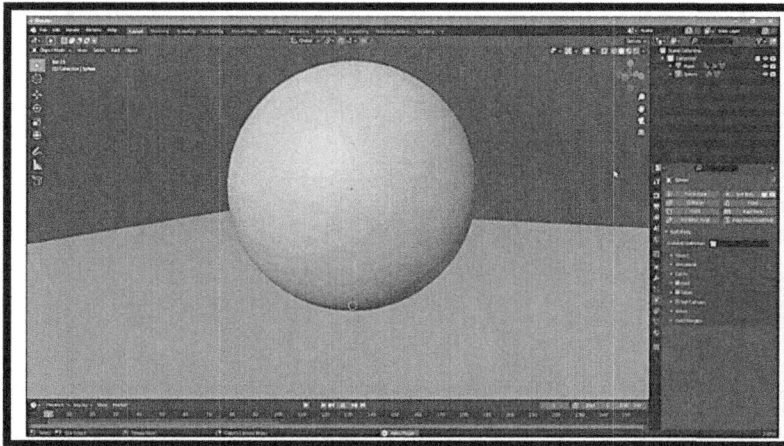

It has several characteristics with the Cloth simulation and can even serve as a substitute for it on occasion. This simulation is incredibly important because other objects besides cloth are soft. A prime example would be our bodies, which are always moving as we go about our daily activities. For this reason, it can be very helpful when trying to replicate the motion of actual bodies.

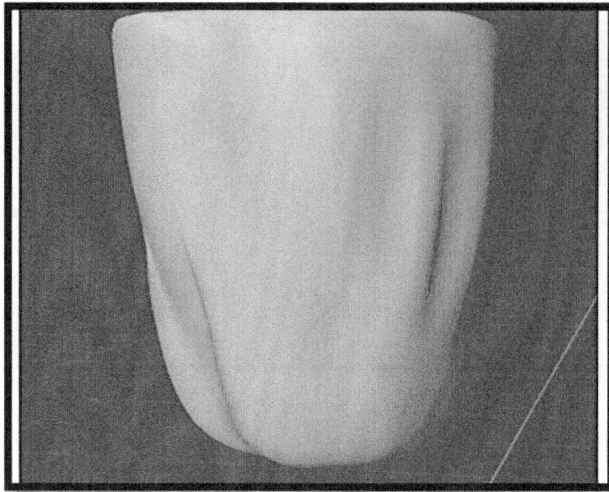

Fluid Physics

Fun and exciting fluid simulation! Plus, it's not that hard if you have the correct information. In addition to liquids, Blender can also simulate smoke. This section contains all the necessary information for you to develop your fluid simulations.

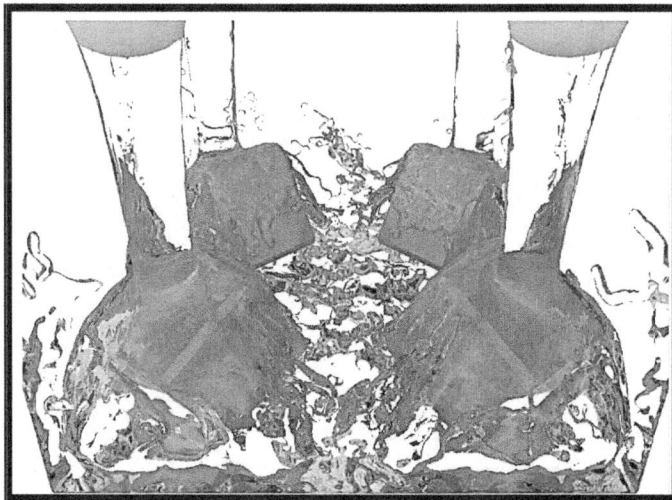

Rigid Body Constraints

Things with a rigid body type are the only ones that can use this one. It links two rigid things, so one can affect the other. Take the cube and the sphere as an example; they're linked. Upon hitting the level surface, the cube is dragged down by the descending sphere.

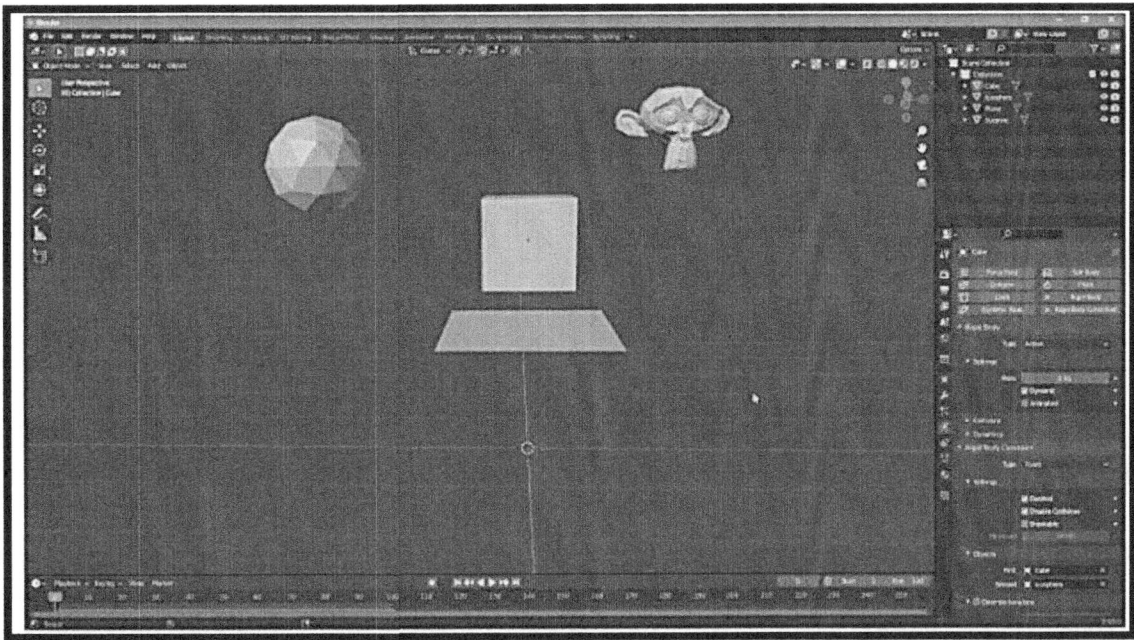

If I make the sphere much lighter than the cube, I can make it such that it can't move the cube. The sphere will be held in position as soon as the cube stops sliding on the ground.

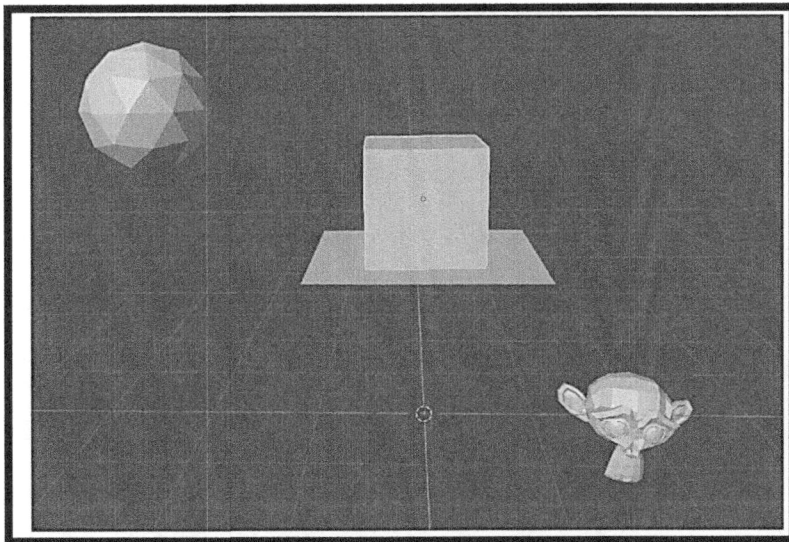

There are also several types of limitations. You can change it from the default one to one that is associated with a certain place. The sphere would spin endlessly, never stopping or falling, to rephrase. It would swing back and forth rather than revolve around the Cube, which is immovable.

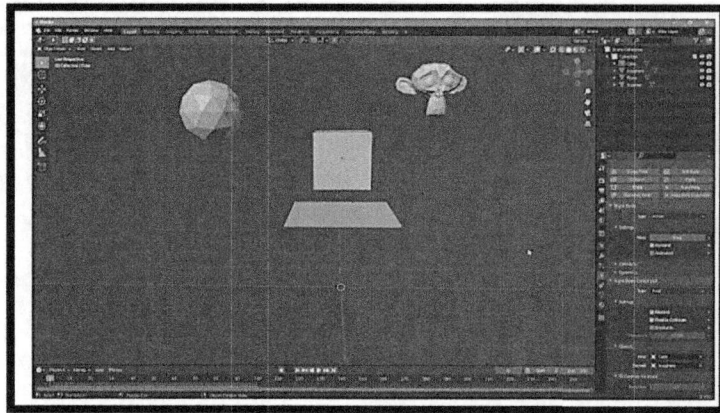

Blender Gravity

Many of the physical principles we demonstrated rely on gravity. In Blender, you may find an Earth gravity option by default. What if you believe that has to be changed? Handled with ease. All that is required for this is to locate the Gravity line in the Scene Properties.

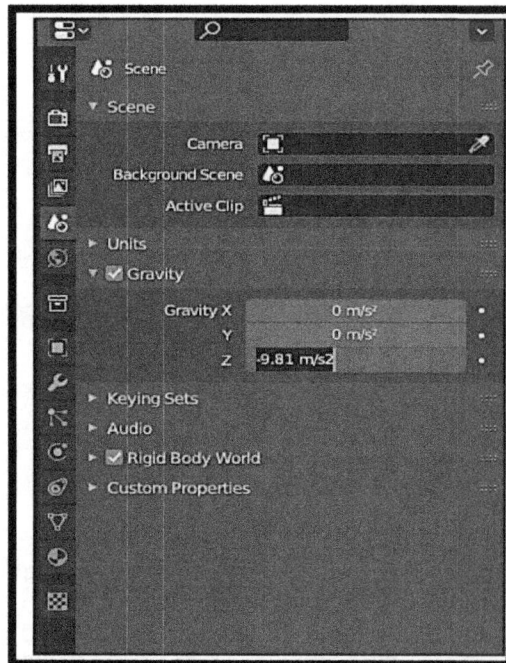

Find out if gravity exists, how it works, and how strong it is right here. All it takes to see the results is to add moon gravity to the scene:

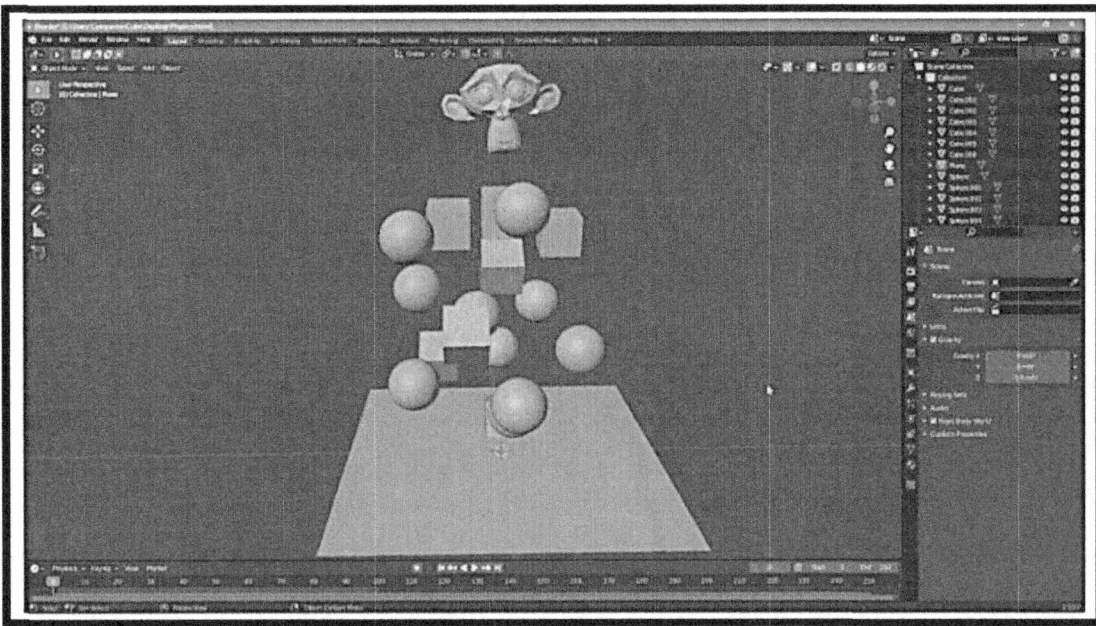

Baking Blender Physics Simulation

Keyframes can be built from specific types of models. Because of this, you may save the simulation as an animation and make changes without having to recalculate it. In most cases, you will find this option in the Cache section of the Physics Simulation box.

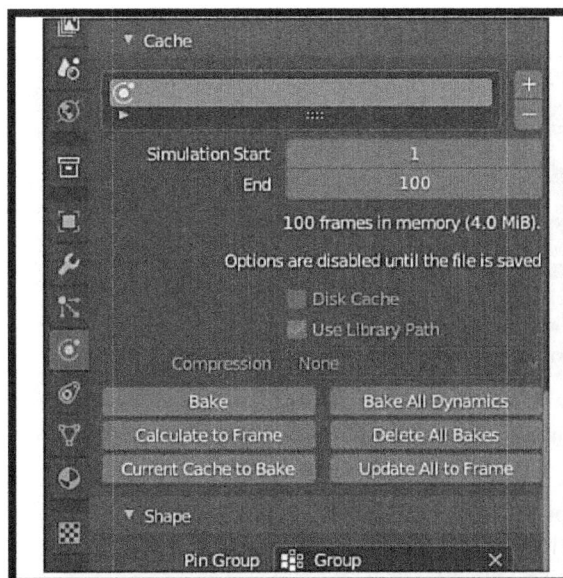

However, this component is omitted from some models. Well, that's just the more perplexing ones, like Fluid and Soft Body. In this window, you can choose the beginning and ending frames that you want to keep, and then click "Bake."

The simulation will continue until you delete the cache, after which it will disappear. After finishing a simulation, you should always bake it. If you follow these steps, they will look more finished and less prone to bugs.

Blender Cloth Brushes

With this detailed guide on cloth brushes, you'll learn the ropes of Blender's brush system. For your convenience, we will give you some basic examples to help you understand the principles. In Blender's Sculpting Editor, you have the option to use fabric brushes. Objectually, a fabric Brush mimics the feel and look of real fabric. You may create a realistic and highly controllable hybrid effect by combining the elements of Sculpting and Cloth Simulation. Anyway, it's not ideal and won't take the place of either feature.

How to Use a Cloth Brush

We require an item before applying a Cloth Brush on anything. No object can be considered valid unless it contains many polygons. A simple subdivision plane was my choice for this. The desired effect mimics the wrinkling of the fabric.

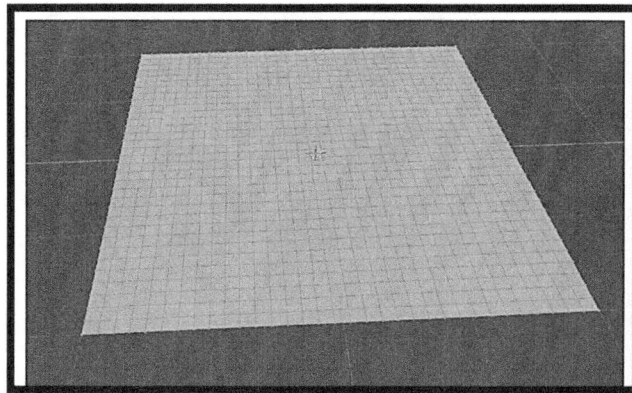

The subsequent step is to proceed to the Sculpt Mode. You can modify the status of the current window or start a sculpting workspace. Here you will find all of the tools and brushes. A swatch of fabric is seen beside the Cloth brush in this collection of icons.

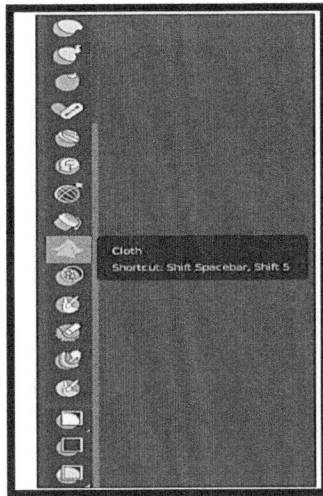

The brush is prepared and waiting for you here. A fabric simulation can be applied to an object by dragging and dropping it.

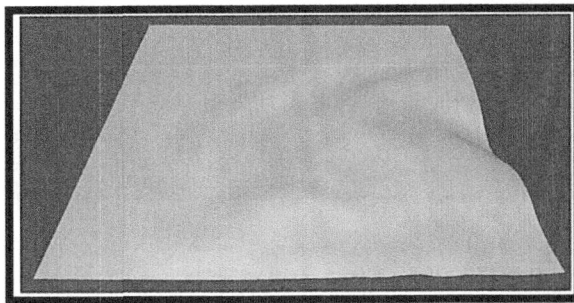

Blender Cloth Brush Interface

On top of the Sculpt Editor, you'll find most of the brush-related information you need.

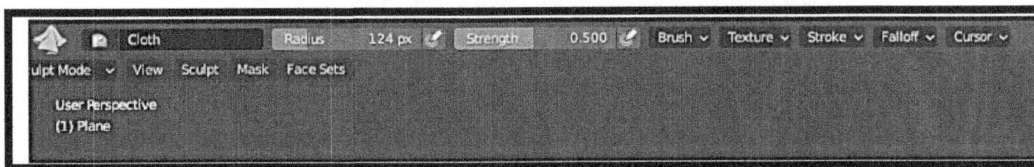

Navigate to the Active Tool tab to gain access to additional settings and data. The Properties Editor is accessible via the Active Tool tab as well as the tool menu on the side.

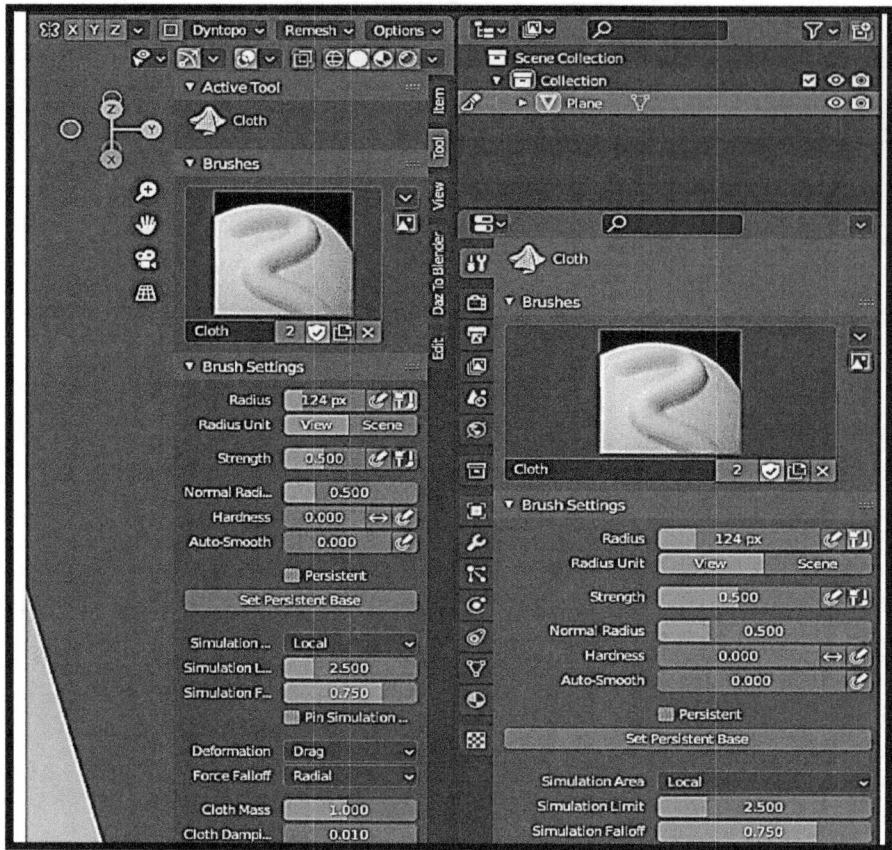

There is only one change, and that is that anyone can access the same window from wherever. They aren't required to be equally accommodating, so pick the one that works best for you. Here you can adjust the brush's strength and radius. These two factors are crucial for every brush. Not to mention the abundance of additional choices. Later on, we can go back to the original plan of switching out the cloth brush we have. It is time to look at the brush crosshair in its natural state. This is what the object looks like when viewed from a distance:

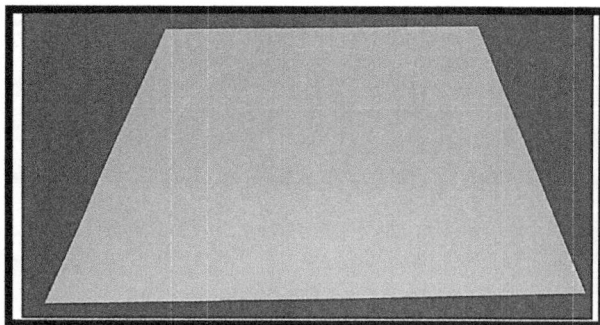

Four complete circles. Right in the middle are two orange orbs, but the two further out appear gray. Two are located in the center, as is typical with most sculpting brushes. When a brush fades, it exposes its weakest or most powerful point. The faster decline in power as you near the line is indicated by the brighter one. Also, the gray rings in the simulation region. When you press on an object, the simulation only uses the gray area. It will be unable to make changes to the section that is changing until it stops changing.

As can be observed in the image, the simulation changed all data inside the gray rings that encircle the picture's borders but did not affect data outside of those areas. The variations in the lighter grayscale tones stand out. Blender will show the same red outline if you try to use simulation outside of the gray area. Repositioning your mouse within the circle will allow you to make the necessary modifications.

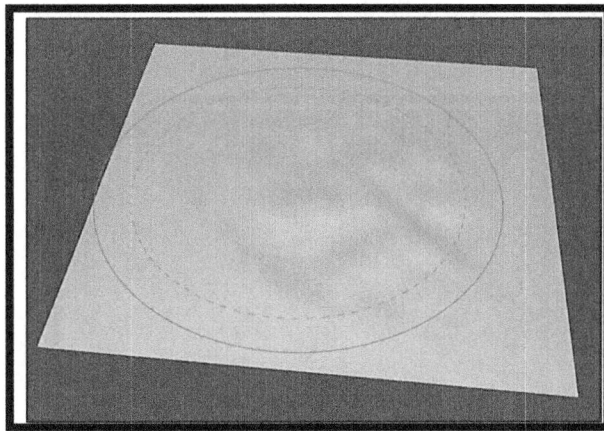

This is crucial to keep the object's physics model to a minimum. Discovering the answer in this way will be much faster. This can be avoided by repeatedly tweaking the object's small details. Altering the Simulation Limit can also be done by going to the Brush menu. This causes calculations to take longer, which, as previously said, might create substantial delays.

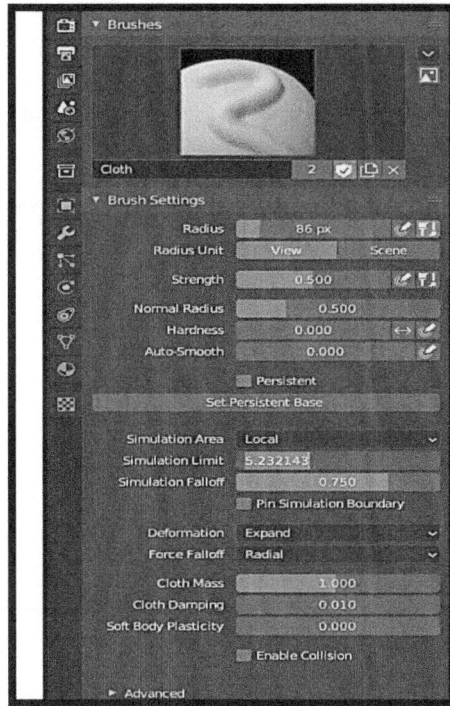

Different Cloth Brushes

Although it may seem like there is just one Cloth Brush there are quite a few. Blender cloths are another name for brushes like this. You can locate all of them in the Tool Settings box, namely in the distortion option.

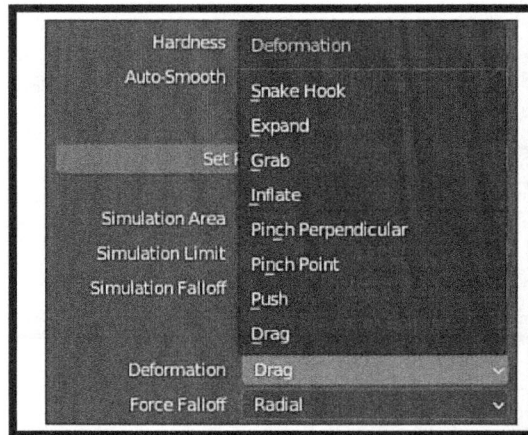

As far as technology is concerned, it's essentially the same Cloth Brush; it has only been shaped differently. Alternatively, its main use is as a kind of fabric brush. Given that this is the beginning, we will go through the choices in descending order of price. Simply running your hand over a piece of cloth is all that is needed to practice drag. Typically, it merely produces a small number of wrinkles. But if the radius is big enough, it can change the object's shape completely.

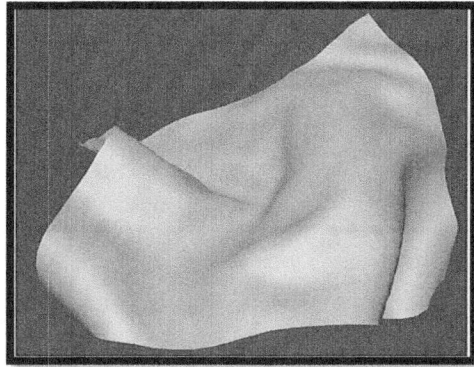

"Push Deformation" is the answer to all of your questions. From above, something is pressing on the fabric, causing it to wiggle.

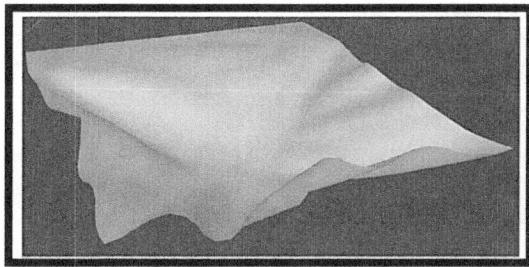

As the name "Pinch Point" suggests, two competing pressures are at work here. The common outcome of this is a prominent wrinkle.

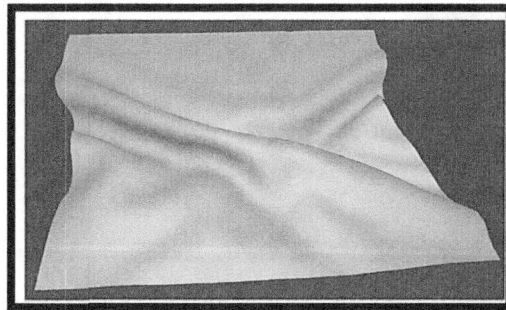

Pinch Point and Pinch Perpendicular are functionally similar but have different names. Since Pitch Point was more reliable and easier to use, I generally favored it.

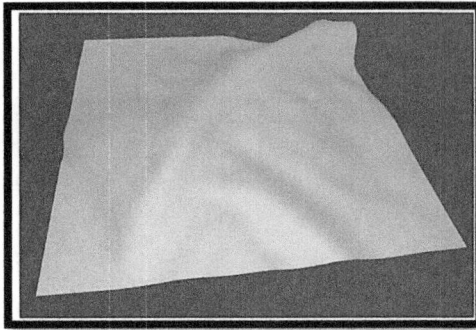

Proceed by inflating the brush. The item is propelled by an internal force in this one. It makes more complicated items look inflated when used on them, yet it wraps around anything when applied to the plane.

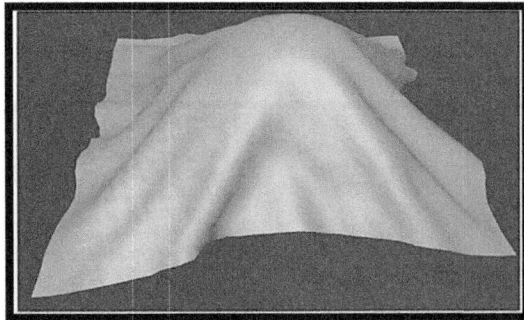

Both the Inflate and Push deformations are present at the same time. This is illogical because you can undo changes in progress by pressing [CTRL]. On closer study, though, you might be able to spot a few small changes.

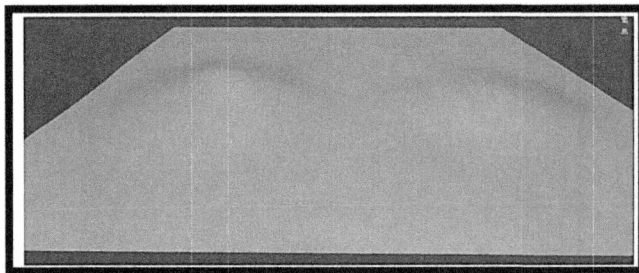

Grab is easy to use. This is the only way to determine if the item was picked up and relocated. Although it serves a different purpose, a Grab brush is still present in Regular Sculpting. There is nothing more it can do, like making clothes wrinkle, except from altering an object's shape. You can see a cloth grab on the left side of the picture and a simple grab on the right side of it. You can't possibly confuse the two.

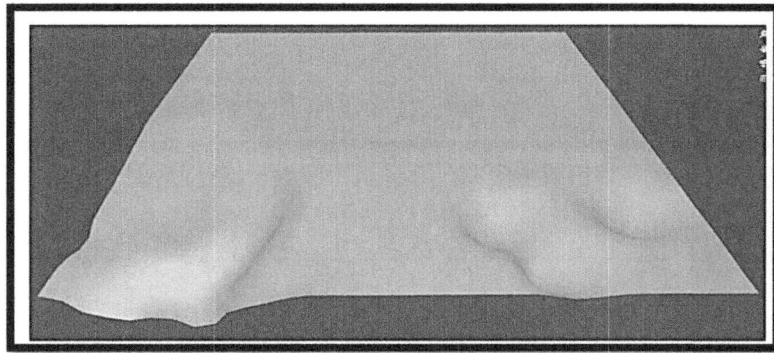

You can add more details to your garments by clicking the Expand button. It somewhat distorts the object, incorporates new characteristics, and bestows certain haphazard flaws on it.

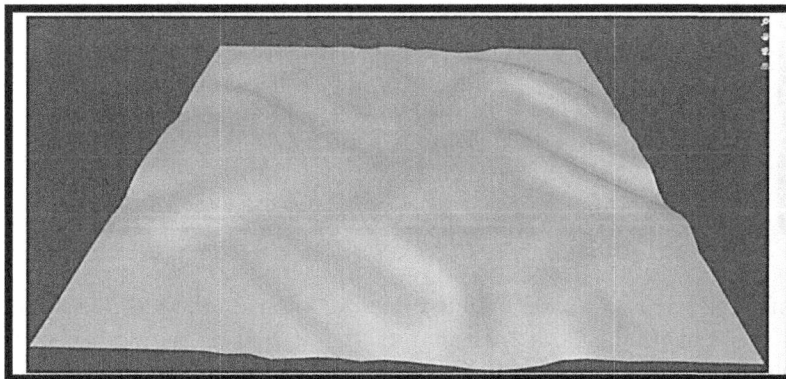

The Snake Hook is the final brush. Equal in principle to the grab brush but substantially kinder and gentler. Another option is conventional modeling Snake Hook, which, as a refresher, completely changes the contour of the object, giving it a completely different look.

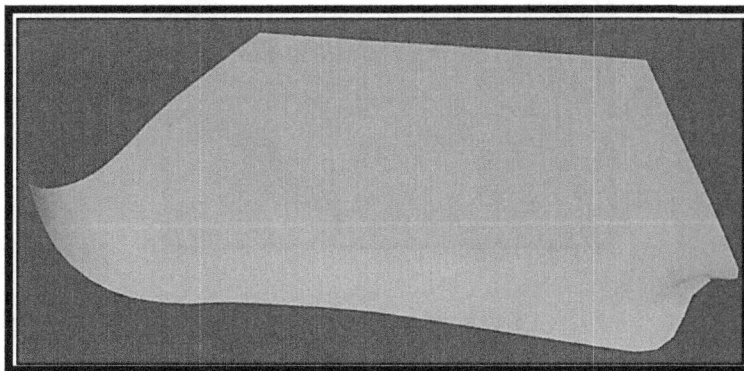

Cloth Filter

The Cloth Filter is another "Cloth" brush in the Sculpt Editor, as you might have seen upon closer inspection.

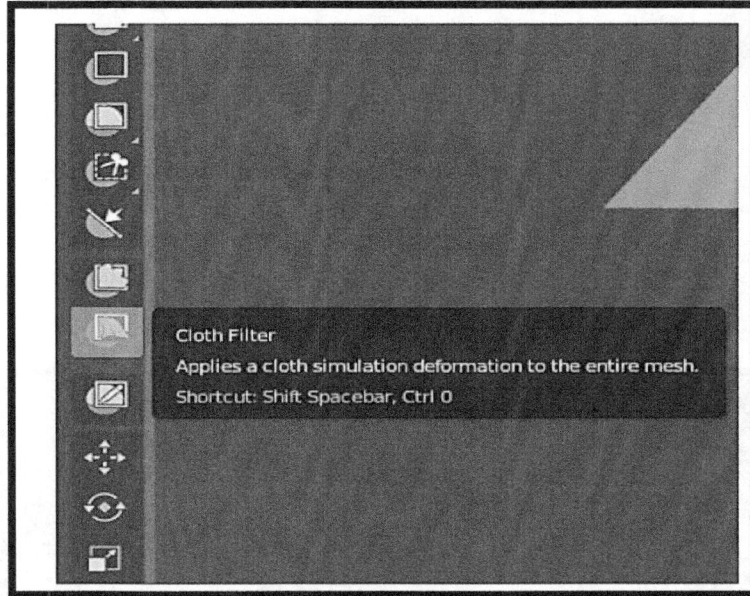

It changes the form of the fabric, but other than that, it's the same as the Mesh Filter up there. Whatever, I say we check it out. Kind of like the Cloth Brush, but it lets you simulate the cloth all over an item at once, which is a huge plus. After failing miserably on the Plane, I've decided to try my luck with a high-poly spherical this time around.

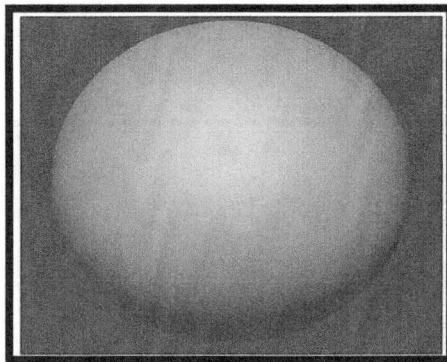

The Filter Type option can be found in the Tool menu. Each of these variants of this brush is fully functional.

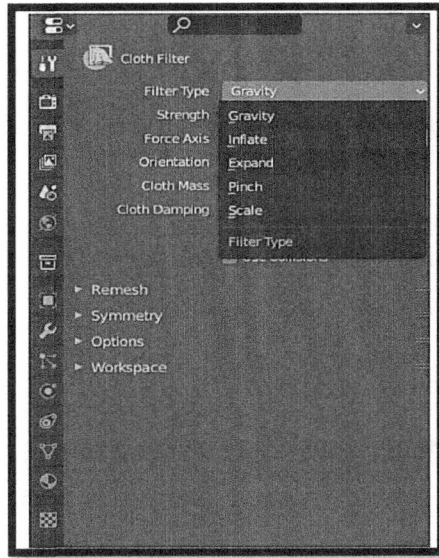

When the gravity filter is applied, the item will naturally descend or ascend following the principles of physics.

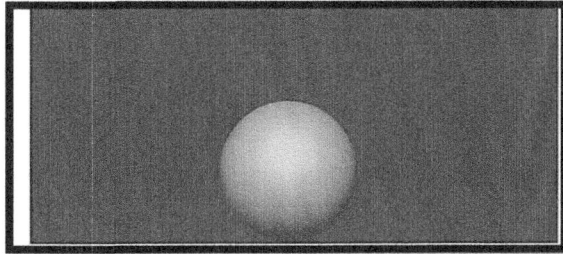

Inflate Filter – inflates an object. I have deflated the sphere by inverting the filter as it is already inflated.

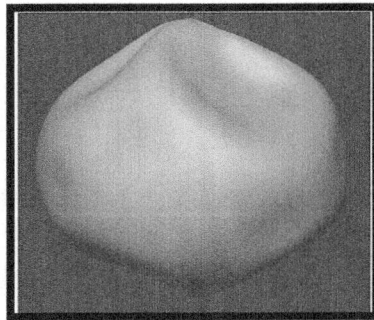

After that, the program goes to Expand and does what you asked it to do. True to its name, it gives the impression of somewhat magnifying the object when applied uniformly throughout.

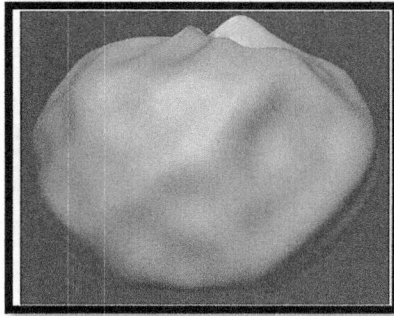

Two opposite directions of pinch force were applied:

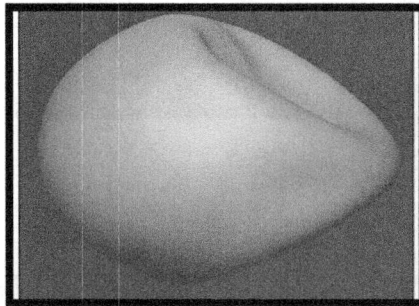

How to Simulate Cloth in Blender

This is going to start with a breakdown of our Blender Cloth Simulation. We need an object, of course, for this to work. Since it applies to any object, I'll test it on a typical cube. After you've chosen an object, head over to the Modifier Properties. One can incorporate cloth physics with that.

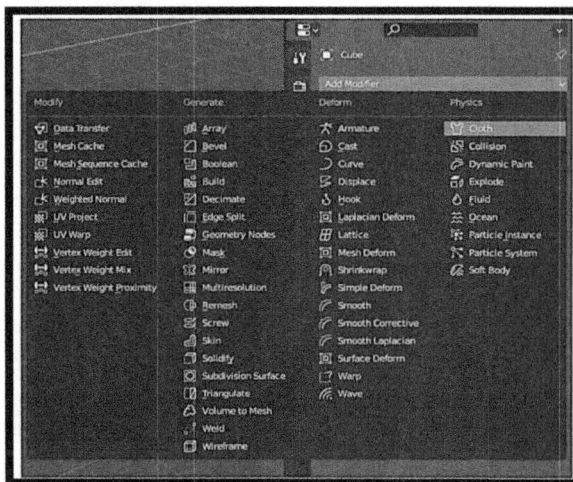

The same can be achieved in Physics Properties. Instead of using the Modifier Properties, which won't show all of the simulation's parameters when you add them, you can use the Physics Properties instead.

Several extra settings will appear in the Physics Properties box when you apply Physics Simulation to an object. Later on, we shall go back to them. To observe the results of this simulation, look at the entire scene. What will happen when I click "play"? Hence, very little occurs that is significant. All it takes is for the Cube to fall to pieces.

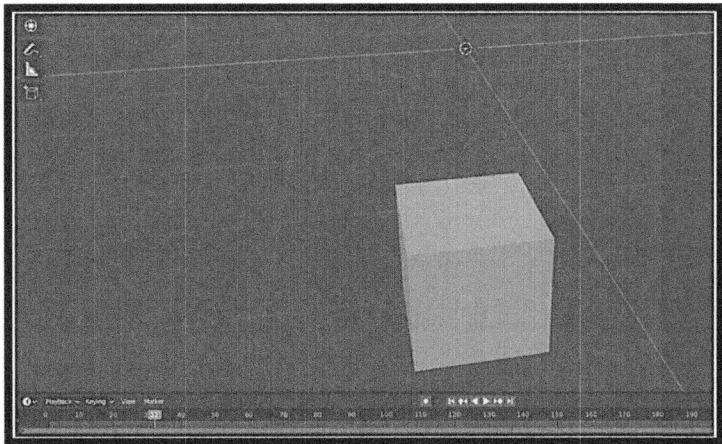

This scenario can't work without an additional object. The Cube will become motionless when it is ensnared by a solid item. Going back to frame 0 will allow you to change scenery. I placed the plane object just underneath the cube, so now it will strike it. The moment I press "play," Cube begins to fall significantly more.

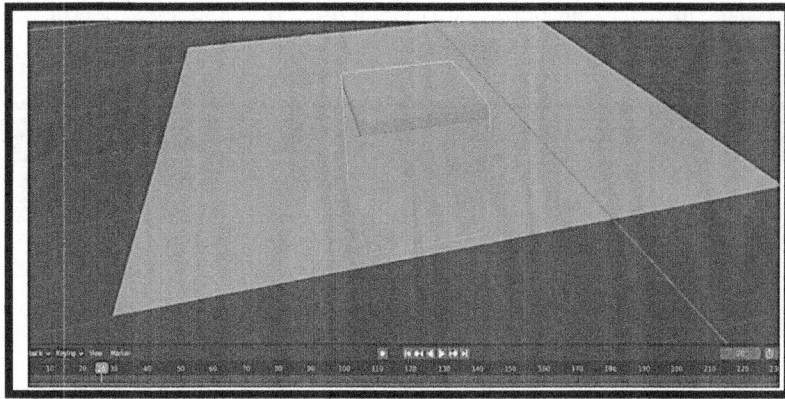

Now since the Cube doesn't have any physics, we need to add them to the flat object even more. Set the Plane to Collision in the Physics Properties for this to occur. It is a real-life simulation that causes this thing to collide with other objects. Do not even bother. No additional adjustments are required either. Finally, the plane halts Cube's plummeting. However, it stays on the plane and does not change at all. Cloth simulation has not been detected.

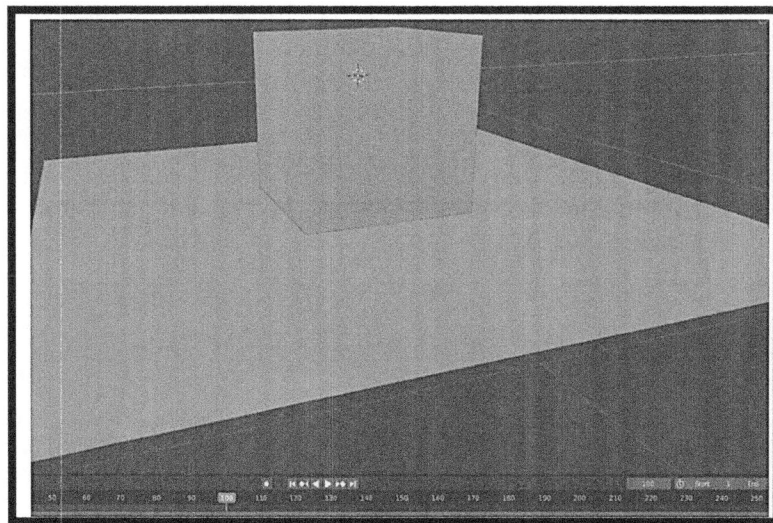

Therefore, because geometry is malleable, it is crucial to any simulation. Plus, there are just 8 points on this basic cube. Because there aren't enough of them, Cloth Simulation can't utilize them. Enhance the object's form so it might be used to resolve this issue. The simulation will seem more realistic with the addition of additional geometry. On the other hand, more time will be needed to make and show this simulation. As a result, you need to make an effort to find a middle ground. I gave the Cube some form by repeatedly dividing it with Subdivide.

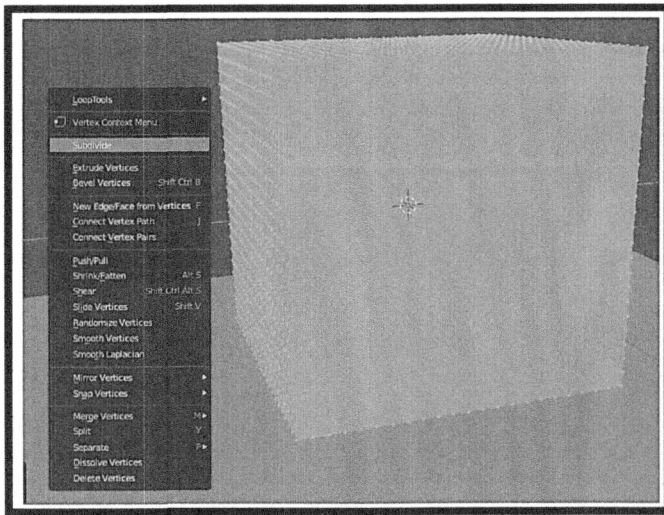

Once you hit "play," the Cube will finally distort and fall to the floor. It seems to be made of a cloth-like material.

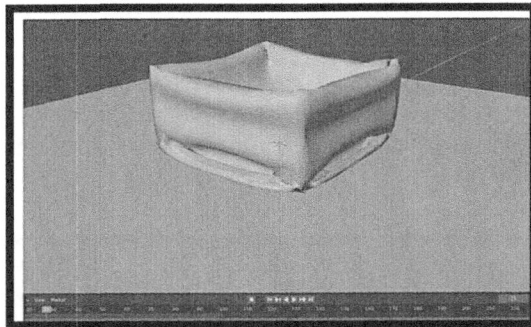

Once you've made a scenario, you can edit it in any way you like. Keep an eye on the scene as the height of the cube changes. The simulation may be fine-tuned with a simple twist.

Still, the Cube isn't the simulation's ideal item overall. Can you find any fabric containers? It is possible to think of spheres and planes as superior objects. Because of its fabric-like behavior, the plane is ideal for use in virtual garment simulations. When applied, it will simulate collisions with other objects and encircle them beautifully.

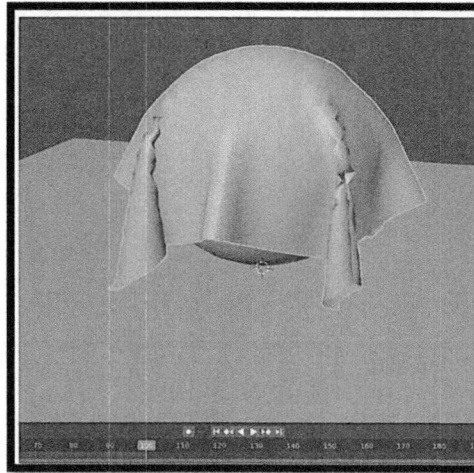

Blender Cloth Simulation Settings

Next, we'll go over the Physics tab in the Properties Editor and the options it gives you. Although numerous, just a small number makes a difference. I will thus focus on the ones that I think are most crucial. Start with the Quality Steps setting at the very top.

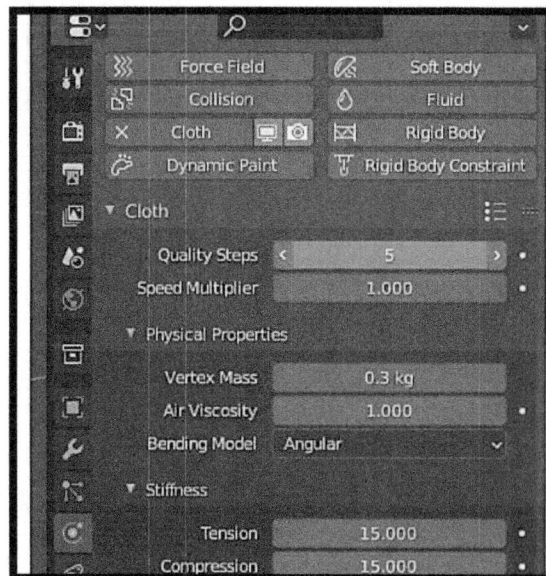

Changing this parameter can change the overall simulation accuracy. The lower the range, the worse it gets. Obstacles, malfunctions, or delays can occur for a variety of causes.

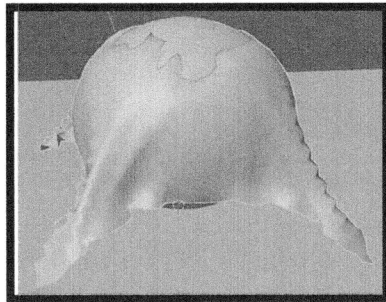

They believe that the simulation will work better if you crank this up. It is already much better at value 2.

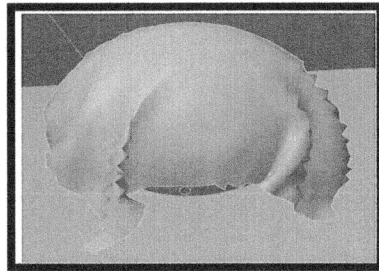

You mustn't take this too seriously, as is the case with many other things. A higher value for this parameter will result in a higher simulation power usage, as the two variables are related. Going overboard is usually not necessary. At Quality Steps 5 and 10, we may see the same simulation. Nonetheless, it would seem that they are not too dissimilar. Instead, they have a lot of commonalities and issues. Step 10 of Quality takes a very long time.

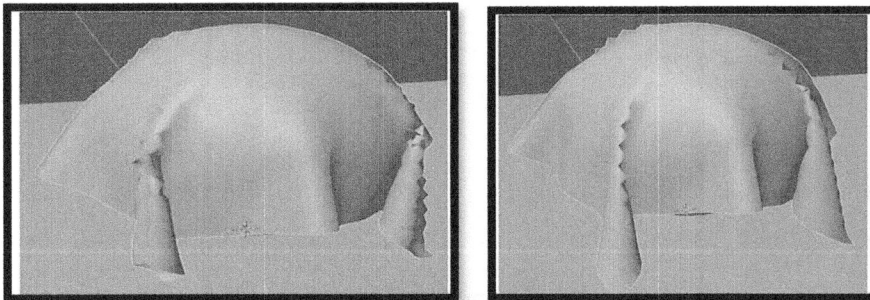

Down below, you'll see the Speed Multiplier. It controls the simulation's calculating speed, as expected. An increase in value will make it appear as though the identical item is occurring much more rapidly. Another option is to reduce the Speed Multiplier, which will drastically slow down the simulation. You won't be able to capture a frame with such fine detail when the Speed Multiplier is set to 1.

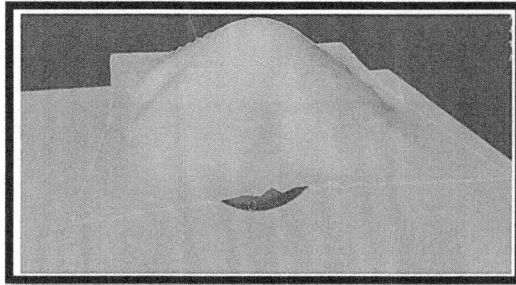

You can change the object's vertex weight using the Vertex Mass property. Due to the compression of the air, an object with very little weight will descend at a slow rate. Even when I make my plane light, it won't be able to wrap the sphere in its entirety.

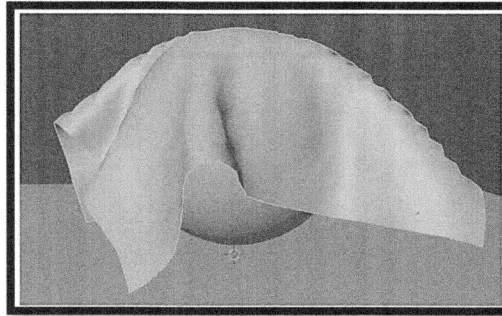

A **Heavier Vertex Mass** will fall faster and wrap around objects more easily. From this picture, you can tell that my plane hit the sphere and stayed there because of the sphere's weight.

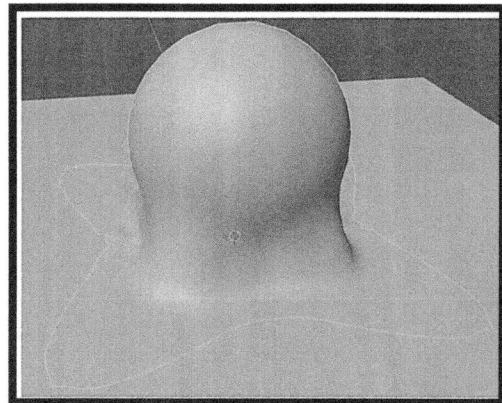

The viscosity of the air affects the deformation resistance. Changing the shape of an object is an easy operation if its air viscosity is low. Without any effort, my plane circled the sphere after swooping down on it.

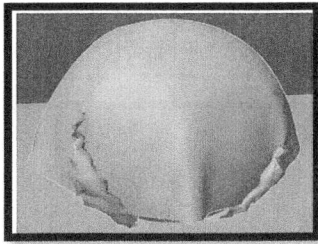

On the other hand, a high air viscosity will make it less malleable. The object's shape remains remarkably unchanged as it gently descends, in contrast to its lighter state.

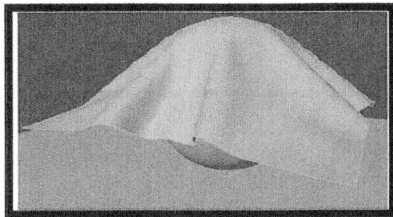

Internal springs are the next settings. The simulation will now have springs added to it, allowing it to bounce, just as promised. A spherical, rather than a plane, would be more suitable for this application. Using Cloth Simulation with its default settings yields the following result:

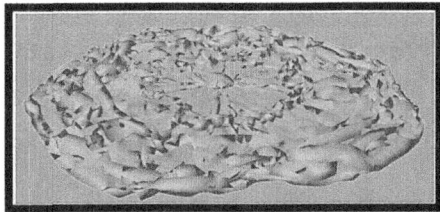

The terrain has been leveled. It has completely lost all resemblance to a sphere. However, its behavior changes significantly after I enable the Internal Springs setting. It doesn't compress and collapse but rather acts more like a spherical. The item appears to be driven by springs because it bends slightly as it hits the ground before leaping up. Every other option works with this one. In this case, adding mass causes a dramatic shift in the object's leaping behavior.

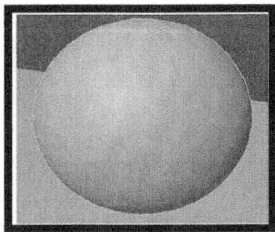

Next, you'll find the pressure setting. Due to the plane's re-occlusion, we should consult our old friend, the split default cube. When using the default Cloth settings, it looks like this, in case you forgot:

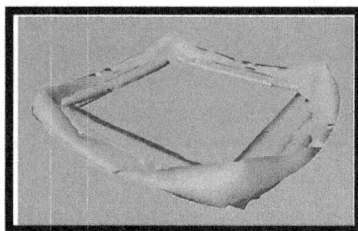

A deflated and deformed object. Behold, the moment I activate the Pressure setting, the entire situation transforms.

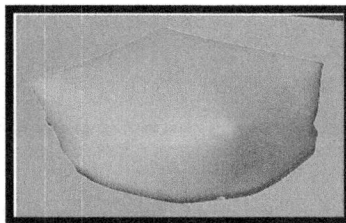

It looks like a piece of the cube just exploded. This is the basic operation of it. Comparable to compressed air, the internal pressure acts as an internal force pressing down on the object. More pressing will cause it to look more like an expanded cube:

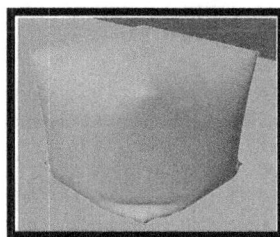

You might have observed that several of the examples fail to adequately illustrate the things we work with. By this, I mean when students meet as a group and work out their math problems. As follows:

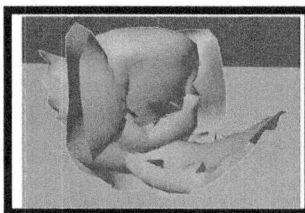

It looks ugly in certain scenarios and can be a big problem. Luckily, fixing it won't be a problem. Get to the "Self Collision" menu item and turn it on. There will be an increase in computing time, but the result will be of greater quality:

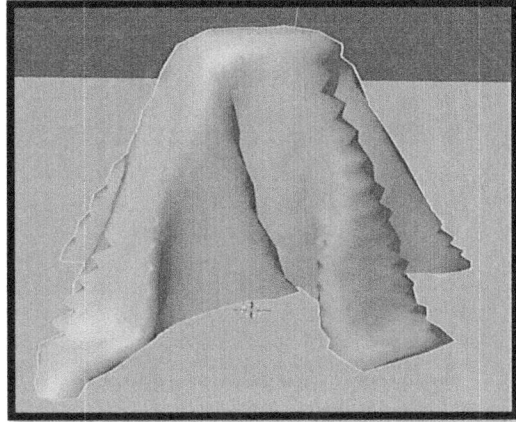

Pinning Parts

Maybe it would help to zero in on the Cloth simulation. The majority of fabric items are attached to something, rather than just letting them float aimlessly. Think about the rope that holds a flagpole to the ground. Making pinned vertices allows you to do this again in Blender. Select the edges you want to pin in Edit mode. After that, go to the Object Properties and make a new Vertex Group. After that, simply include the points you selected in this section.

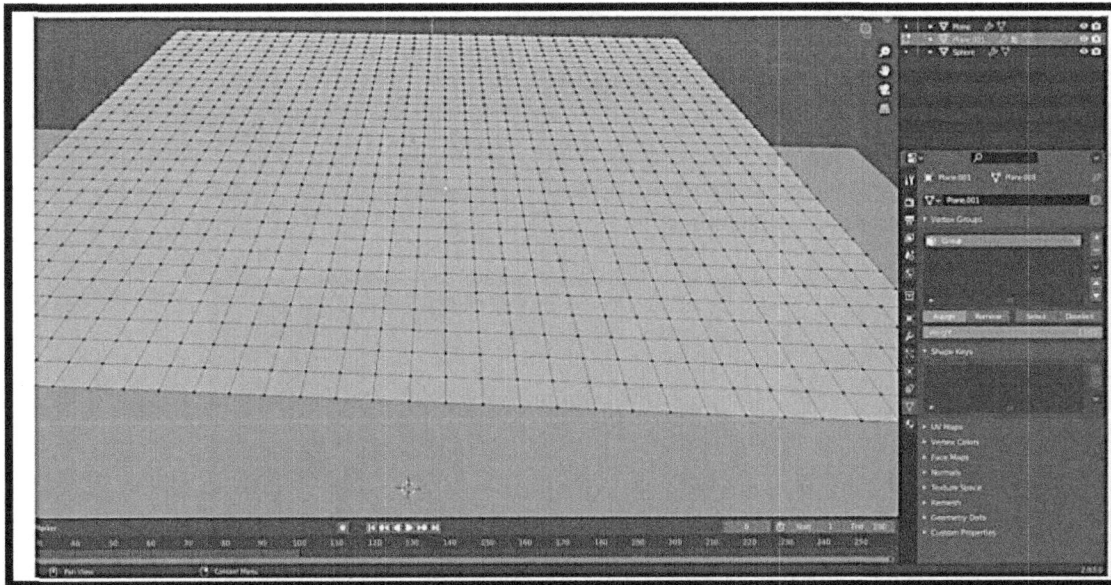

The next thing to do is go to the Physics Properties box and look for the Pin Group option under Shape. Which vertex group you made here is entirely up to you.

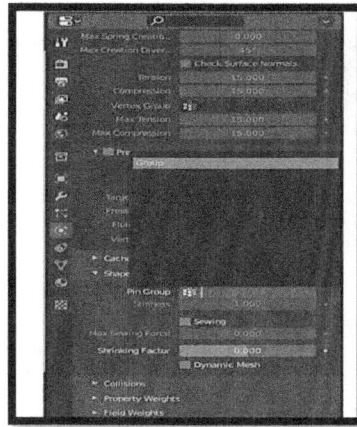

It is complete. Now, when I hit "play," the entire game will play out, except the pinned areas.

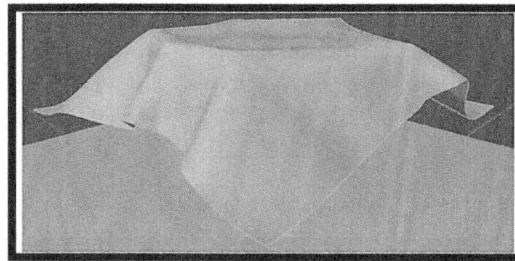

Hooking Simulation to an Object

Continuing from the last example, here is a method that requires more work: connecting the entire simulation to a single item. This approach should assign a complete edge loop to a group rather than utilizing random locations. **Delete the previous selection**.

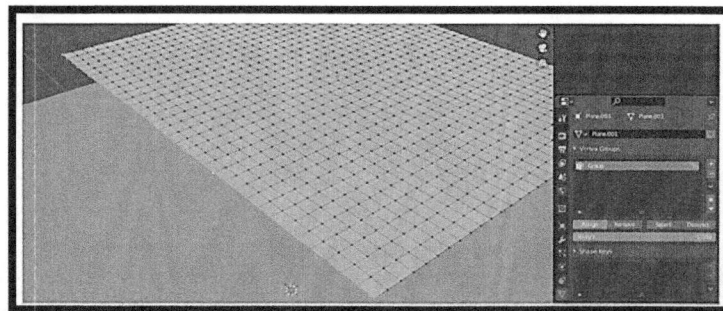

Selected newly generated vertex groups can have hook modifiers applied to them. Make another empty object and join it to the first. In contrast, Blender can automate the entire procedure. Choose the desired vertices, and then go to the Vertex menu, where you can choose Hooks and finally Hook to New Object.

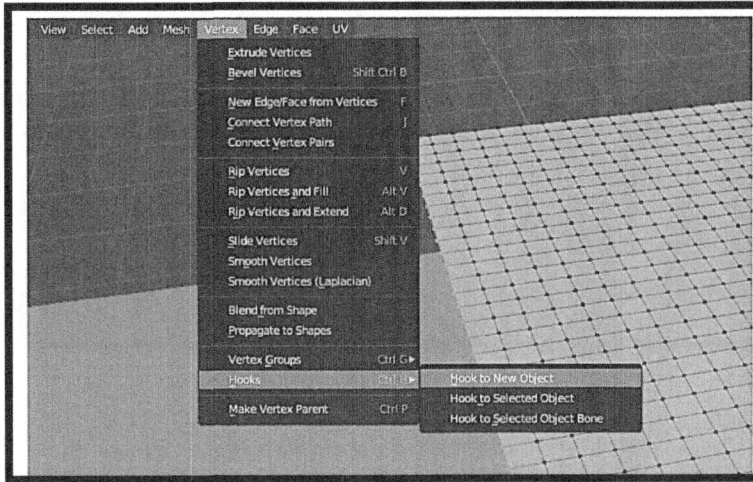

This is how you make the right connections, an empty, and a modifier. Among all the various modifiers, the Hook Modifier probably wouldn't be very high on the list. You have to put anything on top for it to work properly.

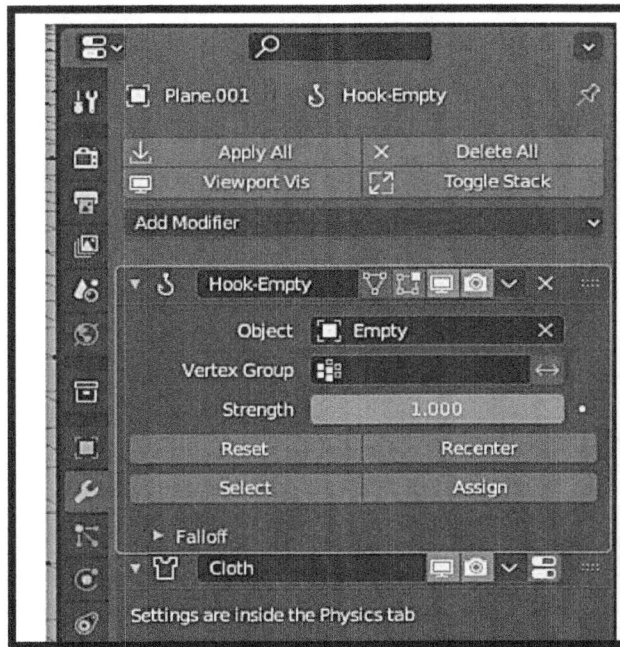

As a result of our connection to an Empty, the vertex group we created will likewise change position after the task is finished.

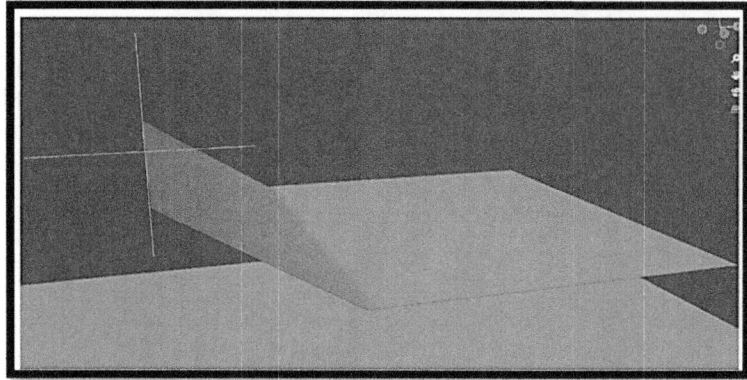

It certainly doesn't seem like a viable solution, does it? In such a case, I could be wrong. The calculations will continue uninterrupted until you try to move this inanimate object while the video is playing. As the fabric simulation runs, that will turn the item into a static silhouette.

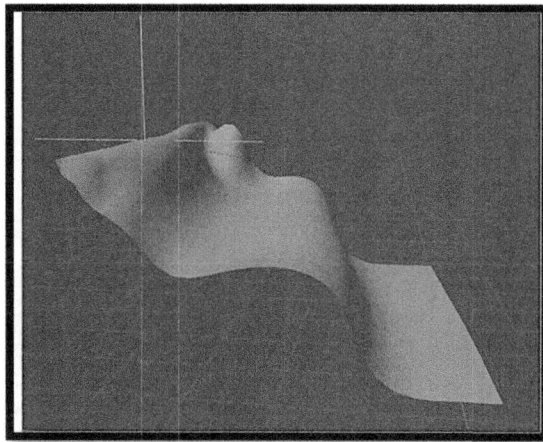

This animation method makes it easy to move your clothing item to a different spot.

Baking Simulation

The complete simulation will be reevaluated every time you play back your animation after making changes. Hence, each time you make a change, you'll have to recalculate everything. It may appear reasonable, but it's not the best choice because models can become very complicated, which makes the computation take a long time. To save yourself the trouble of repeatedly doing the math, you can "Cache" your Blender Cloth Simulation. The **Physics Properties' Cache part** is the proper place for this.

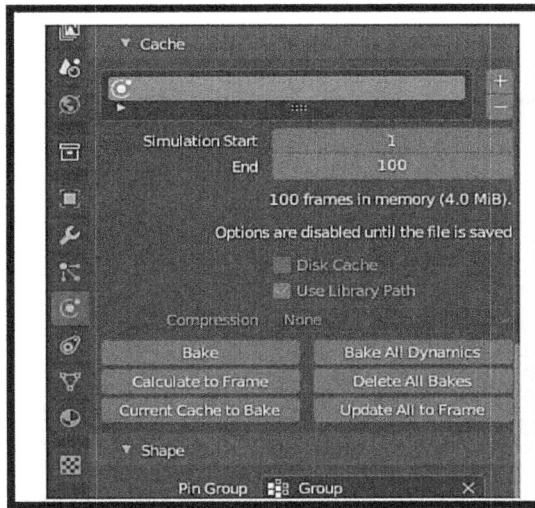

After selecting the beginning and ending frames for your simulation, you may bake it by clicking the **Bake** button. After that, you may see Blender's progress meter at the bottom of the software.

Your simulation will be "Cached" once you finish, so there's no need to worry. Since your accomplishments will be intangible, they will be pointless. The extent to which I modified the initial form is plain to observe here. It has been rearranged and twisted by myself. Additionally, it changed its shape on frame 0.

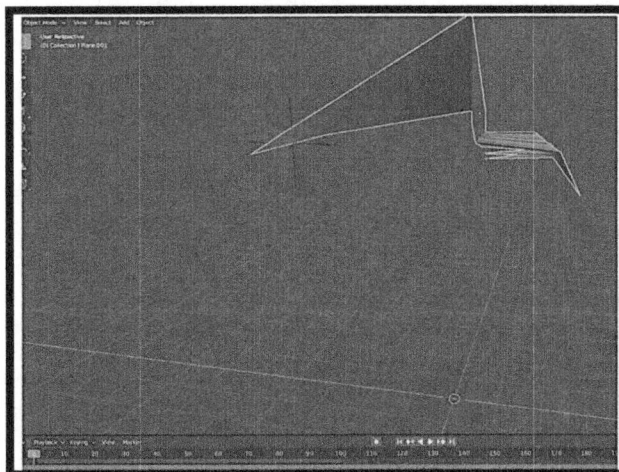

But as soon as the animation starts, it goes back to how it was before storage. Frame 2 clearly shows that it is in a completely different spot.

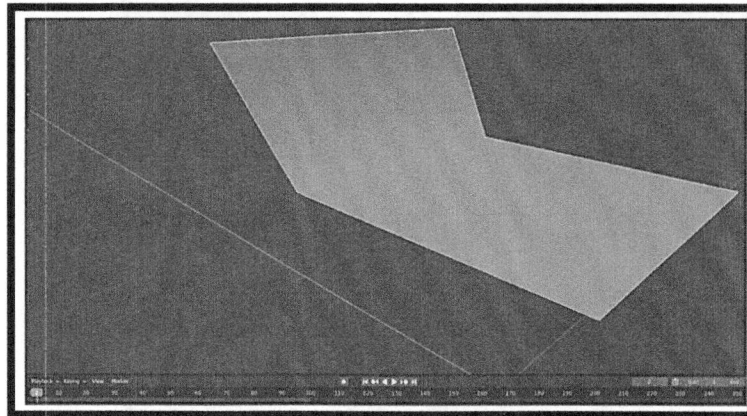

Furthermore, I am unable to move it from its present spot. Taking out the baked cache is now your sole option for making changes to this simulation.

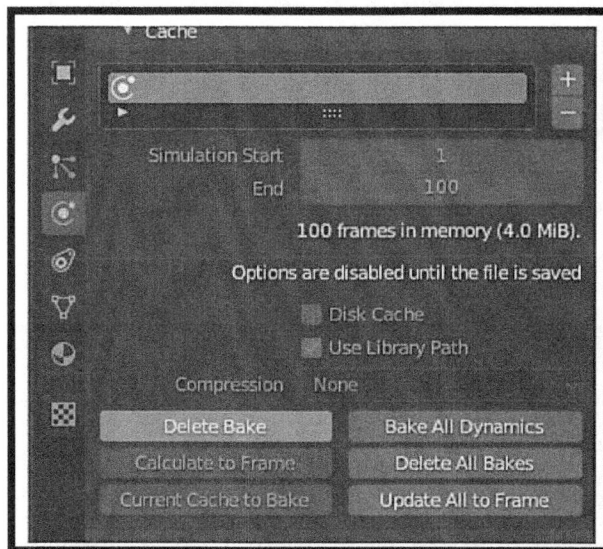

Blender Fluid Simulation

It is interesting to hear about the Blender Fluid simulation. These models allow users to create breathtaking outputs and are entertaining for the most part. You already have these in Blender, and they're good. However, there are several reasons why newcomers could find them difficult to use. The Blender guide for simulating smoke and liquids is worth checking out.

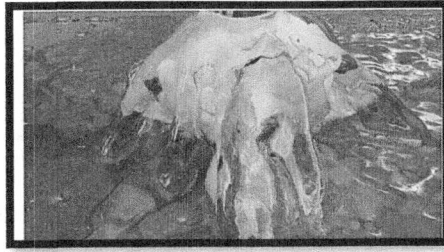

Creating Liquid Simulation Domain in Blender

Establishing liquid boundaries is the initial stage. We can't simply put it in Blender and disappear. The fluids must remain contained at all times, making this step extremely important. The use of an object is required to establish these limits. Right now, anything will do, but a bit-sized cube will work.

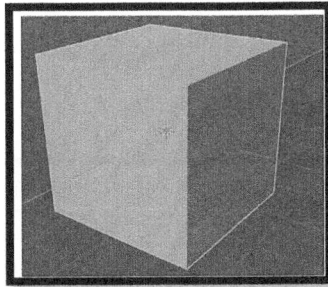

After you've checked the box, go to the Physics Properties and click on the name of the fluid simulation to activate it. Next, switch to the Fluid Type option and select the Domain. What this means is that our Fluid Simulation will house it. The Cube will change its look instantly.

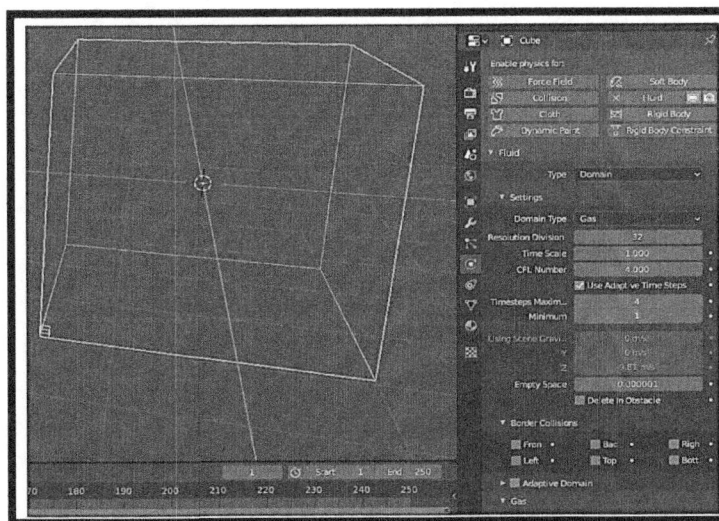

Right now, it would be more accurate to specify the Domain Type as Liquid rather than Gas. For the time being, it is crucial to note that it will not work with liquids. The Cube should return to its stable state after that.

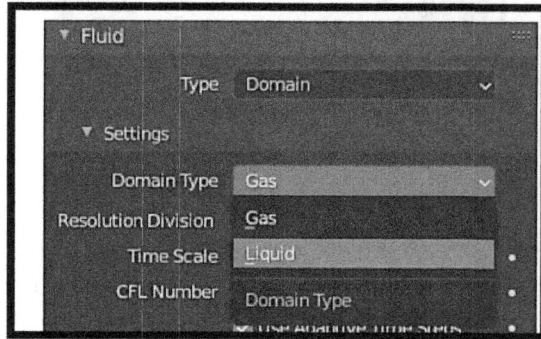

Additional modifications are required. First, you need to turn on the Diffusion feature. This one is crucial because it determines the look and texture of our drink. Three distinct choices are available for the honey, oil, and water. It is now set to "Water," so I will not alter it.

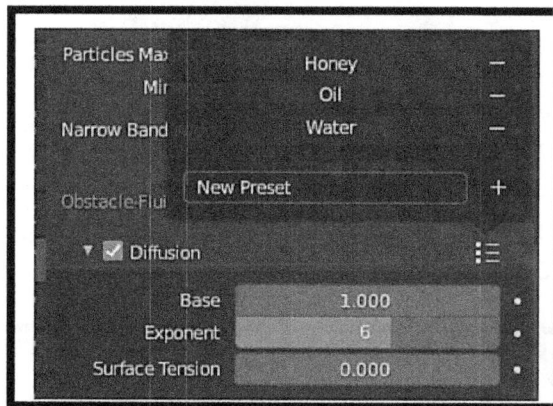

Additionally, be sure you turn on the nearby Mesh feature. This will allow us to construct a Fluid Mesh in the future.

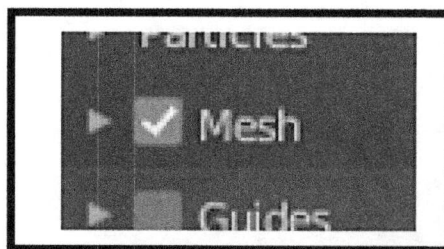

The last step is to change the cache type from Modular to Replay in the Cache section. I believe everything is functioning well as it is, but I wanted to make sure. It might be impossible to detect liquids at the same time if that isn't the case.

Creating Liquid Simulation Flow Object in Blender

Adding liquid is the next step after creating the bound object in Blender Liquid Simulation. We also need to make something to add liquid to the scene. Right now, a UV Sphere could be the best thing to use for this job. Drop it into the Cube once it's finished. You can simplify things by enabling the Wireframe Viewport Shading or the X-Ray function (Ctrl+Z).

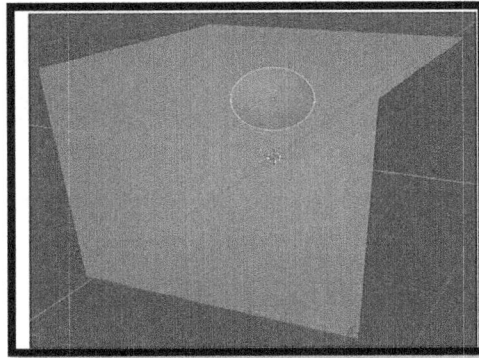

Go to the Physics Properties to activate the Sphere's Fluid Physics Simulation. This time, change the Type to Flow instead.

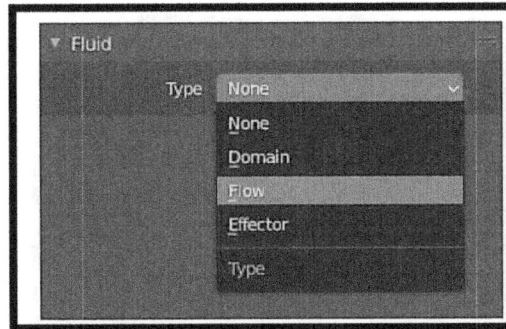

Selecting the Flow Type, in this case, Liquid is the next step. Also, in the Flow Behavior menu, you should see an option to enable Inflow. Consequently, fluids will be added to the simulation. You should be able to play the animation and see the fluids move now that the objects are set. Just press the Spacebar. However, the likelihood of anything happening is low. There's an error in that. Have no fear; I can resolve this issue quickly. Changing the Resolution Division is as easy as re-selecting the Domain Object. At any moment, you have the option to revert your modifications. If you want to fix the issue by beginning the simulation again, this is your only option. Also, remember to start your animation at frame 1.

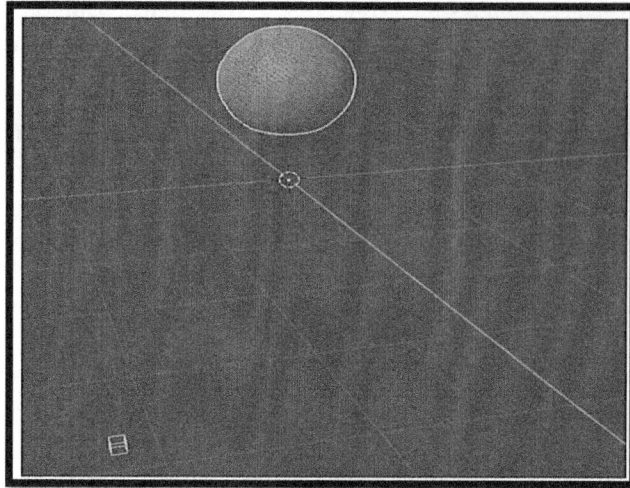

If everything is working as it should, the X-Ray particles surrounding the Flow Object should become visible and the Domain object should become translucent.

Simulating Liquids and its Settings

Pressing the [Spacebar] should now start playing the animation. Theoretically, this should be useful for physics. It may take some time for the calculation to complete because this can put a strain on your computer, especially its CPU. After you finish the first set of numbers, the second set will go by much more quickly.

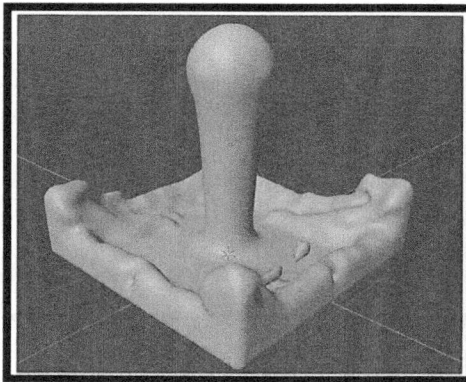

Consequently, the outcome is imprecise, as is evident. The water's low level of detail is made up of large chunks of water. The Resolution Division option in the Domain Object settings is to blame. The more you play about with these settings, the more exact your drink will turn out, and the opposite is also true. Nevertheless, this will also drastically change the periods for computation. The highest possible value is 6, which is quite unusual. It lacks the natural fruitiness and more closely resembles jello. No matter how quickly the figures pop up.

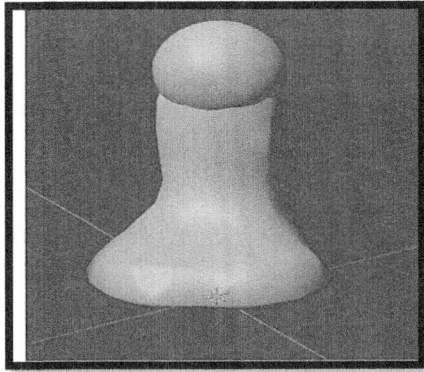

This is just a preview number and not the actual value. You can anticipate the liquid's behavior with just the barest minimum of information. Always turn this option up to its maximum before printing. An obvious improvement becomes apparent as soon as the width is increased to 50 divisions:

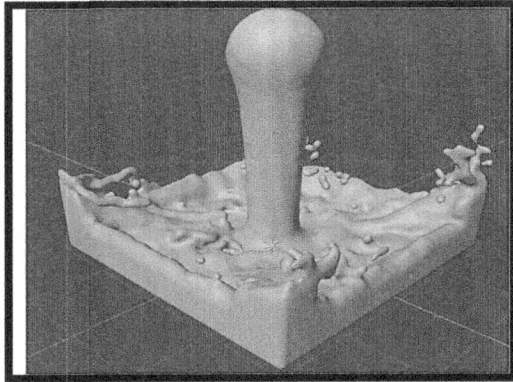

I noticed a substantial improvement in the simulation quality after raising the Resolution Divisions to 100, as shown in the image below. It has the most details compared to all of them, and there are innumerable little drips of liquid everywhere it hits the ground and walls. The others were lightning fast, but this one was snail's pace. After all that, though, the majority of individuals go considerably higher.

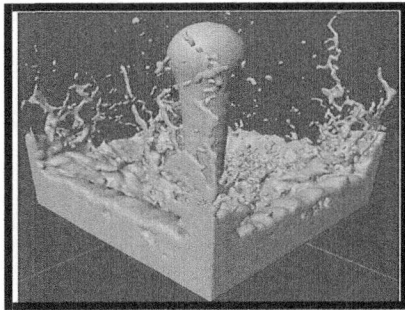

Another important characteristic is the **Time Scale**, which is situated under the Resolution Division. The simulation rate of the liquid is adjusted by it. That is the difference between the original and each subsequent frame. So far, the default value of 1.0 has been used for everything. This, like the last two images, is the result of the Resolution Division 50 calculation. But the Time Scale is at 2.

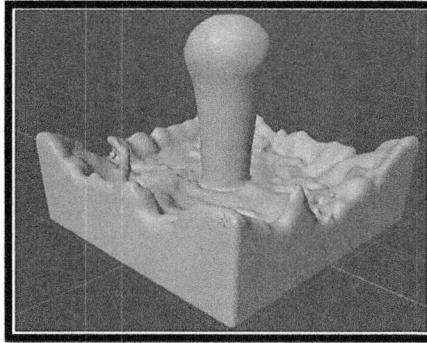

The distinction will stand out when you compare. The one with the bigger Time Scale is far farther along in the animation. There is more liquid and less noise already. Regardless, it's the same animated frame. Reducing the value of the Time Scale is the standard practice. The animation will move at a more leisurely rate, but each picture will have more information. Some people use this to make their final render motion more detailed. If you want to make the motion look more realistic, you can post-process it after you severely reduce the Time Value.

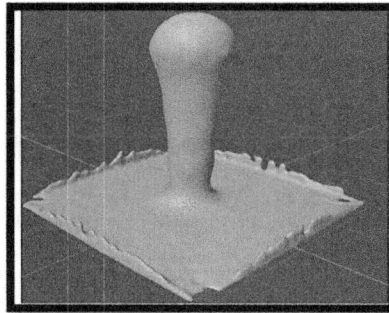

How to Add Collision Objects to the Fluid Simulation

It is not very interesting to just simulate plain old liquid in a box. Making these fluids able to communicate with anything is a huge improvement. You can wrap some other things around them. Before you may add this type of object, you must first create it. No particular kind of mesh is required or even allowed. Additionally, after reading our Blender Physics Simulation, you could think that we should use Collision Physics, as it proved to be the most effective when mixed with other physics.

I'm afraid that won't be successful. What you see before you is liquid. The two types of rigid bodies, active and passive, are identical.

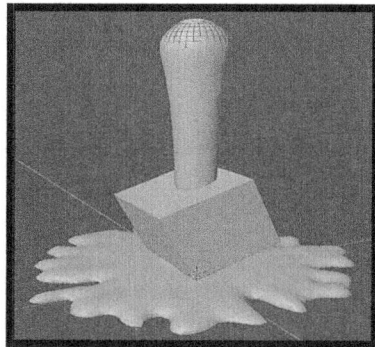

A Fluid Physics component must be re-added to the item. On this specific occasion, nevertheless, we shall choose the Effector Type.

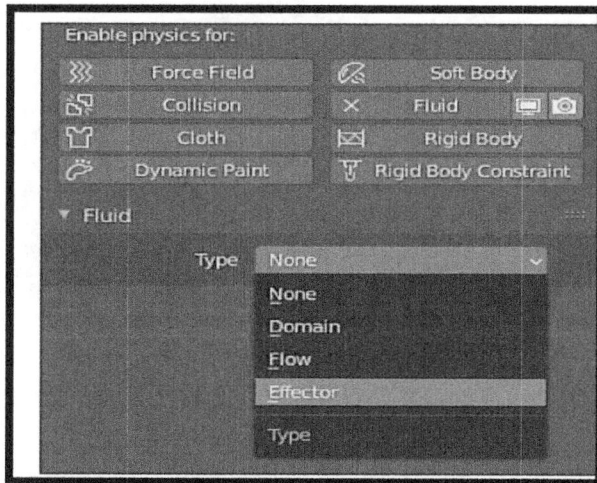

The "object" is whatever it is that our bodily fluids may irritate. Yes, you read it right. By default, the Effector Type is set to Collision, which is precisely the desired outcome. It is going to crash into our item right now. Typically, you'll have to restore the Resolution Division to its default settings and then restart the simulation to get it going again. Thereafter, it needs to be finished:

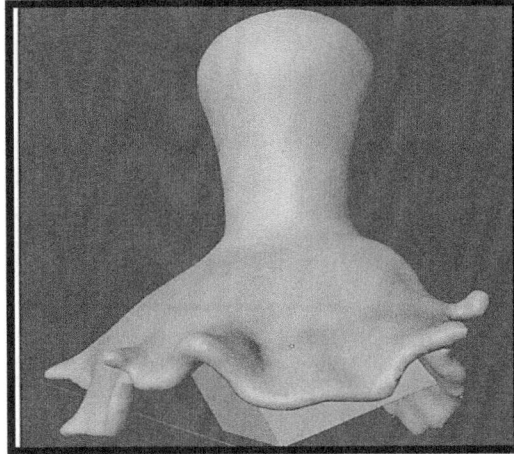

How to Simulate Smoke

The Fluid Simulations feature in Blender, though, can do much more than that. I am now going into detail on Smoke Simulation. First, let's make a little scene using the Smoke Simulation. Given that we have previously finished the Liquid Simulation, this amounts to nothing more than that. We should merely make little changes to our choices. So, I'll stick with the scene I had before, which is a big cube with a sphere within. I would like to start by reverting my Cube's Domain type to Gas, the default configuration.

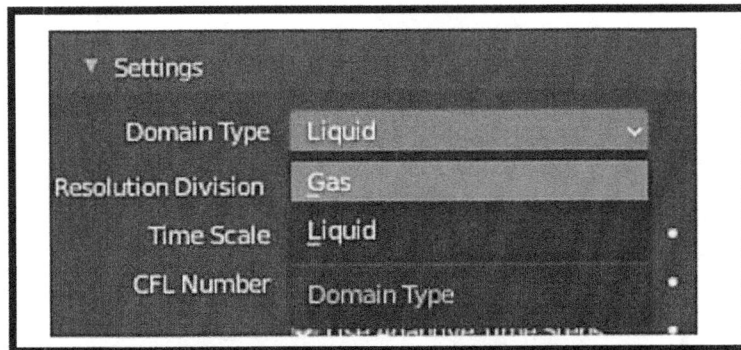

Thereafter, switch the Flow Type of the Flow Object from Liquid to Fire + Smoke or Smoke.

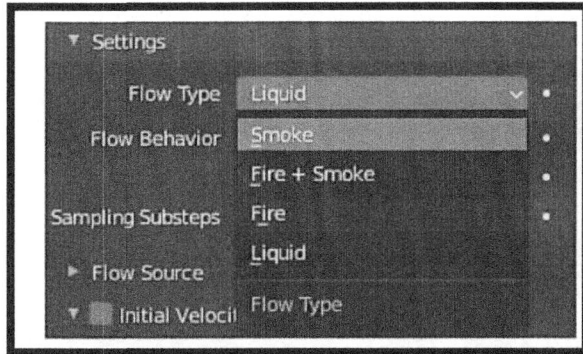

By pressing the space bar once this is done, you can start the animation and see how smoke interacts with the Cube's "roof" as it emerges from the sphere.

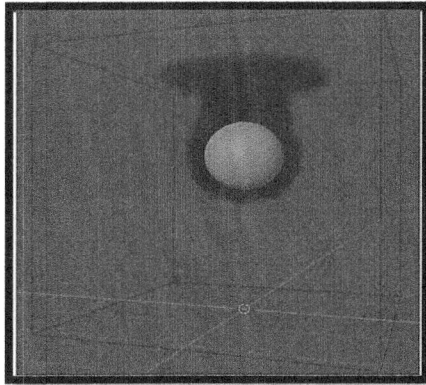

When it comes to the rules and restrictions, it's the same as the Liquid Simulation. In other words, the Resolution Division changes the amount of information in the smoke, while the Time Scale changes the rate at which it arises and flows.

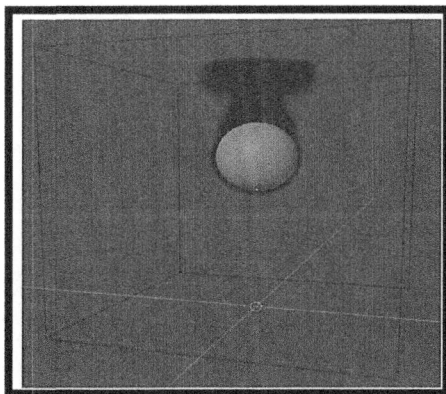

Effector Objects can be made to interact with smoke in the same way they did with liquids if you so desire.

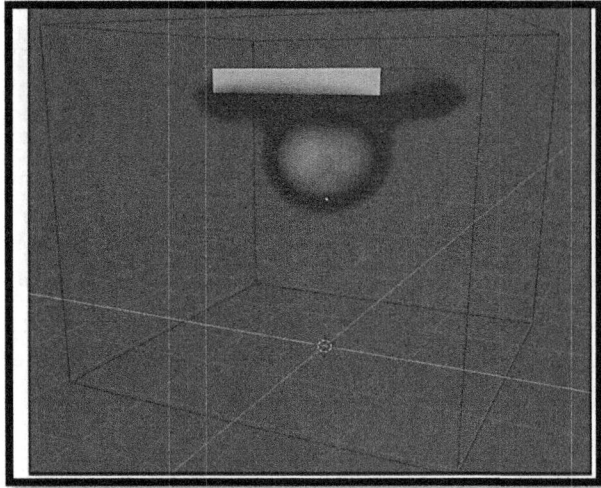

CHAPTER 8
UNDERSTANDING CONSTRAINTS

Introduction

You may control the position, rotation, and size of an object among its many attributes with the use of constraints. You can use them with predetermined values or point to another object (the "target") to apply them. Constraints are useful in static projects, but they come into their own when it comes to animation. In the form of indirect animation, controlling an object's motion is possible by making use of the targets used by its constraints. The owner of the constraint can be indirectly animated by manipulating these targets, which can alter their attributes. The option to animate the constraints' settings exists. When animating with the bone of an armature, it's important to think about the position and influence of the target point for the best results. Think about where the real target point is along the bone, between the root and the tip. As they track the path of a bouncing ball across the court, they can enthrall a tennis player. They make sure that a bus's wheels turn in unison. Because of this, dinosaurs were able to gracefully bend at the knee. They let you hold a sword with ease and make the hilt swivel with your hand. When using Blender, you can use constraints on Objects and Bones alike.

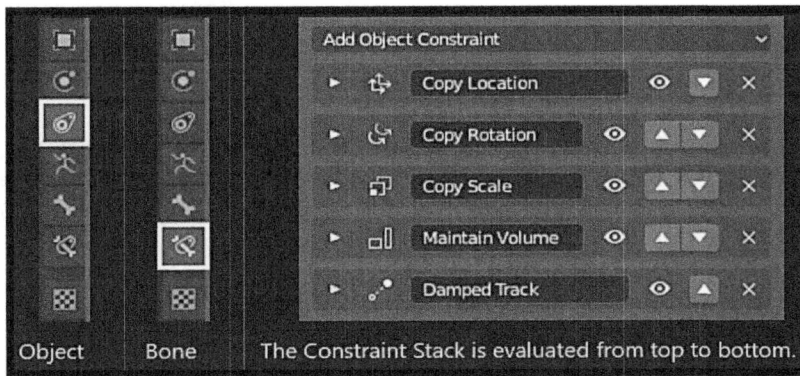

Starting at the top and working our way down, the Constraint Stack is evaluated sequentially. To form a Constraint Stack, constraints must cooperate.

NOTE

- A rig's sophistication and complexity can be significantly improved by implementing constraints.
- It's crucial to proceed cautiously and not impose numerous limits at once without thinking about how they could interact with one another.
- Start by taking a direct approach. Acquire a thorough understanding of one limitation. With its accompanying animation example, the Copy Location Constraint is an excellent starting point for investigating other constraints. If you put in the time and energy to understand each core idea, the rest of the limitations will become a lot easier to see.

How to Add and Remove a Constraint

You can also use the knowledge about Object Constraints to understand Bone Constraints. To add a constraint, simply navigate to the **Constraints tab** and access the **Add Object Constraint** menu.

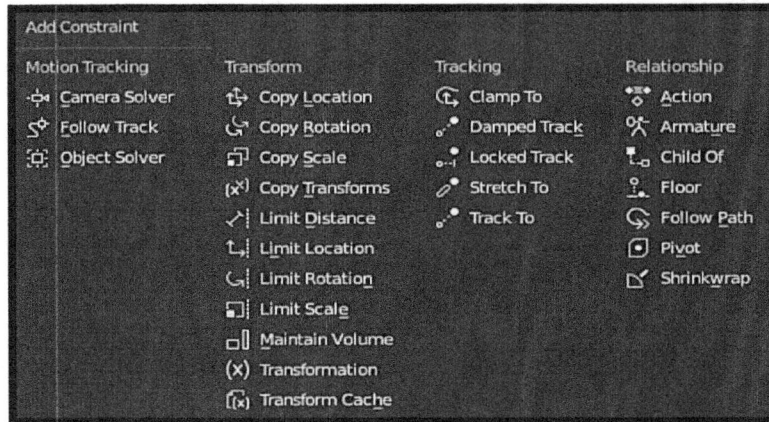

You can delete a constraint by clicking the "**X**" button in the header.

Apply Constraint (with Targets)

Places constraints on the item in question. A pop-up menu lets you choose the constraint type, and the Add Constraint (with Targets) Adjust Last Operation panel makes it easy to make changes afterward. If the chosen constraint allows for targets, another object will be used as the constraint target if it is selected alongside the active object. If you set a constraint to use a bone from another armature, and that armature is in Pose Mode, the tool will look inside the inactive armature for the active bone and use it.

Copy Constraints to Selected Objects

- **Mode**: Object Mode and Pose Mode
- **Menu**: Choose Object > Constraint from the menu, and then click the option to Copy Constraints to Selected Objects. By doing so, you can efficiently apply restrictions to numerous objects simultaneously.
- The constraints of the active item are applied to the other objects that were selected.

Clear Object Constraints

Gets rid of any constraints on the selected item(s).

Track

A tracking constraint is applied to the selected items using these technologies. No further constraints will be applied to the active object; it will just act as the target object for the constraint.

Clear Track

Removes the selected objects' Damped Track, Track To, and Lock Track constraints.

Clear and Keep Transformation (Clear Track)

Removes all current Track Constraints from the selected objects while keeping their change.

How to Transform Cache Constraint

If your animations were made in the transformation matrix, like rigid bodies or camera motions, and you're streaming them from Alembic or USD, you'll need to apply the Transform Cache Constraint. Working with dynamic meshes, like those used in deforming animations, requires the use of the Mesh Sequence Cache modification.

Options

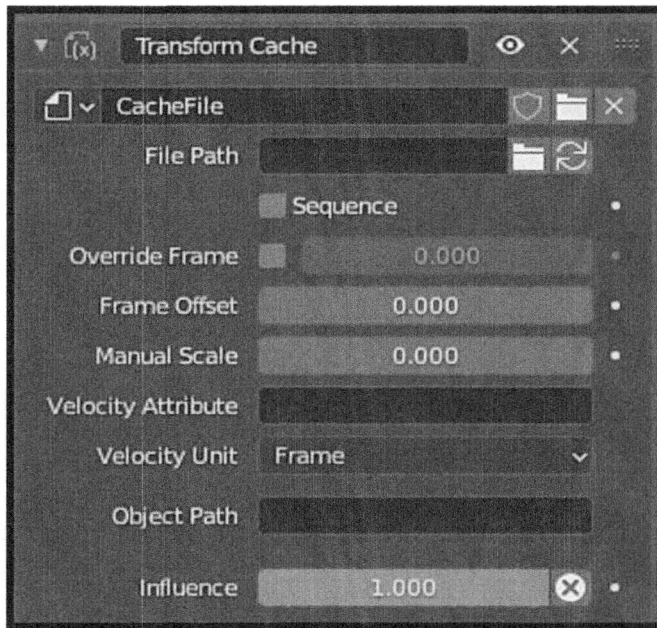

Cache File

To choose between the Alembic and USD files, use the data-block menu.

File Path

The address of the file is either in Alembic or USD format.

Sequence

Finding out if the cache is split into different files is crucial.

Override Frame

Instead of depending on the current scene frame to retrieve data from the cache file, you might want to think about using a custom frame. When choosing the right file in a sequence or correctly recovering data from the cache file, the Frame value is critical.

Frame Offset

Subtracted from the current frame to determine the file sequence or conduct data lookups in the cache.

Manual Scale

To change the object's size relative to the starting point of the universe, use the scale factor.

Velocity Attribute

The "velocities" Alembic attribute is commonly used to generate motion blur data and is the default for the majority of Alembic files. Only Alembic files currently include the Velocity Attribute option.

Velocity Unit

Describes how to read time-dependent velocity vectors.

Frame

The velocity unit can be scaled independently of the frame rate because it was encoded in frames.

Second

It is recommended to modify the velocity unit from seconds to frames per second (FPS) based on the scene's frame rate. For the time being, the Velocity Unit option is only compatible with Alembic files.

Object Path

Whatever part of the archive or performance space contains the Alembic or USD item.

Influence

Controls how much of an effect the restriction has on the item.

How to Maintain Volume Constraint

Options

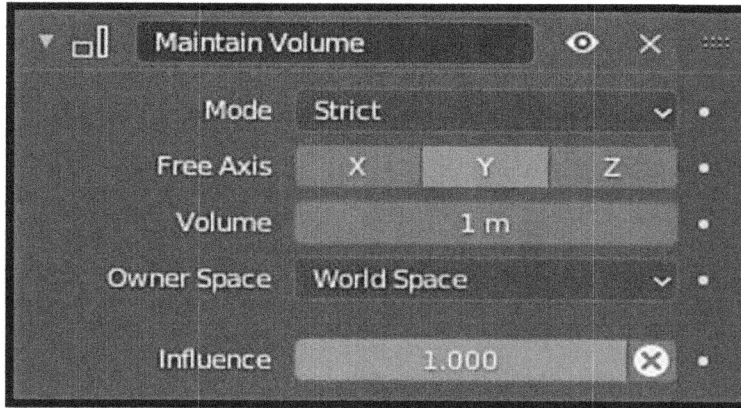

Mode

This method specifies how the constraint changes the size of the non-freely changeable axes.

Strict

This setting prevents non-free axis scaling and forces the given volume to be maintained. Only the ratio of the scales of the non-free axes is taken into account.

Uniform

If the pre-constraint scaling is uniform, this mode will keep the volume constant. We take into consideration any non-free axis scaling that deviates from uniform scaling.

Single Axis

When the item is resized along its unconstrained axis, this mode keeps the volume constant. We apply any extra scaling that goes beyond the standard axis boundaries.

Free Axis

There are no restrictions on the object's axis adjustment.

Volume

At rest, the volume of the bone.

Owner

You can choose the exact region in which to evaluate the owner's transform characteristics with this restriction.

Influence

Controls how much the restriction affects the thing.

How to Track Constraint

By default, the Track To constraint will rotate the owner such that a specified "To" axis always points in the direction of the target, and it will also retain another "Up" axis perpendicular to the global Z axis. The "billboard tracking" in three dimensions is analogous to this tracking. Because of its effective and controllable limiting mechanism, this tracking constraint is highly esteemed. In some ways, this constraint is quite similar to the Inverse Kinematics constraint.

Billboard Tracking

The word "billboard" has a specific meaning in the context of real-time computer-generated programming. This term describes flat objects that maintain a steady angle of view toward the camera, functioning as "trackers" that aim to capture the image. Within the context of video games, this idea takes on further significance. To bolster textures of mist or trees is their principal function. Your trees would often shrink to nothing or your mist would convert into a layered paste if they weren't facing the camera consistently. Even if it doesn't hold much water, this would be hilarious nonetheless.

Options

Target

If the Data ID is not allocated, it becomes non-functional (red state), which is problematic because it is critical for picking the restrictions target.

Track Axis

When talking about tracking, the local axis is the owner's axis that points in the direction of the target. Because of the bad decisions, the relevant axis is now pointing in the opposite way of the goal.

Up

The global Z-axis, or the target Z-axis if the Target button is turned on, should be lined up with the top-most local axis as precisely as feasible.

Target Z

In most cases, when tracking rotations, the owner's up axis is positioned as closely as feasible to the global Z axis. Pressing this button will bring the Up axis into optimal alignment with the local Z axis of the target.

Target/Owner

Using procedures that are typical in the industry, convert spaces.

Influence

Adjusts the degree to which the object is affected by the restriction. When the Tracking Axis and Up axes are the same, the constraint will no longer work (become red).

Using Clamp to Constraint

To precisely align an item with a curve, use the Clamp To constraint. In the same way that the Follow Path constraint does its job, the Clamp To constraint does the same. Clamp To "maps" its owner's location along the target curve to find its optimal position, rather than depending on the evaluation time of the curve. This information is shown in the Transform panel. The 3D Viewport is useful for Clamp To because it allows you to see your owner's movements more accurately than when you were using an F-Curve and repeating the animation over and over again. One disadvantage of the Clamp To constraint is that you can't adjust your rotation such that it follows the banking of the targeted curve, unlike the Follow Path constraint. Because rotation isn't always essential, a Clamp To constraint can be useful in some cases so that you can get the rotation you need in other ways. **While not perfect, the following simplified procedure is used to convert the object's initial position to its position on the curve:**

- A "main axis" is chosen, either by the user or by default as the longest axis of the bounding box of the curve.
- Along the main axis, the position of the item is contrasted with the bounding box of the curve. In this case, the result will be zero because the object is perpendicular to the left side of the curve's bounding box and X is the principal axis. The outcome will be 1 in the opposite case when the item is perpendicular to the right.
- This value can only be between zero and one when the cyclic option is not chosen.
- The final position of the object along the curve to which it is clamped is determined by using this value as the curve time.

Due to the imprecise mapping of curve time to the main axis location, this technique fails to produce the intended result. For example, regardless of the shape of the curve, an object positioned exactly in the middle will be strongly bound to a curve time of 0.5. The reason behind this is that it is positioned halfway along the bounding box of the curve. However, the 0.5 curve time position is not limited to just one location inside the bounding box!

Options

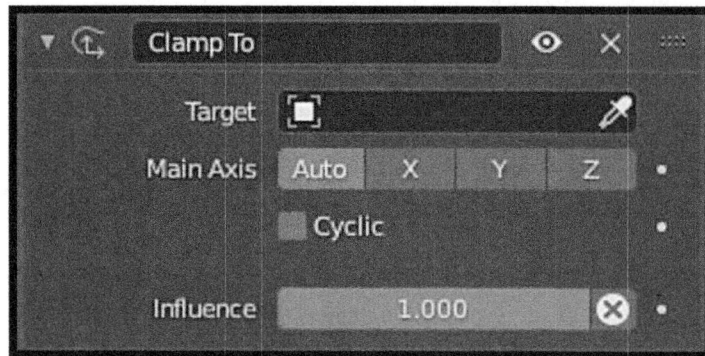

Target

The object of the curve that the Clamp To constraint will follow is determined by the target Data ID. Make sure the object type of the target is correct.

Main Axis

The primary axis of the path, which can be the X, Y, or Z axis, can be chosen from this set of buttons. There will be very little movement along this axis when the object is secured to the target curve. Because of how this limitation works, there might be a little shift along that axis. Since the main trajectory of a rocket launch is upwards, the Z axis is utilized in rocket launch animations. As a default, the Auto option will use the axis with the longest curve, or X in the case where they are equal. This is usually the best option.

Cyclic

The default behavior is to lock the item in place as it approaches the target curve's halfway point. As soon as it reaches one end of the curve, it is sent to the opposite end, provided that the Cyclic option is activated. This is designed to be used on closed curves, like circles, so your owner can easily go around them.

Influence

Controls how much the restriction affects the thing.

How to Copy Transforms Constraint

To make sure the owner's transforms match the target's, the Copy Transforms constraint checks if they are identical.

Options

Target

In its absence, the Data ID becomes non-functional (in a red state), which is problematic because it is essential for choosing the restrictions target.

Mix

Details the process of merging the copied transformation with the existing one.

Replace

The present transformation will be superseded by a new one.

Before/After Original (Full)

An imaginary parent or child of the constraint owner undergoes a fresh transformation, either before or after the current transformation. Combining a non-uniform scale with rotation leads to the development of shear, as the scale is regulated similarly to the fundamental Full Inherit Scale mode of bones.

Before/After Original (Aligned)

Any hypothetical offspring or parent of the constraint owner can have a new transformation applied to them, either before or after the current transformation takes effect. To avoid the creation of shear, the scale is controlled in a manner analogous to the way bones control alignment and the inheritance of scale. This is identical to the use of the Split Channels option; however, the outcome of Full is utilized instead of the location component. The result is the same as Full when a uniform scale is utilized exclusively.

Before/After Original (Split Channels)

This procedure takes the transformation's position, rotation, and scale parameters and combines them. This constraint works in a manner analogous to a combination of the following: Copy Location, Copy Rotation, and Copy Scale (with Offset). Keep in mind that if the inputs contain sheared modifications, the outcome can be slightly different. The input transformations' rotation and scale components do not affect the resultant location in this mode because the location channels are added together.

Target/Owner

Conversion between spaces using industry standards.

Influence

Manages the degree to which the constraint impacts the object.

CHAPTER 9
VIDEO EDITING AND COMPOSITING

You can edit videos with Blender, in addition to using it for modeling and animation. To accomplish this, you can use either the Compositor or the Video Sequencer. You may combine numerous video channels and add effects to them with Blender's Video Sequencer, a powerful video editing system. When combined with Blender's animation features, these effects can make for some powerful video edits! You can put numerous video clips into the Video Sequencer and then arrange them end-to-end or overlay them to create a seamless whole. Fades and transitions, which allow you to move fluidly from one clip to another, can also improve the overall flow. Finally, you can add sound and time to the video sequence precisely.

How to Set Up Your Project

To achieve success, it is essential to create an ideal work atmosphere and customize your project according to your tastes. Keep in mind the following distinctions while you plan your video project:

- **Settings and activities related to the work environment:**

At a high level, as when you install add-ons, these settings apply to all of your projects. They may also influence your work on projects other than videos. These settings should be configured once and then kept constant for all of your projects.

- **Project-related settings and activities:**

Your project's unique needs, such as the format you'd like the final product to be in, dictate the exact configuration that will be used. It is crucial to thoroughly evaluate these environments and tasks before beginning a new project. There are a wide variety of contexts and activities at both levels. You can customize it on a per-project or even per-strip basis, for instance, by activating automated proxies globally.

Directory Structure

It is common practice to combine multiple components into a single video project. In general, there are three ways to classify them.

- **Video files** include video clips, photos, graphic files, and Visual Effects (VFX) like masks, lens flares, and animation.
- **Audio files:** dialog recordings, voice-overs, music, and a variety of Sound Effects (SFX) like environmental sounds and swooshes...
- **Project files** include the blend files and backups, as well as (partial) render results and documentation like scripts and storyboards.

When they pool their resources, they can rapidly amass a library of digital files. It is advised to organize all the assets into suitable subdirectories and store them in a single project directory. Why? If you follow good file management methods, you won't have to worry as much about erasing files by mistake or leaving out critical ones when you transfer projects. As a result, you will be less likely to see the annoying "file not found" or "file is missing" messages. First and foremost, having a well-structured directory will help you keep track of all your assets. Certain files can be included within Blender files. Due to their enormous file sizes, video files cannot be processed using this method. Make sure all the necessary files are in your project directory.

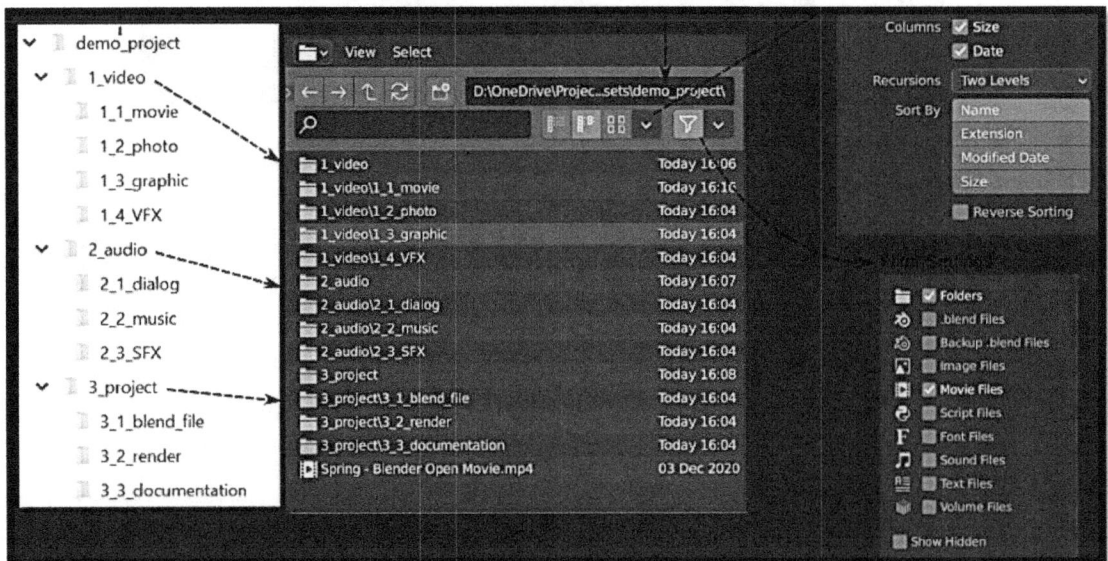

How to Edit Your Project

When it comes to video editing, there is no cookie-cutter method. Although there are certain niche applications, like editing tutorials or wedding films, everyone agrees on four core functions.

- **Montage**: Starting with the raw material, you must arrange the segments in a way that successfully tells your story. Sorting, merging, dividing, and editing clips is necessary.
- **Effects**: Some of the effects available to you are smooth fades and dynamic animations like rolling end credits, which you may select from when making your transitions.
- **Color grading**: If your timeline has a variety of shots, color grading is a must. The colors may appear drastically different from one camera to the next because of differences in lighting and camera settings. Achieving a harmonious perception of color is possible through the use of color grading and color-correcting techniques.

- **Sound**: Music, voice-overs, and unique sound effects are all part of the sound. For even more advanced audio editing, you can use third-party programs like Audacity.

Montage

Montage is a technique for expertly assembling disparate media elements—such as video, audio, text, and effects—into a unified whole. It was Russian director Lev Kuleshov, working in the 1910s and 1920s, who first demonstrated montage's importance. Importing or adding strips is, of course, the first step in establishing your timeline. There are several approaches to this problem, and they all have their advantages and disadvantages. Picking a strip is the first step before doing anything with it. Picking outstrips can be done in several ways. Within the display, you may effortlessly alter the strips in both the horizontal and vertical directions. After a strip is cut or split, it will be separated into two halves: the halves that were there before and after the split. Both Split and Hold Split are at your disposal. Trimming is a method of video editing that entails adding or eliminating segments from the beginning or finish of a clip. The length of the video will be altered as a result of this. When you group strips, you're essentially making a Meta strip.

Selecting

Presented here is the active sequence strip with its sleek outline. By clicking the left mouse button in the middle of the strip, you can pick the entire thing.

Select Menu

There are several choices for selecting strips in the Select menu.

All A

Pick all the timeline strips.

None Alt-A

Clears the timeline of all strips.

Invert Ctrl-I

Flip the current picker over.

Select multiple items by dragging a box around them, including the handles Pressing Ctrl-B

Selects all strip handles in the specified area; works similarly to Box Select but also offers other options. To change the length of a strip, all you have to do is move the handle that is now chosen. (Instead, the entire strip will move when you choose both handles.)

Frame Orientation Left/Right [/]

Pick the rows that span the complete width of the current frame, either left or right.

Current

Choose the strips that intersect the current frame.

Handle

- Both, Left, and Right
- Choose the left, right, or both handles of the selected strips.

Both/Left/Right Neighbor

- To the left, right, or on either side of the chosen strips, choose the handle of the strip that is next to it.

Channel

Pick out all the strips that belong to the same channels as the ones you're using right now.

Linked

- You may access all of these options by pressing Ctrl+L, Ctrl+NumpadMinus, or Ctrl+Add on the numeric keypad.
- You can change the choices by putting or taking away adjacent strips.

Grouped Shift-G

Pick out several strips that are very similar to the active one. You can adjust the default setting in the Adjust Last Operation section to select different strips.

Type

Pick out a set of strips that are comparable to the one you're using right now. As an example, if the current strip is a Movie strip, then all Movie strips will be selected.

Global Type

Pick out strips that are comparable to the one you're viewing right now in terms of content kind (music or images).

Effect Type

It will choose all effect strips if the active strip is one of those. Otherwise, select all strips that do not have an effect. (No matter the label, this operator isn't checking the effect type.)

Data

Pick out other strips that share the same file, scene, movie clip, or mask as the one you're presently working with.

Effect

Find out what kinds of effects are being applied to the active strip right now, and then choose all the other strips that have the same effects. If you apply a Gaussian Blur effect on the active strip, for example, it will pick all the other strips with that effect.

Effect/Linked

Pick out several lower-channel strips and overlap them in time with the one you've picked. After that, you can add effects to the associated content strips. Finally, link the content strips to the effect strips you choose.

Overlap

Pick out time-overlapping segments, either partially or entirely.

CHAPTER 10
GEOMETRY NODES

With Geometry Nodes, a complex system for node-based operations, one may easily change the geometry of an object. Including a Geometry Nodes Modifier will get you access to it.

Any set of geometry nodes that are linked to a modifier is called a Node Group. This state's geometry, whether it was the initial geometry or the modified geometry, will be sent to the Group Input node. After that, the geometry can be efficiently handled by the node group, and the output can be passed on to the next modifier without a hitch by way of the Group Output node.

Numerous kinds of geometry can be altered via geometry nodes.

- Meshes
- Curves
- Point Clouds
- Instances
- Volumes

How to Use Inspection

Geometry node trees are useful for building or understanding them and looking at intermediate values might help you figure out why something isn't working. If you're having problems understanding or fixing a node tree, Blender has several tools to help you out. Data from the most current node tree evaluation is often displayed by the inspection tools.

Socket Inspection

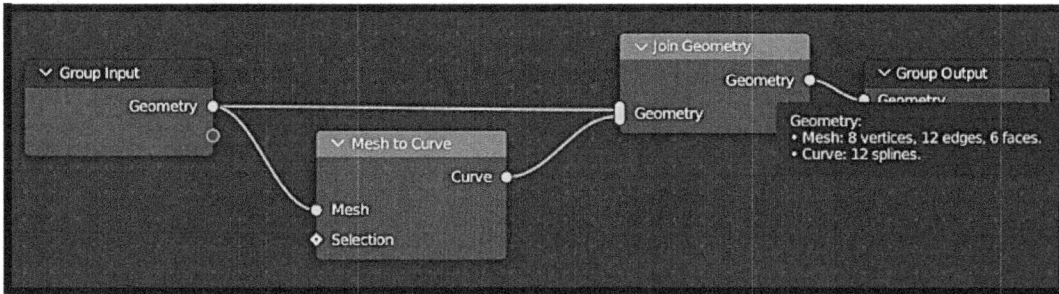

Information on a socket's worth from the most recent assessment can be found in the inspection report. For basic data types such as integers, vectors, and texts, the value that is shown is the one that exists. Geometry sockets only keep the most basic information about the geometry, including the number of elements and the data types it includes. Only during the execution of the node tree are socket values recorded. Nodes can't access values unless they're linked to the Group Output. To improve efficiency, values are not saved while rendering.

Attribute Search

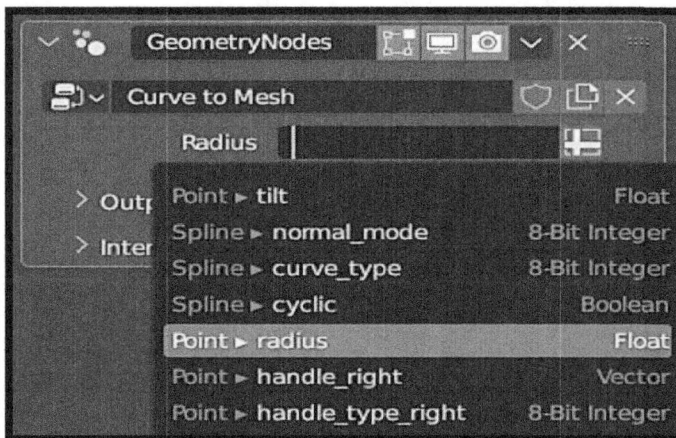

The attribute's search attribute is shown when you click on its input in the modifier. A complete inventory of all characteristics accessible throughout the node or modifier's execution is provided on this page.

Viewer Node

Both the Spreadsheet Editor and the Viewport make use of the Viewer node to display intermediate geometry.

Node Warnings

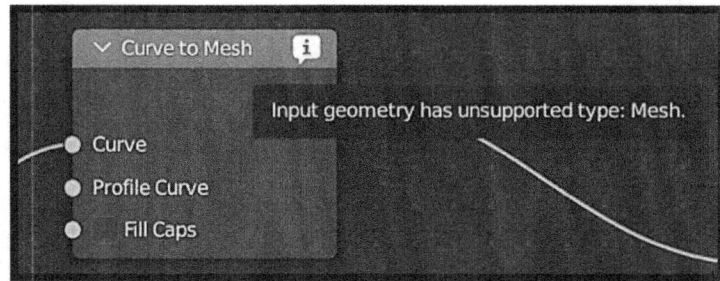

A warning will be displayed in the title when the inputs to a node are invalid. The error message will be shown when you hover over the warning icon. To receive warnings, you must link a node to the Group Output, as they are generated during the node's execution.

Node Timings Overlay

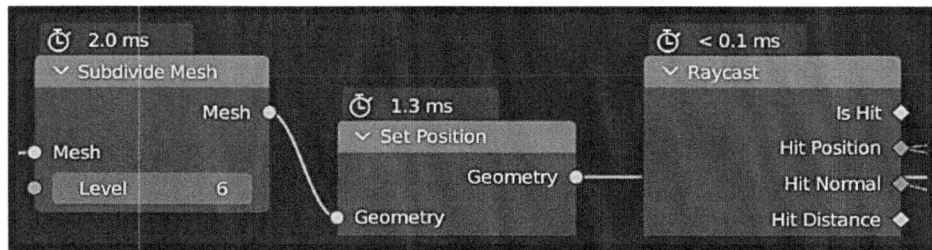

When we look at the node timings, we can see how long it took each node to execute at the last time we evaluated the node group. To enable them, open the overlays popover in the node editor's upper right corner. Multiple uses of a node group cause the timings to be affected by the node editor's context, as shown in the path in the top left corner. When viewing a group of nodes, the Group Output node displays the total time, whereas frame nodes display the sum of all the nodes within them. Keep in mind that the timestamps shown are only estimates and might incorporate extra steps like removing or replacing a geometry input that has nothing to do with the node's actual operation. Furthermore, other nodes can be processed concurrently by the evaluation system when a node requires several CPU cores. In most cases, the execution time of field nodes is dependent on the data-flow nodes to which they are linked; in other words, field nodes do not operate autonomously.

Named Attributes Overlay

A node or collection of nodes can have their custom-named attributes shown using the "Named Attributes" overlay. Nodes like Capture Attribute Node, Named Attribute Node, and Remove Named Attribute Node can make use of attributes with specific names. As required, these properties can be read, written to, or erased. There may be issues with using named attributes if the source geometry already has attributes with the same names. In such a case, a geometry node group can overwrite important data. The problem can be more easily detected with the help of the overlay. In the Named Attributes panel of the modifier's user interface, you can locate the identical data.

Geometry Randomization

Depending on the node, the items they produce might not always be in the same sequence. The sequence of edges that branch out from the triangulate node, for instance, is consistent but not precisely defined. Depending on the version of Blender you're using, the elements' order can be changed. As a result, changes to the Blender implementation can render node setups useless if they depend on a particular order. To fix issues or improve efficiency, it may be necessary to reorder the sequence. Temporary enablement of "geometry randomization" can aid in the identification of blend files that depend on unstable indices. When turned on, several internal algorithms reorganize the components of the generated shape, making it useless. Make sure your configuration works with randomization enabled when you build it for long-term use. To begin, go into the settings and turn on Developer Extras. Find the option to Set Geometry Randomization after that. You can choose to activate or deactivate the randomization feature in the popup.

How to Use Attributes

The data recorded for each element in a geometry data block is sometimes referred to as an attribute. To illustrate, a number or vector can be assigned to each vertex. By setting a value at the Group Output node, values can be changed, and multiple nodes can change the values of individual attributes. Whenever feasible, data types and domains are converted implicitly, just as node sockets.

Named Attributes

Several parts of Blender, including shaders, painting, and UV mapping, make use of attributes. To input a named attribute in the modifier panel, click the corresponding icon to the right of the value button. By entering a string, users can browse the input geometry of the modifier and choose certain properties to work with.

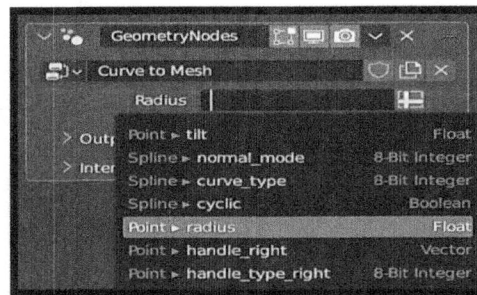

For every attribute, the search attribute gives some background information. The domain of the attribute appears next to its name in the menu. The data type of the displayed attribute is located next to the menu.

Anonymous Attributes

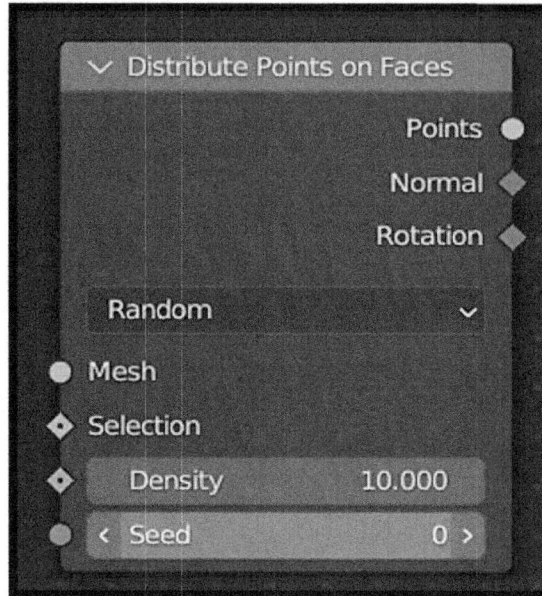

Any set of generic characteristics kept on a geometric object but not assigned a particular name is called an unidentified attribute. Every property in Blender's interface usually has a name. However, characteristics can be transmitted easily via node sockets in geometry nodes. As a result, nodes can access attribute data inside an input geometry using an output known as an Attribute Field. The geometry still stores attributes, including those that aren't explicitly named. Interpolation of these anonymous properties occurs automatically, with a few exceptions, whenever the geometry changes with other nodes. The attribute it references will typically likewise be accessible so long as the node link stays accessible. However, a separate geometry from some other source cannot be associated with anonymous attributes.

Data Types for Attributes

Every element stores data according to the type of the attribute.

- **Boolean**: Is it true or false?
- **Integer**: A 32-bit integer.
- **8-Bit Integer**: A more compact integer within a range of -128 to 127.
- **Float**: Floating-point value.
- **Vector**: 3D vector with decimal values.
- **2D Vector:** A 2D vector containing floating-point values.
- **Color**: Color represented using 32-bit floating-point values.
- **Byte Color**: Color represented by RGBA values using 8-bit positive integers.

- **Quaternion**: Quaternion rotation using floating point values.

In this list, we've included both the simplest and the most complex items. Integers, for example, are more complicated than Booleans because they can store more data. It is recommended to utilize the more advanced data type when merging distinct geometries, provided that there exist matching names. The Join Geometry Node's ability to link geometry with named attributes is vital to keep in mind.

Data Conversion

The use of Geometry Nodes allows for the smooth conversion of data kinds.

Valid Conversions

- To convert color data to its grayscale equivalent, it is first converted to float data.
- It's worth mentioning that integers are transformed into floats and floats are trimmed while discussing the difference between float and integer.
- Each component receives the value of the modified float when it becomes a vector. A vector's average of its components is computed when it is transformed into a float.
- Notably, in float and Boolean data types, true is defined as values higher than 0. To be more precise, the value of true is 1, whereas the value of false is 0.

Attribute Domains

An attribute's domain is defined by the kind of geometry element it is associated with. The interpolation and usage of a property in nodes and shading are determined by its domain, therefore understanding it is vital. Determine the attribute domains using the Spreadsheet Editor.

1. **Point**: Domain attributes are linked to specific locations in space, each with its position.

- Points on a mesh
- Elements of a point cloud
- Control points for curves
2. **Edge**: Edge domain attributes are linked to the edges of a mesh.

3. **Face**: Domain attributes for faces are linked to the faces of a mesh.

4. **Face Corner:** The attributes of the Face Corner domain are linked to the corners of the mesh's faces. A UV map attribute is a prime example.

5. **Spline**: Domain attributes for splines are linked to a collection of interconnected control points on a curve.

6. **Instance**: The Instances that make up geometry have the attributes of the Instance domain. On duplicates of geometric data, they can store a variety of values. Nodes in the geometry only work with properties in the instance domain.

Several domains incorporate attributes without a hitch. The values are transferred from the Point domain to the Face domain smoothly when the Position Node is linked to the selection input of the Set Material Node node. Basic averages are usually used for values in domain conversions. The following rules govern the interpolation of attributes of the Boolean data type, though:

Custom Attributes

In geometry nodes, you can find properties like vertex groups, UV maps, and color attributes. Their name is enough to identify them. To keep things organized; don't use the same name for a vertex group and a UV map, for example. Geometry nodes can only access one of the characteristics if there is a naming collision. Attributes can be created by nodes with different names the first time they are used. Keep in mind that when using a geometry node like Join Geometry, vertex groups aren't necessarily generated. The same is true for vertex group attributes; if you change their data type from "Float" to something else, the attribute will no longer be a vertex group.

Attribute Conversion Operator

You can change an attribute's domain or data type with this operator, which is under the property editor's Attributes panel. The ever-evolving nature of Blender's attributes has rendered some features incompatible with the flexible attributes utilized by geometry nodes. These attributes, which can be stored on any domain with any data type and are characterized by a name, are presently incompatible. When working with data produced by geometry nodes, this operator becomes vital in specific contexts.

Mode

- **Generic**: Quickly and accurately convert and extrapolate properties from one domain or data type to another.
- **Vertex**: Create a Vertex Group using the property that maps to a float property in the domain of points.

Without taking modifier changes into account, this operator works only with the initial object data. Therefore, geometry nodes will not affect any properties that they have added or changed. It is required to use modifiers to change the type of a procedurally created attribute.

How to Use Fields

A field is essentially a function that, given a set of instructions, takes in several inputs and, in response, returns a single value. It is possible to use different sets of input data to compute the same field result several times. For calculations that produce unique results for each element (e.g., mesh vertices, faces, etc.), they are extensively utilized in geometry nodes.

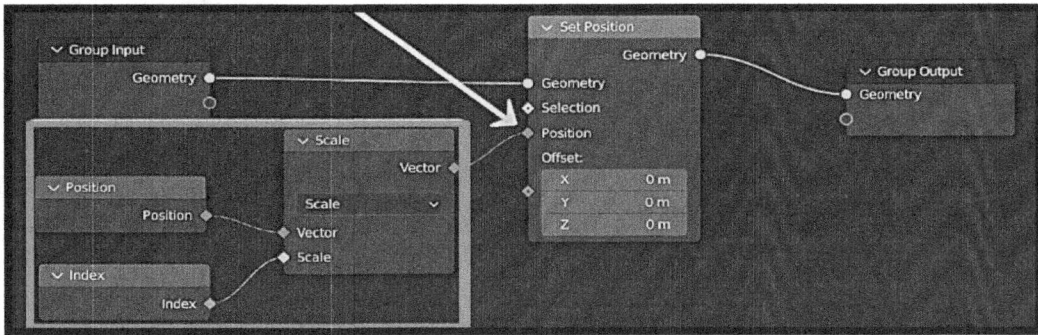

Field Visualization

Field sockets and normal data sockets are distinguished by their forms. The three different socket shapes stand for the different "field status" options.

- **Circle**: The socket is limited to accepting only one real value and does not allow field inputs. There is just one value that the node reliably outputs to the output sockets.
- **Diamond**: The socket can take a field as an input or output, depending on the diamond shape. If you connect a single, constant value to these sockets, the output should be the same for all of the elements.
- **Diamond with Dot**: The socket in a diamond with a dot can be a field, however at the moment it only has one value. The ability to precisely track individual calculations, as opposed to working with a field that generates several outputs, is a great benefit of this feature. On top of that, Socket Inspection will show the value instead of the input fields' names.

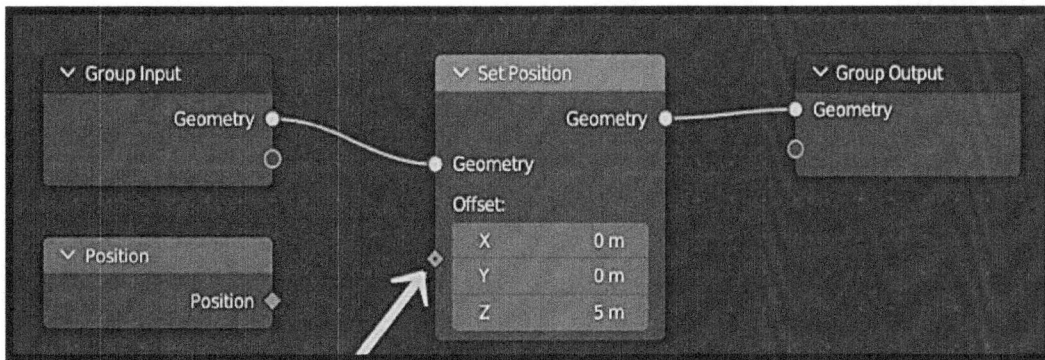

174

The socket shape is a consistent diamond with a dot, indicating that the field maintains a uniform value for each element. All points will be elevated by 5 meters.

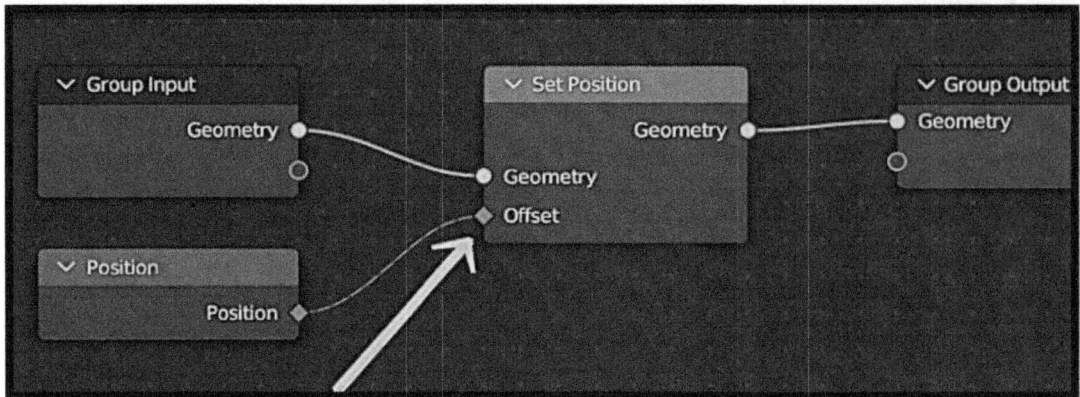

The socket shape is a diamond and the field input currently has a fluctuating input. Put simply, the value may vary for each element. In this scenario, the position will be multiplied by two, as the offset for each point corresponds to its position. The dashed line represents the node connection that has been formed between two field-supporting node sockets. A solid red line indicates an error when a non-field socket is linked to a field socket.

Types of Nodes

Geometry is usually handled by data flow nodes, whereas operations on data per element are performed by field nodes. The geometry data can be inputted into the node tree by field nodes, or the data can be processed by function nodes.

Data Flow Nodes

The standard definition of a data flow node is a node with two geometry-related inputs and outputs. This would imply that they change the geometry data that the Geometry Nodes modifier will produce.

Input Nodes

For field evaluation, input nodes provide data. These principles might not amount to much on their own. When taken into account alongside a data flow node (geometry) and their role in producing an output, however, their actual value becomes apparent. Nodes that accept attributes, such as ID and Position, are examples of input nodes. Nodes that allow selection, such as Endpoint Selection, are also instances of input nodes. The Distribute Points on the Faces node and other geometry-handling nodes can also provide field inputs as Anonymous Attributes.

Field Context

All field nodes function according to the rules set by the data flow node to which they are connected. In most cases, the attribute domain and geometry component type make up the context, and the former dictates which input node data is obtained. It is often believed that data output will be the same when using the same field node tree in different places. Keep in mind that each data flow node will evaluate the field node tree, which could lead to data retrieval from a different or altered geometry.

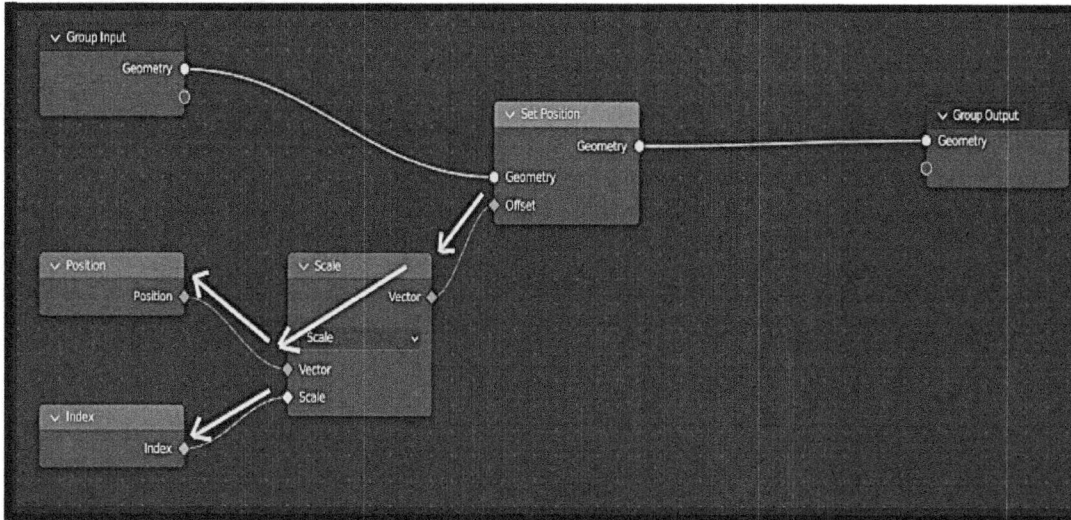

There will be a single evaluation of the Set Position node's input field in this scenario. To evaluate the field, the node retrieves the inputs from the nodes that make up the field and then goes through a process of reverse traversal.

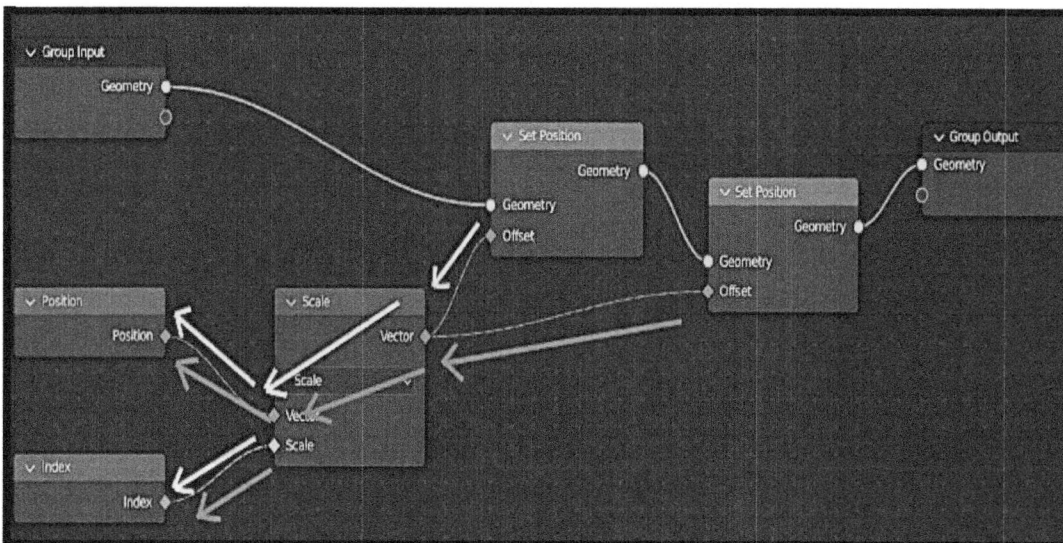

Each data flow node must be evaluated twice to add a second Set Position node; this is because the field node tree is identical. The second Set Position node takes in geometry data that already reflects the changed position from the first node; therefore the output will be different.

But even after changing the geometry, it's usually required to keep using the same field values. A copy of the initial location can be saved using a Capture Attribute node in this scenario. You should know that evaluating the Capture Attribute node's field input is an independent procedure. A later version of the code substitutes a copy of the position attribute for the real position in the input fields of the **Set Position nodes.**

How to Use Instances

Instances stored by objects don't only hold actual data like a mesh or curve; they also allow references to other geometries, objects, or collections. You don't have to duplicate the underlying data to duplicate geometry and its storage in an object thanks to instancing. By implementing this optimization, render engines like Cycles can effectively manage geometry data that is utilized in various places without requiring duplication. The exact transformation performed on each instance concerning the source geometry is

177

precisely recorded. Each instance also keeps track of its related geometry. The geometry node's Instance on the Points Node makes creating instances a breeze. It is currently not possible to combine instancing from geometry nodes with instancing from the property editor's Instancing panel.

Nested Instancing

It is possible to implement nested instancing because instances may store geometries and geometries can include instances. To put it plainly, you can make an instance or multiple instances. Instances on real-world points will automatically build nested instances when you use the Instance on Points Node.

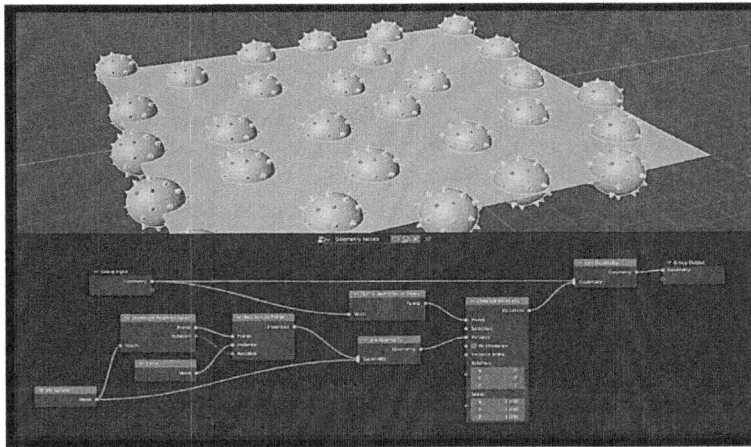

An advanced node group that enables the creation of nested instancing through the use of Instances on Point nodes in a sequential manner. Here, we use nested instancing to distribute the geometry, which consists of a mesh and instances, evenly. A set of instances and a **"real"** mesh make up the final geometry. The geometry of each instance consists of a sphere mesh and numerous cone instances.

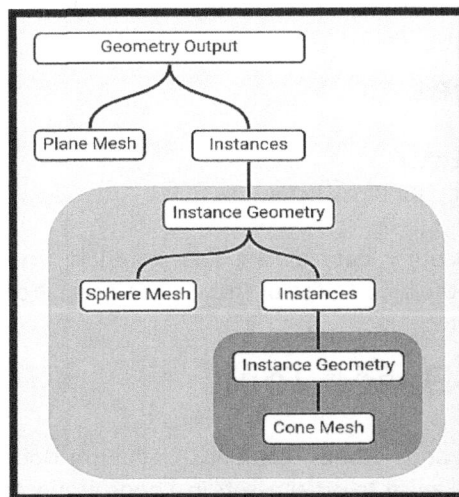

Here is the tree of instanced geometry for the example above. The method is practical since it produces only three different meshes: a plane, a sphere, and a cone. Improving the meshes' complexity would lead to a noticeable performance boost. Rendering and viewing in the viewport are both limited to eight levels of nested instancing. Geometry nodes allow for the creation of more complicated instances, however, these instances must be executed after the node tree.

Realizing Instances

The act of "realizing" instances entails converting them into unique geometric forms. It is not possible to process the complete instance of geometry simultaneously when it is realized; instead, it requires additional memory and individual processing for geometry manipulation.

Instance Processing

Instead of processing the realized geometry as a whole, most geometry-handling nodes usually process each distinct geometry independently. It would be sufficient to subdivision three meshes rather than each instance of a mesh if a Subdivision Surface Node were to be added at the end of the example. The processing of the String to Curves Node's output, where each character is treated just once, is another important example. For each given geometry, this method guarantees consistent results, which can greatly improve performance. To achieve diverse consequences for each occurrence, the Realize Instances Node node is a great tool.

How to Use Baking

Baking facilitates the retention and retrieval of intermediate geometries. Parts of the node tree can be "baked" to improve performance. It is not common practice to think of the data format utilized to store geometry data as an import/export format. For easy portability, objects with volume can be saved in the OpenVDB format. **When it comes to baking data, you have two options:**

- **Bake Node:** This is a tool for baking specific parts of the node tree.
- **Simulation Zone Baking** is a technique used to bake animations, allowing the result of one geometry state to influence the next state.

Data-Block References

- **Editor**: Geometry Node Editor
- **Panel**: Sidebar Node and Data-Block References

Baked geometries that refer to other data blocks, like materials, are included here. Following data processing, this panel allows for the adjustment of these references. Presently, the only data-block types that are supported are material ones.

How to Use Node-Based Tools

By utilizing the tools defined by node groups, Blender's Geometry Nodes enable users to improve the program's fundamental features. Similar to other assets in a node group, they are easily shareable.

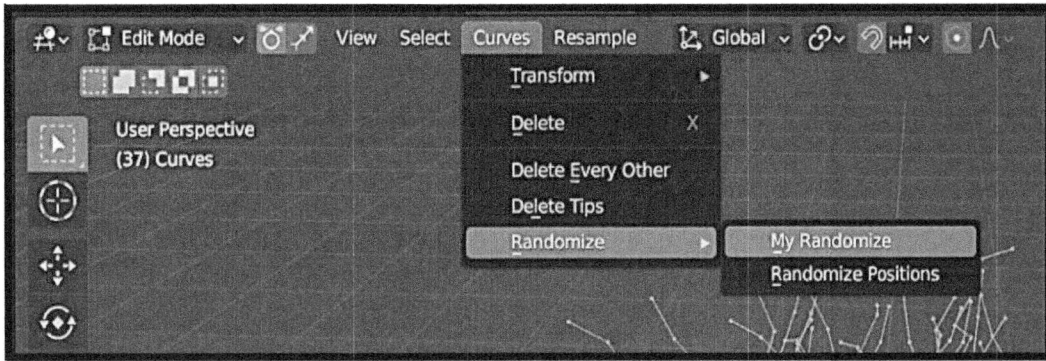

Tool Context

By changing the editor's context to "Tool," you can build Node-based tools. All newly created node groups in the tool context will be enabled as Tools by default. Users will have to explicitly add them as Assets before they may share them. Viewer Node and Socket Inspection are not accessible in the Tool context.

Asset

Node groups, like standard node groups, use the asset catalog to decide which menus to appear in. You can easily add the tool to an existing menu if its name is a match for an existing catalog. The "Unassigned" option displays assets that do not have a catalog or local tools. Verify that the Asset Browser is set up with the appropriate asset settings.

Supported Modes & Data-Types

Groups of nodes must define the kinds of modes and objects they may handle. With this data, we can better pinpoint where the tool is located in the UI. In the Tool context of the Geometry Node editor, you may access the popover menus where you can change these properties. Currently, the only supported modes for the Mesh and Hair Curves object types are Object, Edit, and Sculpting. You can't use Shape Keys on mesh objects. Shape key data will be deleted from a mesh if the node tool is used on it.

Tool-specific Nodes

These are the only nodes that can be used in a Tool context:

- Face Set Node
- 3D Cursor Node
- Set Face Set Node
- Set Selection Node
- Selection Node

When a group of Tool nodes contains the Self Object node, it fetches the Active object from within.

180

Unsupported Nodes

The Modifier context is the only one that supports these nodes.

- Simulation Zone
- Viewer Node

Modifiers

What are the common modifier options?

There are a handful of settings that are consistently used by a large number of modifiers. You can use vertex groups and textures, among other things, to fine-tune and regulate the effect on certain vertices.

Vertex Group

With Vertex Groups, you can easily regulate the effect of a modifier on individual vertices by assigning weights to them. You can always reach them when you need to make changes to meshes or lattices.

Vertex Group

The vertex group's name. The moniker has made the group famous. That means you'll have to go through and pick the right group for every single modifier that depends on the renamed vertex group; otherwise, their fields will become red and you won't be able to use them anymore.

Invert <->

Changes the modifier's effect on the selected vertex group such that it now shows which vertices will be unaffected. The group's weight values are altered oppositely by the setting. Some modifiers have it.

Texture

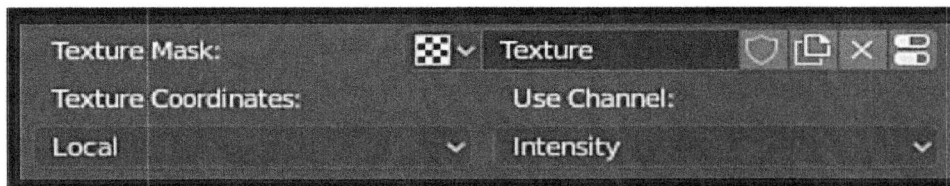

These parameters allow you to alter the modifier's effect using a variety of image kinds, including parametric ones. The texture's grayscale value is usually utilized in numerous cases. On the other hand, the full RGB color space is usable in specific cases, including with some Displace modifier settings. You may add motion to textures by moving the mapping coordinates or adding movies.

Texture

Choose the texture data block that best suits your needs. Clicking the button on the right side of this field will take you to the Texture Properties tab, where you can easily access the parameters for the selected texture.

Texture Coordinates

The texture's coordinates are necessary for obtaining the vertex values.

UV

Find the coordinates of the texture using the face's UV coordinates.

UV Map

Coordinates for textures are stored in the UV Map. In the absence of UV coordinates, the object will revert to using the Local coordinate system. If this field remains blank and a UV map is accessible, such as immediately following the initial UV map's addition to the mesh, the active UV map will be utilized.

Note

The only faces that are ignored are those that employ that vertex. When UV coordinates in the mesh are not adjacent to each other, artifacts can form.

Object

Using the coordinate system of another object, get the texture's coordinates.

Object

The texture coordinates the origin. The texture mapping coordinates will change as the item is moved. When this box is not filled out, the Local coordinate system will be used as the default.

NOTE

The texture coordinates will also be updated when you move the original item.

Global

Get the texture's coordinates using the world's standard coordinate system.

Use Channel

Make sure you're using the right channel as the value source. Be aware that there is a restricted set of modifiers that grant access to this feature. Unless otherwise specified, the channel will behave as the Intensity in all other situations.

Intensity

Simply adding up all of the RGB channel values yields the overall average. Using the RGB values (1.0, 0.0, 0.0) as an example, we can see that the average is 0.33.

RGB/RGBA

A number representing a color channel.

Hue

The shade inside the HSV color model corresponds to the color on the conventional wheel (for instance, yellow has a lower hue value than blue).

Saturation

The hue determines the HSV color model's saturation level. As an illustration, the saturation value of pure red is 1.0 while that of gray is 0.0.

Value

It is the HSV color model that provides the value.

Note: Except Intensity, all of the previously listed channels have been calibrated for gamma correction.

CHAPTER 11
TIPS, TRICKS, AND TROUBLESHOOTING

Optimization Tips for Complex Scenes

In Blender, processing high-resolution models, texturing, and lighting can be taxing for your computer, especially when you're working on intricate or large-scale scenarios. Particularly for animation and rendering jobs, improving your scenes' optimization guarantees a better workflow and faster performance. Here are some doable things you may do to streamline your scenes without lowering their quality.

Reduce Polygon Count

Your scene's polygon count is one of the primary performance determinants. To reduce an object's polygon count in Blender without drastically changing its look, use the Decimate Modifier. You can get away with even less detail if the subject is far away from the camera; tiny flaws won't stand out.

Use Instances and Linked Objects

Pressing Alt + D will bring up instances instead of duplicating things. Blender can save time by not treating duplicates as distinct objects because instances share data. Things like trees, furniture, and tiles tend to repeat, thus this comes in handy for those situations.

Optimize Textures and Materials

If your scene has large, high-resolution textures, it may run more slowly. Use compressed formats or reduce the resolution of the textures. Keep procedural texture sampling levels low unless required, and simplify materials by lowering the number of nodes in your shader sets.

Adjust Lighting and Shadows

Lighting complex scenes with many sources of light or very high shadow resolutions might put a strain on your equipment. If you can, reduce the number of light sources and use baked lighting or lower the quality of shadow maps to make shadow calculations easier, especially for static objects.

Use Proxy Models for Large Scenes

Opt for low-poly proxies rather than their full-detail counterparts when dealing with distant or unoccupied objects. Even while you're editing fine-grained elements of your scene, the viewport remains responsive.

Bake Physics and Simulations

Things like fluid, fabric, or smoke can add a lot of processing power to physics models. Once you're happy with the findings, bake the simulations. The simulation is then transformed into a static animation, allowing the system to allocate its resources more efficiently.

Simplify Viewport Settings

Make performance a top priority by adjusting the Viewport Shading settings. Instead of Material Preview or Rendered mode, choose Solid or Wireframe mode while working on complicated scenes. Under the Render Properties tab, you'll find Simplify, which, among other things, allows you to manage detail levels, subsurface subdivisions, and more.

Use Render Layers and Collections

Divide your scene into smaller parts and focus on each one separately. To facilitate rendering, divide your scene into layers using render layers; then, when compositing is complete, combine the layers. Previewing and rendering will be easier on your PC as a result.

Update Drivers and Blender Versions

Performance issues may arise if you are using outdated drivers or an older version of Blender. Always use the most recent stable version of Blender, which usually has performance improvements, and make sure your graphics drivers are up-to-date.

Use an SSD for Storage

A solid-state drive (SSD) upgrade can greatly improve the performance of your scene files and textures stored on a hard drive. When dealing with big texture files, it also makes things more responsive.

Troubleshooting Common Issues

Blender Crashes or Freezes

Among the most common complaints is that Blender will unexpectedly freeze or crash, particularly when dealing with demanding tasks. Possible causes include out-of-date drivers, inadequate hardware resources, or incorrect configuration settings. Make sure your PC can run Blender by reviewing the system requirements. If the crash happens when rendering, try lowering the sample count or changing to a less resource-intensive rendering engine, such as Eevee, instead of Cycles. Blender crashes are commonly fixed in newer versions; therefore it's a good idea to upgrade your graphics drivers and Blender version as well.

Viewport Lag or Slow Performance

Your system can be overwhelmed by the scene's intricacy if traversing the viewport becomes sluggish. To begin, make the viewport display settings as simple as possible. To alleviate the stress brought on by previews of materials and lighting, switch to Wireframe Mode or Solid Mode. For the time being, use lower-resolution placeholders for any high-resolution textures you may be using. Improving performance can also be achieved by disabling some effects in the viewport and reducing subdivisions by activating the Simplify option in the Render Properties tab.

Objects Not Rendering Properly

Several things could be causing items to look deformed, missing, or undetectable in the final render. To begin, choose the object in question and use the Outliner's camera icon to double-check that it isn't hidden in the render. The object will not be rendered if this is left unchecked. Also, check that the materials used to make the item are properly assembled. Things can appear black or translucent if their textures are missing or if their materials are assigned incorrectly. To recover deleted texture files, go to File > External Data > Find Missing Files.

Lighting and Shadows Look Off

Mistakes in positioning or settings frequently lead to lighting and shadow problems. Make sure all of your lights are turned on and in the right places if your scene seems too flat or gloomy. Make sure that the shadow settings, including shadow resolution and contact shadows, are properly configured on the Render Properties tab. using high dynamic range (HDR) photographs or turning up the light intensity might help with this if it doesn't work.

Unexpected Object Behavior

Possible causes of an object's unpredictable behavior include parentage, modifiers, or hidden constraints; for instance, an object may move when it shouldn't or not react to transformations. To find out if there are any limitations, go to the Constraints page. If you think another item is affecting the object's behavior, you can check its parentage in the Outliner. To make sure that the problem isn't caused by any unforeseen effects, such as array or displacement modifiers, check the modifiers stack as well.

Render Times Are Too Long

Complex scenes in particular can cause lengthy render times. Make sure the render parameters are optimized first. To keep quality while using fewer samples, reduce the sample count for both the preview and final renders. Denoising can be used for this purpose. For scenes that don't call for Cycles' superior realism, switch to Eevee. Lessen the amount of shader nodes and stay away from high-resolution textures to make materials easier to work with. If your graphics card is up to the task, you may speed things up by enabling GPU Rendering in the System preferences menu.

Missing Add-Ons or Tools

The functions or tools you require could appear to be absent at times. In most cases, this is because the related extensions are disabled. Just find the add-on you require by going to Edit > Preferences > Add-ons. To activate it, locate it and then check the box. Check that you have the correct version of Blender and that the add-on is installed successfully if the add-on isn't shown. To manually install custom add-ons, go to File > Install and choose the file extension (.zip or.py).

Materials or Textures Not Displaying

Verify that you are in either Material Preview or Rendered Mode if you are unable to see textures in the viewport; textures are not displayed in Solid Mode. Make sure the textures are applied appropriately by checking the object's UV mapping as well. If you've imported a model but can't see the textures, try going to File > External Data > Find Missing Files and relinking the texture files.

Issues with Animations

Keyframes, restrictions, or rigging could be at the root of an animation's unexpected behavior. Make sure the timeline is properly aligned with all keyframes and that the interpolation types (found under Keyframe Properties) are suitable for the motion you want. When it comes to rigging, make sure the bones are properly weighted concerning the mesh and see if any constraints are getting in the way of the animation.

Blender Fails to Start

Blender won't launch at all? It could be because your hardware isn't compatible, the installation files are faulty, or blender dependency files are missing. The first thing you should do is reinstall Blender, making sure you download the 64-bit version that is compatible with your OS and hardware. If the problem continues, try running Blender from the command line. This will allow you to examine any error messages, which may provide information about the problem. Update your graphics drivers and make sure your PC satisfies the system requirements.

Corrupted Files or Projects

Try accessing a previously saved or backup version of the Blender file if the original one becomes corrupted or won't open. The File > Recover > Auto Save option allows you to access the backups that Blender automatically saves of your work. For any unfinished versions of your project, you can also look in the temporary files folder on your computer.

Keyboard Shortcuts Not Working

Conflicts with custom keymaps or add-ons could be the cause of certain keyboard shortcuts not working. To return the keymap to its default state, navigate to Edit > Preferences > Keymap. To temporarily disable an add-on to determine if it's the cause of the issue, try installing it again.

Keyboard Shortcuts for Efficiency

General Navigation

In Blender's 3D viewport, you can navigate and manipulate your view using these shortcuts.

- **Middle Mouse Button (MMB):** Rotate the view. Hold and drag the MMB to look around your scene.
- **Shift + MMB:** Pan the view horizontally or vertically.
- **Scroll Wheel:** Zoom in and out.
- **Numpad 1, 3, 7:** Switch to front, side, or top views, respectively. Press **Ctrl + (1, 3, 7)** for opposite views.
- **Numpad 0:** Switch to the camera view.
- **Home:** Center the entire scene in the viewport.

Object Selection and Manipulation

You may quickly manipulate items by using these shortcuts to move, rotate, or resize them.

- **A:** Select all objects. Press **Alt + A** to deselect everything.
- **B:** Box select. Click and drag to select multiple objects.
- **G:** Move (grab) the selected object. Press **G**, then X, Y, or Z to constrain movement to a specific axis.
- **R:** Rotate the selected object. Use X, Y, or Z to rotate along a specific axis.
- **S:** Scale the object. Combine with X, Y, or Z to scale along one axis.
- **Ctrl + A:** Apply transformations (location, rotation, scale) to finalize an object's changes.
- **X or Delete:** Delete selected objects.
- **Shift + D:** Duplicate the selected object.
- **Alt + D:** Create an instance of the selected object (saves memory by sharing the same data).

Editing Mode

To access Edit Mode and deal with objects' geometries, use these shortcuts.

- **Tab:** Toggle between Object Mode and Edit Mode.
- **E:** Extrude. Use this to create new geometry by pulling out edges, faces, or vertices.
- **Ctrl + R:** Add a loop cut. Hover over the model to see where the cut will be made.
- **I:** Inset faces. Shrinks or grows the selected face(s) inward or outward.
- **Ctrl + B:** Bevel edges. Adds rounded edges to your geometry.
- **M:** Merge vertices. Use this to combine selected vertices.

- **K:** Knife tool. Allows you to cut new edges into your mesh manually.

Viewport and Camera Control

Quickly change your perspective and work in three-dimensional space.

- **Z:** Toggle shading modes (Wireframe, Solid, Material, Rendered).
- **T:** Show or hide the tool shelf on the left side of the screen.
- **N:** Show or hide the properties panel on the right.
- **Shift + Spacebar:** Maximize or minimize the selected viewport.
- **Ctrl + B:** Set a render region (limits rendering to a specific area in the camera view).
- **Alt + B:** Clip the viewport to a specific region (only show what's inside the box).

Modifiers and Object Properties

A faster way to deal with modifiers and apply modifications.

- **Ctrl + 1-5:** Add a subdivision surface modifier with a specific level of detail.
- **Ctrl + Shift + B:** Bevel selected geometry or objects.
- **F3:** Search for any tool or command by name. Useful if you forget the shortcut for something.
- **Shift + Ctrl + Alt + C:** Set origin (move the object's pivot point).

Animation Shortcuts

These shortcuts make it easier for animators to create, edit, and manage keyframes.

- **I:** Insert a keyframe for the selected property (like location, rotation, or scale).
- **Alt + I:** Remove keyframes from the selected property.
- **Spacebar:** Play or pause the animation timeline.
- **Left Arrow / Right Arrow:** Jump to the previous or next keyframe.
- **Shift + Left Arrow / Shift + Right Arrow:** Move to the start or end of the timeline.
- **Ctrl + Tab:** Switch to the Dope Sheet (animation timeline).

Rendering and Output

Rendering and previewing scenes become much faster with these shortcuts.

- **F12:** Render the current frame.
- **Ctrl + F12:** Render the entire animation.
- **Shift + Z:** Toggle between Rendered and Solid viewport shading (useful for previewing your scene lighting).
- **Ctrl + S:** Save your project.
- **F3 (after rendering):** Save the rendered image.

Miscellaneous Shortcuts

Blender has additional helpful shortcuts for many tasks.

- **Shift + C:** Reset the 3D cursor to the center of the scene.
- **Ctrl + Z:** Undo the last action. Use **Ctrl + Shift + Z** to redo.
- **Shift + F:** Enter fly mode to navigate your scene with WASD keys like in a video game.
- **Alt + G / Alt + R / Alt + S:** Reset location, rotation, or scale, respectively.

How to Learn Shortcuts

This is not an exhaustive list that you must commit to memory. Make it a priority to master the ones you employ frequently. If you want to know what the shortcut is for a certain tool or menu item, Blender will show you when you hover over it. You may greatly increase your productivity and efficiency in Blender by becoming accustomed to these shortcuts.

Conclusion

Blender isn't just another 3D tool—it's a powerhouse of endless possibilities, designed to cater to everyone from beginners taking their first steps into 3D to industry veterans crafting stunning, groundbreaking creations. Mastering Blender isn't about overnight success—it's about patience, consistency, and a willingness to experiment.

With every tool at your fingertips—modeling, animation, rendering, scripting—you have the power to bring your wildest ideas to life. The key lies in understanding the fundamentals, diving into Blender's thriving community, and harnessing powerful efficiency tools like keyboard shortcuts to maximize your workflow.

What makes Blender truly exceptional is that it never stops evolving. With regular updates, a passionate global community, and an ever-expanding toolkit, there's always something new to learn, a fresh technique to master, and a creative boundary to push.

So, take your time, embrace the learning curve, and don't hesitate to seek help from the vast Blender community. The more you use it, the more its limitless potential will unfold before you, taking your skills—and your creative vision—to unimaginable heights.

Now go forth, create, explore, and push the boundaries of what's possible. The world of 3D is yours to shape. 🚀

INDEX

Groups of nodes must define the kinds of modes and objects they may handle, 180

S

Made in the USA
Las Vegas, NV
01 April 2025